101
Inspirational
Stories
of the
Sacrament of
Reconciliation

101
Inspirational
Stories
of the
Sacrament of
Reconciliation

Sister Patricia Proctor, OSC

A Called by Joy Book

Franciscan Monastery of Saint Clare
Spokane, Washington

www.calledbyjoy.com

ISBN-13: 978-0-9728447-5-8
ISBN-10: 0-9728447-5-9

ATTENTION SCHOOLS, UNIVERSITIES, COLLEGES
AND CHARITABLE ORGANIZATIONS:
Quantity discounts are available on bulk purchases of this book for educational, gift purposes or as premiums for increasing magazine subscriptions or renewals. For information, please contact:
St. Anthony Messenger Press at 1-800-488-0488.

Dedication

to Father George Morbeck

Before I entered the Monastery, Father Morbeck was our parish priest. I was impressed by his solid faith and fearlessness in proclaiming God's message. Didn't matter whether the topic was popular or not—he preached solid Catholic doctrine in season and out of season. At one point he decided to preach the sacraments. Each week he covered one in his sermon. That's what I am doing…working my way through the sacraments, one book at a time.

When I was discerning entering religious life, I went to talk to Father about it. After some very helpful discussion and as I was getting ready to go, I suddenly remembered to ask him to bless a miraculous medal I was wearing. So he blessed it and then I said, "Oh! I should have asked you to bless me as well." He smiled and said, "I already did. I blessed the whole package."

Our Church is full of many good, Catholic priests; strong men who lead prayerful, quiet lives of faithfulness, in season and out of season. In my opinion, Father George is one of the best.

Thank you, Father Morbeck.

With Prayerful Thanks

When I was a child, I read a book about a little red hen who tried to get the duck, the cat and the dog all to help her plant and harvest some wheat. She didn't have any luck—they all said, "Not I." No matter what she asked of them, they couldn't help her, so in the end she would say, "Very well, then I will do it myself!" And she did.

Well, that didn't happen with this book! Every step of the way I got, "Sure, I'll be glad to help," or "No problem, I can do that" or "Thank you for the opportunity, I would love to help!"

So this is my page of prayerful and grateful thanks to all who made this book possible.

The beautiful sisters I live with: the most generous and loving women on the earth. I am so blessed to be a Poor Clare Sister in community with you!

The friends who subscribe to my daily mailings and respond time and time again with stories, suggestions, information, and lots of prayer. So many wonderful people responded to my efforts, and though I could not use everything that was submitted, I appreciate each and every one so much. The hardest thing with this series of books is not being able to use each story that comes in. Everyone is so special and puts so much prayerful time and energy into contributing, that I feel like a heel having to say, "Yes" to this one and, regretfully, "No" to another. What makes it easier is the love and understanding from those who receive a "No" but respond with prayers and support anyway. You are so appreciated! You are the unsung heroes in the book, and I hope your story will be used next time!

My book production friends who pull each book together from start to finish—Barb Ries, Anne Marie Schroeder, Virginia Schmuck, Dale Duncan, and Cynthia Landeen—my faithful friends who are always willing to go the extra mile to make it happen on schedule when I'm not!

For the beautiful cover and illustrations by Theodore Schluenderfritz, and for Kathy Czeck and all the printing people at POS—THANK YOU!

All the great people at Saint Anthony Messenger Press, our Franciscan Family in Ohio! God bless you over and over for your help, support, care, and willingness to work with all the new ideas I come up with! I know that every Catholic publishing house is doing the work of God, but in my book you stand out above the rest!

With grateful thanks,
I ask God to bless each of you with, "All Peace and All Good!"

Sister Patricia Proctor, OSC

Contents

Appendices

Foreword

In my practice of counseling, I have been most amazed at the opportunities for counseling that confession offers to the penitent, and for free! I have seen the benefits as I performed my humbling duty of hearing confessions in Rome, where I now work at the Pontifical Biblical Institute; in India, where I am originally from; in Germany and the U.S. where I studied; and in Zambia in Africa where I worked for many years.

Many practicing Catholics have moved away from the rigid notion of "no communion without confession," to one of asking God's pardon for their sins as being enough, without seeking absolution from a priest. To this I can only repeat the words I heard from a born again pastor on the radio telling his congregation that, "Even if God has forgiven you, you still need to find a friend, even if he lives a thousand miles away, and tell him what you did, so that your forgiveness is not just from God but also in community."

Catholic teaching, understood from the words of Christ to Peter in which He asked Peter to forgive in God's name with his power to bind and loose both on earth and in heaven, integrates both the concept of forgiveness of God and that happening in community in the rite of confession.

The sacrament of reconciliation, or confession, has gone through a lot of changes in its presentation in recent years thanks to the stimulus given by the Second Vatican Council. With the attempt to move away from the confession box and bring in a more pastoral and face-to-face approach, there has been a lot of learning going on. However, many Catholics miss the point of these changes, and so they do not benefit from the powerful gifts that the sacrament of reconciliation has to offer both for their spiritual growth as well as for better lives at home and at work.

Sr. Patricia Proctor, OSC, in her book, *101 Inspirational Stories of the Sacrament of Reconciliation,* looks at what is actually happening in the use of the sacrament of reconciliation in the life of the Church today; through her collection of personal narratives and teaching she brings those stories into their theological perspectives. They will help those seeking to know more or to practice a more fruitful Christian life to see reflections of their own lives in these stories, and also changes that the sacrament can bring into them once they look at their own states of souls in a deeper light.

May God bless all those who read through this book, and may it bring them peace, joy, and unity in love, which the sacrament of reconciliation is all about.

Fr. Eustace Sequeira, SJ
Pontifical Biblical Institute
Rome

Preface

Ever wish you could be perfectly *at rights* with God, yourself, and all beings?

This book brings forth the light of peace available through the sacrament of reconciliation, given to us by Jesus Christ and extended to us in our lifetime by the Catholic Church.

It has been a joyful effort of the Poor Clare community and of our Sister Patricia Proctor in particular, to present these stories of effectual and graced use of the sacrament of reconciliation.

May they find an extended fulfillment in your renewal discovery of the wellsprings of peace waiting to be poured into your life!

Sister Rita Louise McLean, OSC
Monastery of Saint Clare
Spokane, Washington

Introduction

By the Most Reverend William S. Skylstad
Bishop of Spokane

Memories of celebrating the sacrament of reconciliation remain strong for all of us. I still can remember my first time going to confession. My mother would frequently remind all of us children in the family of the need to go to confession. It was a reminder we heeded, and one for which I'm grateful. Later, during my twelve years in the seminary, we had the opportunity to celebrate the sacrament of reconciliation twice a week, during study hall on Wednesday and Saturday afternoons.

In my years as a priest and bishop, the humbling role of serving as someone's confessor leaves me profoundly inspired by those who confess their sins and failings as penitents. Addressing our holiness of life is always a great challenge, and we can never tell when people will allow the movement of the Spirit to bring them to this truly reconciling sacrament. I often wear clerical attire when I travel, and it's not at all uncommon to pass through an airport and have someone approach me asking to go to confession.

The celebration of the sacrament of reconciliation has fallen off somewhat over recent years. Clearly, we need to rediscover the power of this sacrament in our lives. When we look a little more closely at the sacrament, it becomes clear how important it really is to our spiritual growth.

First, we need forgiveness. Every one of us is a sinner, and we know it. At the beginning of every Eucharist, we acknowledge our sinfulness and proclaim God's mercy with one of several forms of the Penitential Rite. During the Our Father, we pray, "Forgive us our trespasses as we forgive those who trespass against us...." The redeeming and forgiving presence of Jesus is always with us. Again and again, we can return—yes, and we need to return—to the wonderful gift of this sacrament, seeking forgiveness and healing with a spirit of gratitude and joy.

Second, it is important to remember that there is always a communitarian aspect to our sinfulness. Whenever we do something positive, in some small way we uplift the entire community of faith and the world about us. But the opposite is also true. Whenever I sin, the quality of the spiritual life of the community surrounding me is somewhat diminished. The second rite for the celebration of the sacrament of reconciliation is the communal rite, including individual confession and absolution of our sins. As we gather in that setting to celebrate the sacrament, we see our solidarity: with one another as sinners, and in our need for forgiveness. Our churches have specific rooms for the celebration of the sacrament of reconciliation. Those spaces are a visible sign to every member of the community.

Third, we need to recognize the full reality of our lives, sins and all. The preparation that we need to celebrate the sacrament assists us in dealing with the spiritual blindness, sinfulness, and dehumanizing patterns that confound our spiritual journey. Whenever we celebrate the sacrament with our confessor, we must take time aside beforehand to assess the condition of our soul. We must ask ourselves, in truth and integrity: For what do I need to be forgiven? This time we spend in the examination of our conscience is truly a time of honesty, grace and blessing.

Fourth, the celebration of the sacrament of reconciliation keeps us humble. Everyone, from the pope to the rest of us in the pews, needs to confess sins. At a recent meeting of the bishops, we have scheduled an afternoon of prayer and reflection. Almost always during those times, there is an opportunity to celebrate the sacrament of reconciliation. Usually this happens during a Holy Hour. One after another, the bishops rise and go to a station, where a confessor waits to celebrate the sacrament. I find it moving to see that common acknowledgment, all of us approaching the celebration of the sacrament as a need in our own lives.

I often wonder: If we celebrated the sacrament of reconciliation more regularly, might not our Catholic family better address our anger, our shortcomings, and our struggles? There is a healing grace from the sacrament. The celebration of the sacrament is an intense form of prayer and encounter with the Lord Jesus. And it is clear to me that if we respond regularly to the sacrament, our call to holiness will be better appreciated and answered.

May we always rejoice in God's mercy and forgiveness, extended to us in the sacrament of reconciliation! That mercy and forgiveness have power without end in our lives. Thanks be to God!

What Are You Doing Here?

I hope this sharing of my experience is helpful, especially to my brother priests and those who prepare people for the sacrament of reconciliation.

I have been a priest for thirty-three years and a preacher of parish missions and retreats. During my first year of priestly ministry, I was sent to a small rural parish to preach a mission. On Saturday afternoon, I went to the church to "hear confessions" as we used to say back then. The church was empty, and I sat in the small, dark confessional wondering why no one was coming. I opened my breviary and began to pray. A long time passed without anyone coming into the confessional.

I was a little disappointed that no one seemed to want to "go to confession" when suddenly I heard a voice: "What are you doing here?"

The voice was so clear that I thought someone was outside my confessional talking to me. I pulled the curtain aside but found no one there. The church was completely empty. I sat back once again and the voice came a second time: "What are you doing here? You have no right to hear what you are about hear. Only I have a right to hear what is said in this place."

I suddenly realized Who was speaking to me. "They are coming to Me, not you. Only I can forgive their sins. You are given a great privilege to share in the most intimate moments between Me and My people."

A great peace came over me and a deep sense of awe. I realized in that moment that celebrating the sacrament of reconciliation was not a *job* a priest did, but an awesome responsibility and privilege.

Since that day, I have always loved to celebrate the sacrament of reconciliation. I find that my knowledge of God deepens through being His instrument. I am amazed at the ways God uses me during the sacrament of reconciliation, and the blessing it is to those who approach the sacrament in faith and hope.

Fr. Edward R. Wolanski, CP   *Shelter Island Heights, New York*

"God waits

He waits for our return. 'But I haven't been to confession for fifty years!' The response is simply…'Welcome back! How good it is that you are here!'"

Lessons for Confession

   by Fr. Pat Umberger

see page 171

Supernatural Magnet

I am currently a postulant for the Capuchin Franciscans in Philadelphia, Pennsylvania. Perhaps the happiest day of my life was at the Easter Vigil in 1999 when I converted to Catholicism. It was also one of the most humbling.

After I was baptized, received holy Communion, and was confirmed, I was so full of joy that I literally could not stop smiling. Having never experienced joy like this before, I was blown away. Following the Mass there was a reception for all of us catechumens and our families and friends. We had a little party and then it was time to go home.

As happy as I was, on the ride home I began to feel truly repentant. I had never felt this way before. I recalled that as I was going through RCIA the priest, Father Whalen, told me that I would not have to go to confession. Boy, was I relieved. I had never gone to confession before and it scared me.

When I finally felt the desire to go to confession for the first time, I was at the Franciscan University of Steubenville for a young adult conference. It was my second time there but my first time as a Catholic. I was scared because I had never told anyone about the dark things in my soul. It was time to be accountable, and it was difficult.

I held my breath and walked (practically without looking) under the tent that was used as a makeshift confessional. I sat down in the chair and told the priest my sins. After I was done, and as he gave me absolution, I felt an incredible peace hovering around me that was affecting me in an indescribable way. It was very powerful and very peaceful. It was as if I could literally feel God working inside me. It seemed as if He was a *supernatural magnet* vacuuming out my impurities and filling me with His holy flame. As I walked out from that confession I thought, "Wow! That was awesome!"

I assumed that God would move like that at my next confession, and when He didn't, I was disappointed. But, looking back on it, I now realize God is not a showman performing parlor tricks. He is our living God and always does what is best for our souls.

Craig N. Glantz   *Philadelphia, Pennsylvania*

Second Opinion

It was my forty-something birthday and I phoned my mom to again thank her and my dad (who is deceased) for giving me life. Somewhere in the midst of the conversation she said to me, "And to think I almost didn't have you…" Not sure if I had heard her right, I asked her to repeat what she said. She said it again, and added, "Didn't I ever tell you that?" I explained that I think I would recall such a statement, and she proceeded to tell me the way I came into being.

It was the mid 1950s and she was the mother of six boys. My mom was experiencing some "woman problems" as they said back in those days, and went to see her doctor. He told her that because she was experiencing some bleeding, and since she already had six children, he would schedule a hysterectomy for her. The operation was scheduled to take place a few weeks later in Johnstown, Pennsylvania.

Saturday arrived and Mom decided to go to confession and mention this operation to her parish priest, Father John Callhan. He advised her to seek a second opinion from a Catholic doctor. Mom called my aunt and got the name of a Catholic doctor. At her appointment, this doctor explained how she was not in need of a hysterectomy at all, and a much less invasive procedure was performed to ratify her bleeding problem.

A week or so later when the hospital called to remind my mom of the operation that was scheduled, she canceled it. Then, about a month later I was conceived! I owe my life not only to my parents, but to the sacrament of reconciliation and a good holy priest at St. Charles Catholic Church in the small coal mining town of Twin Rocks, Pennsylvania.

Mary K. Soyka   *Salem, Ohio*

My Thoughts...

The Beatitudes comes immediately to mind. Have I done anything not in accordance with their intent?

A nightly examination of conscience is good. It makes us aware of our need for daily conversion. Also, the two great commandments: Love God, love my neighbor. Have I done anything today not in keeping with those commandments?

I find pride is my biggest sin. It's so easy to get puffed up. A nightly examination of conscience helps me identify where I most need conversion since many of the same faults keep cropping up.

I make a list of what I want to tell the priest before confession. Then it's easy to just hand it to him, and we can discuss whatever.

This works for me. Hopefully it will help others.

Mary Lou Duncan

Just Ask Mom

While raising a family of five children, I found weekly confession of sins a helpful tool. Each Saturday afternoon, we would change into appropriate clothes and go to Our Lady of Fatima Church.

Msgr. Coleman was pastor at the time. Before we entered the church, I suggested to the children that they look over the past week and see what sins they might have committed. In fact, I suggested to them, that if they could not remember their sins, to just ask me and I could remind them.

I know that the sacrament of penance had a powerful influence on our family and our interactions with one another. It motivated the children to be good for another week!

Joanne L. McGoldrick   *Spokane, Washington*

Cafeteria Catholic

I was raised Catholic, but the emphasis in our home was mainly to live a good Christian life. Going to church regularly or following the catechism was optional. Since religion in my family was mostly about showing Christ's love in our actions, I believed I was a devout Catholic because my arms were stretched wide helping people like nobody's business.

I attended Mass when it was convenient, and had committed my career to teaching in the Catholic schools. It was at one of these schools that I met my dear friend Lauren.

Lauren was a strange Catholic in my eyes. She kept telling me about different saints and their stories, using them as examples to lovingly teach me about my faith. I thought she was a little *out there* and kept asking her, "How do you know that story is true?" or "Where did you get that story?" Her patience with me was amazing.

Eventually she started telling me about the holy days of obligation. Like Sunday Mass, those, too, were optional in my opinion. I was not going to be a hypocrite and attend Mass during the week. Besides, my dad told me that going to Mass so everyone can see you is not what makes you holy. It's how you live that makes you holy.

Poor Lauren. Look what she was up against. I was this holier than thou Catholic teacher who knew nothing about our faith and was convinced I didn't need to know it because I was living it. Bless her heart. Lauren did not give up on me.

Lauren gave me Scott and Kimberly Hahn's conversion stories. You'd think that would turn me around wouldn't you? No, they were neat stories, but I was already Catholic.

As we went through the school year, Lauren invited me to begin praying with her after school. That was really pushing it. Prayer is a private thing. Sharing with a friend, whoa! But I agreed because I loved her and knew I needed to do what interested her.

Wow! What a difference that prayer time made. She taught me how to pray the rosary, how to talk to Jesus rather than just God the Father, and how to call on the gifts of the Holy Spirit for help. That did me in. When she got all three persons of God and Mother Mary working with me, my eyes began to open.

Then one day Lauren used the phrase "cafeteria Catholic" in a story she was telling me. I asked, "What is a cafeteria Catholic?" Lauren explained that a cafeteria Catholic is someone who only follows the rules of the Church that he or she agrees with and lets the rest go. Well, I'm a major rule follower and did not at all like the sound of that. So I began asking questions.

We turned to the catechism, we turned to the Bible, we prayed the rosary, and I was convicted big time! I knew that I was indeed a cafeteria Catholic, and until now I had not even known it. It was time to decide. "What will it be Mary, are you Catholic or not?"

I pondered this for months and in the meantime got pregnant. This affected me deeply. Was I going to teach my children to be cafeteria Catholics? My heart began to ache, my anxiety increased, and at the prodding of Lauren, I decided to go to confession at St. Charles.

I was so scared. I wrote everything down. I listed all the individual sins that I could think of, such as my wrong attitude, and the biggest sin of all which was that my husband and I had used birth control for years, even before we were married. That one killed me. Granted, he was my only one, but I had still sinned against God. That my husband is my one and only made it okay? Right? Not!

It was Saturday and approaching 3:00 p.m. I was so nervous that I was shaking. I picked Father Pat as the priest I would confess to. He is so warm and caring that I felt I could talk to him. So, I went in. "Face to face or behind the curtain?" I decided to face him.

He smiled and said, "Sit down, Mary." Before I lost my nerve, I told him that I wrote down a whole list of things, and that I had not been to confession in years. I don't think I took a breath.

Father Pat was so dear. He touched my knee and said, "Let's start with a prayer." We did, and that calmed me. Then he told me to begin my confession.

I read everything. I explained how I was raised Catholic and how I had changed. I told him about my husband and me. I got it all off my chest. You know what? He did not look disappointed, he did not tell me how bad I was, and he did not even call me a huge sinner and tell me to leave the Church forever. "You know what he said?"

"Mary, you have had a conversion. God has drawn you closer to Him and your life is about to change for the better." I was shocked and so relieved that I started to giggle. Father Pat joined me. He was so happy for me.

He gave me my penance, which was to go and live the life of a good and faithful Catholic and to say the Joyful Mysteries for strength and courage. I did, and now both my husband and I are living a Catholic life and raising our children to do the same. My life changed that day, and I give thanks and praise to God for both Lauren and Father Pat.

"Mary"   *Tacoma, Washington*

A Different Light

I grew up as a Protestant, active in my church until I went to college. I never paid much attention to other faiths until I met my husband-to-be.

Joe was a Catholic from a very Catholic community. I began attending church with Joe and tried to learn about his faith. When we got engaged, I decided to join the Church—mainly because it was important to Joe and his family. I believe I joined the Church with my head and not my heart, which is why things began to fall apart shortly after our wedding.

Within a year after our son, Lee, was born, my mother was diagnosed with ovarian cancer. *Suffering had begun.* I was very confused. I got angry at everything and everybody: my husband, the doctors, and God. All I saw everywhere, including the church, was suffering and I couldn't handle it.

I felt that God had abandoned all of us. I quit going to church. My actions and attitudes became full of sin. I emotionally began leaving my marriage and unknowingly went into a deep depression.

In 1997, a few years after my mother's death, I was diagnosed with breast cancer. I hit bottom. I had never been more terrified in my life. Worst of all, I had no faith. When I checked into the hospital for surgery, I was asked what church I attended, what my faith was. I had no answer. I felt abandoned by God, but He was there watching over me, along with my husband, who never left my side.

After surgery, I turned on the TV trying to calm down, and that's when I found the channel with the camera on the crucifix in the chapel at the hospital. I left that channel on all night. Every time I woke up there was a soft glow from the TV filling the room—and there was Jesus on the cross.

I stared at Him and began to see His suffering in a different light. For the first time I started to see within my heart the beauty and love of our crucified Savior on the cross. My life began to change.

My mother-in-law gave me a tape of the rosary that Joe and I played and prayed together whenever the fear set in.

During this time, I experienced one of the greatest healings of all, through the sacrament of reconciliation. I had only gone to confession once, when I first joined the church fifteen years previously. As a Protestant I had been taught that all I had to do was to tell God I was sorry for my sins, and He would forgive me. I had been doing that over and over since my surgery, but I couldn't stop feeling guilty for the many, many sins of my past.

Finally, I made an appointment to see our priest, Father Daniel Conlon, now bishop of Steubenville, to celebrate the sacrament of reconciliation in his office. Before my confession, I wrote down everything I could think of then, even though I dreaded facing Father with my embarrassing sins. I felt this push from the Holy Spirit, and I couldn't stop. I poured out my past amidst tears and Kleenex. Father counseled me, and then he stood up, laid hands on me and prayed over me. He told me that in the name of Jesus, my sins were forgiven. I felt numb as I left his office.

In the days ahead, I became aware that a change was happening. Every time I would begin to think about the past, my thoughts immediately would turn to something else. Later, I would realize that I had not spent any time thinking about my guilt or my sins. Thoughts and feelings that I couldn't seem to control before were being cleansed completely from my mind. My past was being lifted once and for all!

Linda L. Lochtefeld   *New Bremen, Ohio*

A Spiritual Maintenance Agreement

By Vinny Flynn

If I were to ask you what confession is, what would you say?

My guess is that, for many people, the first thing that comes to mind is *forgiveness of sins.*

And I think that's a problem. Yes, confession leads to forgiveness of sins. *But it's more than that.*

Confession is a *sacrament*—which means it was instituted by Christ to give grace.

I learned that a long time ago, but then I forgot it, and I keep forgetting it. We shouldn't be going to confession just for forgiveness of specific sins. We should be going *to receive grace.*

Many of us are in the habit of waiting to go to confession until we have committed serious sin, and then we go to get it forgiven.

Through most of my life, I would only go to confession when I suddenly realized that I needed it because I had lapsed into specific sin. "Oops, I blew it again. I have to go to confession."

Not a "repair job"

I think most of us tend to view confession the same way we view taking our car to the garage for a repair job. We think that confession is when we need a major overhaul. We're not running right, so we have to get "fixed."

We should instead be thinking of confession as "maintenance." *Confession should be an oil change.*

I remember when I got my first nice car. It was only two years old, and it only had 12,000 miles on it. One of my friends said, "Let me tell you something. No matter what else you do, change the oil every 3,000 miles, and that car will keep running."

And I have found that to be true.

Our maintenance agreement with Christ

If you've bought any major appliances lately, you were probably offered a "maintenance agreement."

It costs you extra, but, with a maintenance agreement, when things go wrong, you can have them fixed. Sometimes the agreement covers parts only, and sometimes it's free parts and labor.

I like to think of confession as part of our maintenance agreement with Christ.

We come with a lifetime warranty. And if anything ever goes wrong, Christ will replace everything free. Parts and labor. Everything's free. Forever. That's our maintenance agreement. And it doesn't cost us a nickel more.

All we have to do is take advantage of that. We come to confession as a part of that maintenance agreement.

If you buy a new car, the maintenance agreement on it is something like 50,000 miles or five years, whichever comes first. But, this agreement only deals with factory defects or things that go wrong in the normal course of events. If you *abuse* the product, you've ruined the warranty.

God even lets us abuse the product. He still fulfills the lifetime warranty. But, in a practical sense, what is necessary is the same thing we find in an automobile agreement: *there are certain required times for regular maintenance.*

A manufacturer knows that if you don't ensure regular maintenance for the product, it's going to break—and then the company has to fix it according to the warranty. So you have to adhere to regular schedule *of preventative maintenance.*

Preventative maintenance

Just from checking the oil, you can see over a period of time that, even if the car is running fine, impurities slip in. They mix with the oil, and the oil gets heavy and thick and dark, and it just doesn't do the job as well. So eventually, the car doesn't run as well and it wears out faster.

But, if you put *fresh* oil in every 3,000 miles and replace the oil filter, you remove the impurities before they create serious problems.

Let's compare this concept with confession. Let's say we have no "mortal" impurities. We are still "running" fine, nothing is "broken"—but the little impurities are steadily building up, and we are gradually wearing ourselves out.

Just as with an oil change, we should go to confession "every 3,000 miles"—that is, regularly!

I remember how surprised I was when I first read that Pope John Paul II goes to confession once a week!

Now I don't know about you, but I am in awe of that man's holiness. It just amazes me!

And *he* goes to confession once a week. Why? Because he puts a lot of miles on! Even literally. So he goes to confession regularly to keep the "oil" of his life pure—to get a fresh injection of the "new life" of grace.

I know that, at certain times, I need to go to confession more often than at others, or else I start to feel a little dusty, grimy, gritty. Things just aren't quite right.

If I don't take advantage of that period of time when there's nothing serious, but I'm just aware of the fact that "the oil needs changing"—that's when sin is going to come in, and then I'm going to need a repair job.

Built-up sin

What we tend to do when we go to confession is confess our *sins*—but not the *root* of the sin. So our sins are forgiven, but what caused us to sin has not been healed. We think that the *sin* is what the problem is. But it's not. The problem is *what's been building up in us* in terms of our attitudes, our habits, our sinfulness, our weakness, our human condition, that needs *regular infusions of God's*

15

SPIRITUAL MAINTENANCE

grace.

We need to look deeper, asking the Holy Spirit, "Come in. Probe my heart. Reveal to me what the *real* problems are. What are the things that lead to sin? What are the attitudes? Where do I need mercy most? Where do I need healing? What are the things in me at a deep level that need to be healed?"

We need that kind of "regular maintenance," so that we don't reach the point where there is a big fall from grace.

Go frequently

The Catechism of the Catholic Church (1458) says, "Without being strictly necessary, confession of everyday faults [venial sins] is nevertheless strongly recommended by the Church. Indeed, *the regular confession* of our venial sins helps us form our conscience, fight against evil tendencies, let ourselves be healed by Christ, and progress in the life of the Spirit."

Next follows the responsibility that comes *out* of Confession. "By receiving more frequently through this sacrament the gift of the Father's mercy, we are spurred to be merciful as He is merciful."

Regular frequent confession, even if we have no mortal sin, is thus strongly recommended by the Church, so that we can become merciful as our Heavenly Father is merciful—and continue to run smoothly, mile after mile, as our Maker intended.

A Spiritual Maintenance Agreement © *Congregation of Marians of the Immaculate Conception, Stockbridge, MA 01263. www.marian.org. Used with permission.*

Won't Go to Confession

I am a priest in the Diocese of Plymouth in England, and for seven years I was the Catholic chaplain in a rather large local hospital there. One day as I was visiting patients, a man told me he did not want to see me. I said, "Okay, that is all right." Each day as I passed his bed, I would greet him and then walk on.

On one occasion he called me and said, "Listen, if I wanted to receive the sacraments again after more than sixty years, I know I would have to go to confession and I cannot do that." I assured him that going to confession would be quite easy, and that I would ask him the questions. We talked for a long time and finally he said he would go to confession. I made an appointment for him for three days later.

The following day as I passed his bed he called to me and said, "Sorry, but I cannot possibly tell you what I have been doing all these years. I won't go to confession."

I sat at the foot of his bed and asked him, "What are you afraid to tell me?"

To my amazement, he told me about all the sins he thought he could not tell in two or three days' time! When he finished talking, I asked him, "Is there anything else you have to tell me?"

He said, "No, that is everything."

I asked him if he was truly sorry for all these faults and failings because he had now confessed everything! Then I told him about God's love for him and for all of us. I gave him absolution and anointed him. He was so happy!

The next day when I went to the hospital, I was informed that the man had died during the night. All I could say was, "God is so great! His love is beyond understanding."

Daniel A. Longland   *Sidmouth, Devon, England*

A Special Memory

St. Peter's Church has been my home since I became Catholic almost six years ago. However, my story begins a few years before that.

In 1996, my best friend and her family moved to Beaufort, South Carolina. It was during my visits to see her that I attended Mass and became familiar with St. Peter's Parish. As I look back now, I can see that every time I attended Mass, I was being called home. I remember knowing in my heart that I would become Catholic if I ever decided to move from Illinois to South Carolina.

At the age of twenty-nine, I bravely traveled 900 miles, with my cat as my only companion, and arrived in Beaufort on August 31, 1999. Although I did not have a job or a home to call my own, I was eager to start my life anew.

In the spring of 2000, five months after I arrived, I celebrated my first Communion and confirmation at the Easter Vigil Mass. At that point in my life, I was feeling unloved and unworthy. I had been struggling hard to see myself as God sees me, and I was seeking a deeper understanding of His love. I was also trying to grasp our Blessed Mother's love for me.

One day after receiving the sacrament of reconciliation, I had an experience I'll never forget. Like all my other confessions, once I was absolved and out of the confessional, I felt lightness within me. Then I prayed my penance as I knelt in front of our beautiful crucifix. The memory of what happened afterwards has never left me and I pray that it never will.

St. Peter's has a beautiful icon of Mary, and I had always wanted to kneel in prayer in front of it, but I had never had the courage to do so because I didn't know if there was a certain code of behavior for doing this. I was afraid of making any mistakes, and I let fear of the unknown keep me from what I now know is a simple process.

As I knelt in front of my Lord after confession on that unforgettable day, I felt called to Mary. I went to her statue, lit a candle and then knelt in prayer. As I was praying, I began to feel the loving arms of Mary wrap around me. I felt her loving embrace and was made aware of how real she is in my life. It was with Mary's hug that I began to see just how much she will help me draw ever closer to her Son and my Lord, Jesus Christ.

I still have struggles and weaknesses, but I will continue to be blessed by the sacrament of reconciliation for as long as I live.

Amanda S. Abbott   *Beaufort, South Carolina*

Time to Return

My last reconciliation had occurred prior to Vatican II. Back then we always confessed our sins to the priest in a darkened confessional. The sound of the sliding window signaled the time for me to shed the usual minor sins of youth. Confession terrified me, not so much because of the darkness of the confessional, but because of the darkness hidden within me.

College in the tumultuous 1960s came along and I was drawn away from my faith. To me, the Church was little more than a building without any real human or spiritual connection. I became convinced that the Catholic Church had little to offer me and drifted away. I went on to pursue my education, a successful career, and the many distractions of the world.

More than three decades passed. I married outside the Catholic Church and despite our intrinsic spirituality, my husband and I rejected church, and all that seemed irrelevant to us.

We had a good life and traveled abroad frequently, appreciating the world from its multiple perspectives. Curiously, in our travels I found myself exploring cathedrals and chapels, pretending that I was just admiring the flying buttresses and stained glass windows. I never dared to admit that what I was really admiring was the faith and passion that could build such things. I also never dared to admit that I was seeking faith and a passionate relationship with the Lord for myself.

It eventually became abundantly clear that it was time for me to return to God. The Catholic Church was familiar and comfortable, and that was where I was being called to return.

Much had changed in the Church during the decades I had been away. I spent weeks looking for the right parish and a priest to whom I thought I might be able to go to fill in those lapses. A kindly bishop literally half a world away directed me to a local parish.

I scoured the internet for advice on how to go about making a good confession. I spent days and sleepless nights examining my conscience and dutifully prepared a list so I wouldn't forget my sins from more than thirty years. What became painfully clear was that I had committed the greatest sin of all. I had turned my back on God.

Not knowing what to expect or even how to actually go about a formal reconciliation at the dawn of the twenty-first century, I waited anxiously in line. It brought back all of those childhood memories of Saturday confessions from so long ago.

The first word I heard from Father Jim when I entered was "Peace." Gradually I settled in and recounted my general sins from the last thirty-plus years. Then it was time for the *big one*.

I had a conversation with the good priest, telling him how I had rejected God all those years. He absolved my sins and blessed me, and ended with gentle encouragement. He told me that I had made his day by laying all the sins of my adult life before him and expressed his joy that I had returned to the Church.

I was relieved that the priest did not act as though my story was unique or horrendous, and was happy that I had recognized the genuine nature of my greatest sin. Both of these points contributed to me having made a good confession.

My penance was to say a prayer for my non-Catholic husband who would have much adjusting to do as I recommitted myself to a life in which God was now the center.

Later that day I realized it was the feast of Christ the King, and the last Sunday of the Year of the Eucharist. Since then, every year I celebrate that feast day as the anniversary of my rebirth.

Candice Francis   *Escondido, California*

Walking on Air

When I was a child, I attended Immaculate Conception grammar school in Rochester, New York, where we were encouraged to go to confession weekly. Father Wood was the dynamic pastor at the time, and he and the other parish priests, Father Dunn, Father Roach, and Monsignor Cameron, were loved by all the children.

We lived about a mile or so from the school, and had to walk there and back four times a day. One Saturday, my mother told me to walk to church for confession. I did as she said, but when I got there I was so scared that I turned around and walked back home. Mother told me to go back to confession, which I did. When I arrived back at the church and talked to the priest, he was so understanding, patient, and kind that I felt as if I were walking on air when I left. I realized then that I didn't need to be afraid of confession after all.

I also fondly remember the nuns walking us over to church from the school and staying with us as each child went to confession. As I think back on it now, it was a wonderful experience to see long lines of children, each waiting to see one of the priests, and then to see the smiles on their faces as they returned to their seats.

Joan M. Beebe   *Rochester, New York*

"Mortal sin is a serious break in a relationship of love with God, neighbor, world and self. We can think of it as a radical no to God and to others. It happens when we refuse to live in a positive, life-giving way. Just as acts of heroism and extraordinary generosity are evidence of our capacity to say a radical yes to God, so calculated acts permeated with malice are evidence of our capacity to say no to God."

Understanding Sin Today

by Richard M. Gula, S.S.

see page 31

Thirty Day Penance

I believe the sacrament of reconciliation is the perfect way to obtain freedom from the state of sin and to become one with God. How fortunate for me that my first experiences of confession were positive and made me feel good. I knew from early on that going to confession was an uplifting sacrament, and knowing this helped me through an especially challenging time in my life.

As an adult, I experienced some very sinful emotions that changed my life and spirituality for a while. Before that point, I never would have dreamed that I could become so enraged about something that it would take over my life and emotions.

It all started when my ex-daughter-in-law was in our family and her behavior and actions infuriated me. My first response was to act with the three sins of anger: revenge, retaliation, and resentment. Morally I knew these thoughts and actions were wrong, but nevertheless, anger was a constant companion of mine. I tried very hard to turn things around and did all I could to make the situation better, but my efforts proved futile.

I knew I had to confess all that I was doing wrong. I was so torn from the griping emotions of guilt, fear, and anger that I could not think of a better way to find peace than through the sacrament of reconciliation. From my childhood experiences, I knew confession would help make me feel better and that I would be in a better state of grace afterwards.

The wonderful priest who heard my confession sensed the fear in my voice and helped calm me. Then, after I got through my list of sins, he wisely knew exactly how to help me return to a state of peace.

As I waited for my penance, I imagined that I would probably have to say several Hail Mary's, or maybe even the rosary. I said, "So, what do I have to do, say the rosary for my penance?" His answer was not what I expected. It was not even close.

The priest said I had to pray for thirty days for my ex-daughter-in-law. My response was, "I can't do that." He replied, "Oh, but you will."

"But when I pray it won't mean anything because it won't be sincere." I told him.

"You will pray for her every time you pray for yourself and your family. At first it will not mean anything to you, it will be just a formality. Eventually you will find that you will truly mean it and want peace for her," he said.

I still had my doubts but I did pray my penance every day. It was the most difficult prayer I ever had to do. At first, praying for her was meaningless. Then, about two and a half weeks into this penance, I began to express meaning in my prayers.

To my complete surprise, I actually began to truly want my ex-daughter-in-law to find peace in her life. I wanted her to be rid of her anger and control. I wanted her to find the God of her understanding, to have God shine in her heart and soul. It was a unique and great experience to sincerely love her without anger.

Lucy O. Scholerman   *Bay City, Oregon*

Monthly Cleaning

After reading about confession on Sister Patricia's web site, reconciliation was fresh on my mind. I had been thinking that it was about time I went to confession again when one Saturday morning the Lord taught me a little something about the sacrament right in my kitchen.

My coffee pot had been dripping very slowly because I had been procrastinating cleaning it.

I knew I needed to take some action, so I found the instructions and started reading. All of a sudden I felt the Lord speaking to me, showing me my own need for cleaning.

The instructions read: "Descaling—We recommend that you descale your coffee maker once a month because mineral deposits can form a coating in the coffee maker, causing slower brewing time and possibly an off flavor in the coffee. Use a cleaner recommended for coffee makers. Wash the carafe and filter with soapy hot water." That was it! The instructions were simple!

I, too, need to be descaled and cleared of those gunky deposits that build up in my life and in my heart. As I clean my coffee pot monthly with water and vinegar, I will be reminded to clean my spiritual coffee pot in the great sacrament of reconciliation.

Often the Lord uses everyday things to teach me, making His will clear for me. On that Saturday morning, in my family kitchen, I learned more than just how to clean a slow dripping coffee pot.

Jane M. Adams   *Fitchburg, Wisconsin*

The Box

As a child I dreaded going to confession. It was always a fearful time as I examined my conscience and wondered, "Am I confessing all my sins? Will I forget some serious sin? Will God punish me if I don't do it right?" I only felt relief when it was over, and I could breathe easier until the next time. I would liken it to a trip to the dentist.

Sadly, I carried this fear into my adult years. I matured, but the sacrament of reconciliation remained a thorn in my side. I found myself attending Mass but avoiding *the box*. Along the way I met some wonderful priests who talked to me and calmed my fears. I slowly began to see this time as a special gift of God's grace. After Vatican II, I began confessing face to face when the opportunity arose. I perceived this as a visible help for me to overcome my bad habits and serious faults.

A few years ago when I was visiting relatives in Boston I would often stop by the Arch St. Chapel to pray or attend Mass. One day I decided to go to confession while making a visit. It had been a long time since I had received this sacrament. I expected a reprimand for being away for so long and a very long penance. Instead all I heard was, "I just want to tell you how much God loves you."

I started crying and instantly felt sorrow, peace, and the knowledge that this is what the sacrament is meant to be. I can't remember the rest of what the priest said but I was so grateful to him for showing me the forgiveness that comes from God through this sacrament.

Suzanne Ching   *Honolulu, Hawaii*

What a Beautiful Gift

When I first started thinking of converting from the Southern Baptist Church to Catholicism, I visited a small parish and had a nice talk with the pastor, Father Sullivan.

I was struggling because my family was against my converting. None of them were Catholic. Finally, after three years, I attended RCIA at St. Mathews in Jacksonville, Florida, taught by Father Brian Carey. I loved RCIA and Father Carey was wonderful.

In the spring of 1990, our RCIA class was preparing for our first reconciliation. I was incredibly nervous. We went to Marywood, in Switzerland, Florida. My sponsor was Mrs. Mary Korson, founder of the St. Francis Soup Kitchen at Immaculate Conception in Jacksonville.

We were standing in line. I felt twenty-three years of sins burning through my brain. I was convinced the priest hearing confessions would hear all my many sins and be horrified. I was sure my penance would be doing the Stations of the Cross seventeen times!

When I entered the confessional, I was too chicken to use the screen. I whispered, "May we do this face-to-face?" I was then warmly greeted by none other than the friendly Father Sullivan I'd met three years before!

After Confession, I stepped out, crying from relief. I felt that the weight of the world had been lifted from my shoulders. I felt so *clean* and light! My sponsor was waiting for me with a big smile on her face.

I thought of how my non-Catholic family had tried to discourage me from converting. I burst out, "After this, I can't understand why *everybody* doesn't want to be Catholic!"

My sponsor cracked up. Years later, as I reflect on that day, and think of the wonderful lightness I experienced for the first time and still feel every time I go to confession, I have to say, "What a beautiful gift God has given us in confession!"

Susan M. Barber   *Jacksonville, Florida*

A Beautiful Card

It was 1981, and I was feeling a call in my heart to seek God. My husband was a fallen away Catholic and I was a non-practicing Methodist, pregnant with our first child.

That spring we went to Easter Mass at St. Catherine's Parish in Quarryville, Pennsylvania. Before Mass began, my husband decided to go to confession. Father Thomas Gralinski heard his confession and told my husband to see him after Mass. They talked, and we soon started meeting with Father Gralinski once a week at the rectory to learn more about our faith. My husband and I have been going to Mass ever since.

When I was pregnant with my third child in 1991, I started thinking deeply about parenthood. My dad died in a trucking accident when I was nineteen years old and I couldn't help but wonder if I would live long enough to see my own children married, and if I would be able to share in the lives of my grandchildren. I prayed that I would.

Shortly thereafter I read a Scripture that gave the promise of a long life to those who honor their father and mother. That Scripture settled into my soul. I had always honored my father when he was alive, but felt there was a wall between my mother and myself.

I was convinced that my mother favored my three brothers. Even though there were times that I didn't feel this way, I always refused to give her loving cards on her birthday and for Mother's Day. The words in those sentimental cards were not how I felt about her in my heart. Although I always loved my mom, after reading that Scripture I knew I was not honoring her.

I went to confession and told Father Gralinski that I was unable to honor my mother as I truly should. Afterwards, it felt as if a heavy weight had been lifted off my heart.

A few weeks later, I was totally surprised when I received a beautiful card from my mom letting me know how much she loved me, and how proud she was to have me as her daughter. Not long after that, the two of us shared lunch together and she told me about the relationship she'd had with her mother. It was not a loving one and I believe it had a subconscious effect on the two of us and how we got along with each other.

God healed my relationship with my mother after I went to confession that unforgettable day. We are very close today, and I can happily say that I can now choose loving cards to send her and that they truly say what I mean with my whole heart.

I never told my mom about my confession that brought healing to our relationship. She was raised to not trust Catholics and was upset when I became one. Over the last twenty-four years though, she has come to accept my family's spiritual commitment to God. Although she believes in God, she has not made a connection to a church. I continue to share our faith with her whenever possible and keep her close in my prayers.

Darlene E. Graver   *Strasburg, Pennsylvania*

A Heavy Burden

As I write this, I have tears streaming down my face; these are tears of joy and gratitude.

Reconciliation?

The Lord had been working overtime on me for the last several years. But my addictions of pornography, lies, and self-importance—won me back almost every time.

On the feast of the Conversion of St. Paul two years ago, He did to me what He did to Saul. God knocked me down from my high horse. My marriage was in trouble.

Driving to my office that morning, I was listening to the radio and happened to tune in to a Catholic radio station, The Station of the Cross, in Rochester, New York. EWTN's Mass broadcast had just started.

As I listened to the readings, the Lord touched my heart. He helped me to see my life and how far I was from Him. I cried like a child in my car. As I was parking, sobbing like an infant, I resolved to find my Ananias.*

Father Peter Abas, a priest at St. Anne's in Rochester, was the first and only priest I could think of. I left voice and e-mail messages asking if he could see me that night.

We played phone tag throughout the day. Father Peter thought if the Holy Spirit wants it, he will come. At six-thirty that night, I got into my car trusting the Lord would lead me to see Father Peter. At seven o'clock, I drove into St. Anne's parking area. Father Peter was waiting and hoping that I would come.

We went into one of the small private rooms in the rectory, and I knelt down and asked Father Peter to hear my confession. I started by telling how heavy the burden was on my soul. My tears were a cleansing flood, as I recounted, amidst sobs, all my sins. It seemed as if my confession lasted almost an hour. Like the Prodigal Son, I told my Father I was not worthy to be called His son.

Father Peter took a clean sheet of paper, crumpled it in his hands, opened it, and said, "See how ugly this is?" I responded, "Yes, it is a very messy looking paper."

Opening it up, he said, "Look at the lines here, and here, and here— don't they look nice? This is how God sees you—so pleasing to Him that He can only love you." And of course, I cried some more, a mixture of joy and shame in my tears. Joy because He did love me and did not throw me away from His sight, and shame for rejecting Him from my life.

When I received absolution, my soul felt light, and I started to see a new path. Unlike Saul, my eyes did not see everything immediately. But He showed me enough to help me walk home to Him.

Leodones Yballe   *Rochester, New York*

[In the story of Saint Paul, Saul (as he was then called) is knocked off of his horse and blinded by a flash of light. A voice speaks to him saying, "Saul, Saul, why are you persecuting me?" Saul is totally blown away and he says, "Who are you, Lord?" and Jesus answers, "I am Jesus whom you are persecuting." As the story proceeds, Jesus advises Saul to go into the town where he will find a man named Ananias who will cure him.]

My Thoughts...

It's quite possible that a person who is striving to live a truly Christian life may not have any sins to confess from week to week or month to month.

In that case one might mention failings against the virtue of humility. Against that virtue every human being fails at least to some slight degree every day.

Also include some sin (already forgiven) for which one is especially sorry. That is important to assure the validity of the sacrament (No sin, no sacrament).

Fr. Daniel Raible, C.PP.S.

Understanding Sin Today

By Richard M. Gula, S.S.

"Bless me, Father, for I have sinned. It has been six weeks since my last confession. I lost my patience three times; I lied twice; I missed Mass once; I had impure thoughts twice and I gossiped about my neighbor four times."

Sound familiar? The above confession reflects an understanding of the moral life and sin that prevailed among Roman Catholics for centuries. But in the last half of this century, many changes have been occurring in the way we think about morality and sin. These changes have resulted in part from new ways of understanding what it means to be human. They also come from rediscovering old ideas that the Bible and Jesus taught about how we ought to relate to God and to one another.

Sin as crime

There was a time when Catholics thought that living morally was mostly a matter of obeying the law—the divine law or the commandments of God, the ecclesial (Church) laws or the natural laws expressed in the moral teaching of the Church. "It's in the Bible" or "The Church says so" were often our most important reasons for being moral.

Sin was like a crime, a transgression of the law. It was akin to breaking the speed limit on the highway. The law is what made an action sinful. Where there was no clear-cut law (no speed limit), there was no question of sin (go as fast as you want).

Catholic theology has since come to realize that the legal model for understanding the moral life and sin is deficient. For one thing, the demands of being a faithful follower of Jesus, of living according to the vision and values of the gospel, stretch us farther than what can be prescribed by law.

But no one is trying to do away with laws. We know that laws will always be necessary to help us live together well. Just as our city streets would be chaos without traffic laws, so our living together would be a moral chaos without laws like those about telling the truth, respecting property and protecting life.

But laws cannot possibly cover all the decisions that we have to make. The legal model of the moral life too easily makes moral living a matter of repeating the same old behaviors even though we—and our world—have changed. The legal model also tends to focus too much on the actions that we do as being sinful or not. Did I miss Mass? Did I cheat on an exam or on my taxes? Did I disobey my parents?

Laws by themselves don't address the important realities of the heart, such as our attitudes (Are we kind or hostile?), intentions (Do we strive to be helpful or self-serving?) and ways of seeing things (Do we look through the eyes of faith? Are we optimistic or pessimistic?). Jesus reminds us that what comes from the heart is what makes one sinful. Sinful actions are like the tip of an iceberg being held above the surface by a wayward heart (see Is 29:13; Mk 7:21; Mt 23:25-26; Lk 6:45).

The legal model also tends to make the moral life too centered on one's self. Sin affects me and my salvation. Saving my soul through obedience is the guiding moral principle according to this model. This leaves out, however, the all-important relational dimensions of sin and conversion. As St. Paul teaches, no one lives for oneself (Rom 14:7). As the Body of Christ, we suffer together and rejoice together (1 Cor 12:26-27). Because we share a common world, we are part of a network of relationships that joins each of us in responsibility to others and to all of creation. We all know that we violate the ecological balance of nature when we put toxins into our air and water or throw hamburger foil wrappers out the car window. We violate our moral ecology when we create discord, dissension, fear, mistrust and alienation in the web of life's relationships.

Sin's new look

A new look at the moral life has been informed by the biblical renewal in the Church and by some philosophical shifts within the Church and society.

For example, the biblical renewal has given us covenant, heart and conversion—not law—as our primary moral concepts. Responsibility has replaced obligation as the primary characteristic of the moral life. Shifts in philosophy have emphasized the dignity of persons and the value of sharing life in society. Together these shifts in theology and philosophy support a relational model of the moral life. The relational model emphasizes personal responsibility for protecting the bonds of peace and justice that sustain human relationships.

What might a contemporary confession sound like that reflects the relational model of the moral life?

"Bless me, Father, for I have sinned. It has been six weeks since my last confession. I am a husband, a father of three teenage children, and I hold an executive position in a large computer firm.

"Over the past month I have allowed love to grow cold at home and in my work. At home, I have been inattentive to my wife and children as I allowed my new projects at work to consume most of my time and attention. I have spent more time at work and little time with the family. At work, I have selfishly neglected to disclose some data which my colleagues needed for a new project. I wanted to gain the glory. I have also failed to support a female colleague who was clearly being sexually harassed and I failed to confront those who were doing the harassing.

"I think a good penance for me, Father, would be to take the family on a picnic this week and to make a special effort to affirm my junior colleagues for the great work they have been doing."

This penitent senses how he is affecting the quality of life and love in his primary relationships. He also knows what he can do to show conversion. His confession reflects contemporary theology's emphasis on responsibility to others over the traditional overemphasis on what is allowed or forbidden by law. Rather than focusing just on committing sinful acts, it shows that sin is also an omission, a

UNDERSTANDING SIN TODAY

failure to do what ought to be done.

Far from doing away with sin, contemporary theology admits that sin is very much with us and touches us more deeply than we realize. Greed, violence, corruption, poverty, hunger, sexism and oppression are too prevalent to ignore.

Sin is just as basic a term in our Christian vocabulary today as it has been in the past. Its root sense means to be disconnected from God through the failure to love. In sin, we simply don't bother about anyone outside ourselves. Sin is first a matter of a selfish heart—a refusal to care—before it shows itself in actions. Because loving God and loving our neighbor are all tied together, sin will always be expressed in and through our relationships.

The Catechism of the Catholic Church affirms that, just as the least of our acts done in charity has some benefit for all, so every sin causes some harm. The catechism quotes Scripture to make this point: "None of us lives for oneself, and none of us dies for oneself" (Rom 14:7); "If one member suffers, all suffer together; if one member is honored, all rejoice together. Now you are the body of Christ and individually members of it" (1 Cor 12:26-27); "Charity does not insist on its own way" (1 Cor 13:5; see 10:24). In this solidarity with all people, says the catechism, "living or dead, which is founded on the communion of saints, the least of our acts done in charity redounds to the profit of all. Every sin harms this communion" (#953).

One of the most obvious changes in a contemporary approach to sin is the emphasis given to how sin affects the quality of life and love in our relationships. Sin is any action or omission that hinders, violates or breaks right relationships which support human well-being. For example, if I spread gossip or fail to correct a false rumor about a co-worker, I am not only failing in my relationship to that person, but also impairing the quality of life in the workplace.

My favorite example of how this relational vision of sin and the moral life influenced another's behavior came from my five-year-old niece, Julia. She listened to a conversation I was having with her eight-year-old sister about what she was being taught in her preparation for first penance. The lesson on sin was filled with stories of relationships and the difference between loving and unloving choices. The next day, when Julia came home from kindergarten, I asked her how her day was. She said, "I had a good day." When I asked her what made it good, she said, "I had an opportunity to make a loving choice. Kenny forgot to bring a snack today, so I gave him one of my pretzels."

Julia learned quite well that right moral living begins with caring for one another: paying attention to another's needs and acting in a way that enhances another's well-being. Sin, by contrast, turns in and sets oneself against another. Self-serving interests destroy the bonds of peace and justice that ought to sustain us.

Original sin didn't go away

In an age when evils on a massive scale frequently make front-page news (wars, ethnic genocide, bombings, terrorism), theologians are trying to revive the doctrine of original sin. This doctrine tells us that there is more evil in the world than that which we cause ourselves. Consider the children being born in Rwanda or Bosnia today. They are affected and infected by the evil that surrounds them before they are ever able to make choices of their own.

Original sin is the face of sin which we recognize as the condition of evil into which we are all born. It is a condition of being human that makes us feel as if our freedom were bound by chains from the very beginning. We feel the effects of this evil in the pull towards selfishness which alienates us from our deeper selves, from others and from God. Because of original sin, we will always know struggle and tragedy as part of our life.

While the power of original sin pulls us in the direction of selfishness and aloofness, the power of grace moves us to be for others and to live mutually dependent on one another. The film Schindler's List shows how Oskar Schindler witnessed to this power of grace in the way he saved thousands of Jews from the death camps. So did the many unnamed heroines and heroes who helped the victims of the bombing of the Oklahoma City federal building in 1995. So do those who open their homes to refugees of war and poverty.

In order to rise above the power of evil, we need to open ourselves to the presence of redeeming love. This love comes to us through others witnessing to justice, truth and peace. While the presence of original sin may make responsible moral living a truly demanding task, the presence of redeeming love makes it possible. This is the sense of St. Paul's conviction that while sin abounds, grace abounds even more (Rom 5:20).

Social sin—a life of its own

Social sin has been around as long as civilization, but it is a relatively new concept for Catholics. We have tended to focus exclusively on personal (actual) sin: lying, cheating, missing Mass. We have not paid sufficient attention to social structures and customs which hold such sinful practices in place. We are changing, however. One clear example of a rising social consciousness can be seen in Pope John Paul II's 1995 "Letter to Women." Here he publicly acknowledges sexism as a social sin and then goes on to apologize to women for the ways the Church has complied in denigrating women, misrepresenting them, reducing them to servitude and marginalizing them from society.

Social sin describes human-made structures when they offend human dignity by causing people to suffer oppression, exploitation or marginalization. These include educational systems, housing policies, tax structures, immigration policies, health-care systems, employment policies, a market economy. Once established, social structures and customs seem to take on a life of their own. The social sin of racism, for example, has continued and still continues long after slavery was abolished. For example, there remain obstacles to adequate education, to housing, to work, sometimes even to voting.

We learn to live in a world with these structures. We presume that the social customs which they hold in place are good, traditional customs. That is what makes social sin so difficult to recognize and to change. Yet the evil of sinful social structures abounds in all forms of discrimination, racism and sexism; in the exploitation of migrant workers; in the illiteracy and homelessness of the poor; in the lack of basic health care for all; in the manipulation of consumers by the manufacturing practices, advertising, pricing policies and packaging of goods; and in many other practices which we continue to support more out of ignorance than meanness. Why does social sin prevail? Largely because we fail to name social evils and seek to correct them.

Christianity could easily adopt the motto of Missouri: "Show me." It is not enough to talk a good game. The moral teachings of the prophets (see Is 58:6-8) and of Jesus (see the Sermon on the Mount, Mt 5—7) tell us that faith and piety without active commitment to justice are not what God wants.

When we become aware of structural evils, we should not be paralyzed by the guilt of self-condemnation, but moved to conversion. Conversion from social sin involves, at one level, changing our own lifestyle in ways that will help reform society. We cannot do everything to end the structures which support sexism, for example, but we can do some things, for instance, curbing our use of exclusive and insensitive language. We can influence others' attitudes through the ways we talk to and about one another. At another level, conversion from social sin involves examining existing regulations and practices, reforming those that offend human dignity.

Actual sin—we all know it

Another face of sin is personal sin. Our traditional way of distinguishing the degrees of gravity of personal sins is to call them mortal and venial sins.

Catholics traditionally have been taught that for sin to be mortal, three conditions have to be met: 1) serious matter; 2) sufficient reflection; 3) full consent of the will. These are still valuable criteria. They are comprehensive in including conditions which pertain to the action (1) and to the person (2 & 3) before we can speak of mortal sin in its truest sense.

The relational model of the moral life helps us to understand actual sin as primarily an expression of the person in relationship, not simply as disobedience to the law.

Mortal sin. Mortal sin is a serious break in a relationship of love with God, neighbor, world and self. We can think of it as a radical *no* to God and to others. It happens when we refuse to live in a positive, life-giving way. Just as acts of heroism and extraordinary generosity are evidence of our capacity to say a radical *yes* to God, so calculated acts permeated with malice are evidence of our capacity to say *no* to God. Mortal sin involves a moral evil done by a person who is supremely selfish and committed to making evil and not goodness the characteristic mark of his or her life.

While we would not be surprised to find mortal sin in those who choose to make crime, extortion or greed a way of life, we must still be wary of judging another. No one can ever know for sure just by looking from the sidelines whether a particular act of malice is a mortal sin or not. We need to know more about the person's knowledge, freedom and fundamental disposition before God. We must refrain from judging others as being in mortal sin, even though we know their acts are permeated with evil. That is why the Church has never taught that anyone is, in fact, in hell. At the same time the Church acknowledges that we all have the capacity to cut ourselves off from the source of life that is God, which is a good description of hell.

Venial sin. These days people are not giving enough attention to immoral acts of less importance than mortal sin. If mortal sin radically reverses one's positive relationship to God, the habit of unloving acts can corrode that relationship. This is why we must take venial sins seriously. Venial sins can weigh us down with the anchor of bad habits.

Venial sin often enters our lives when we fail to show care for others. People can easily become submerged in self-interest. Perhaps we speak sharply to another, revel in our piece of gossip or exercise a power play over another that keeps us secure and in control. While these acts of selfish arrogance do not radically turn us away from God, they are inconsistent with our basic commitment to be for life and for love. They are venial sins.

Contemporary notions of sin emphasize the gospel's call to conversion in and through the web of life's relationships. The more clearly we can recognize God's presence and love in these relationships, the more clearly we can recognize our venial sins, and the more seriously we can take them. Without recognizing our sinfulness, we cannot grow in converting to the demands of love.

God is merciful

These are only some of the significant changes in our understanding of sin. We are talking about sin differently today because the relational model of the moral life has replaced the legal model. One thing that hasn't changed, though, is our concept of God's love and mercy. We do not believe that God wants us to be weighed down with a distorted sense of guilt and responsibility. Rather, we believe that we are called to participate more fully in the creative power of God calling us to reconciliation, to reconnect with our best selves, with others, with the world and with God.

The sacrament of penance and reconciliation is an opportunity and invitation to heal the brokenness in our lives and to set relationships right. We should give more attention to celebrating this gift, especially during the seasons of Lent and Advent.

Originally Published in Catholic Update *by St. Anthony Messenger Press C0197*
©1996-2006 www.americancatholic.org

Richard M. Gula, S.S., a Sulpician priest, is the professor of moral theology at the Franciscan School of Theology of the Graduate Theological Union in Berkeley, California. He is the author of numerous articles and books, including his latest book, Ethics and Pastoral Ministry *(Paulist Press, 1996).*

Confession with Father Joe

About ten years ago, while we were still living in a rural town in West Texas, I experienced a profound conversion. Still, there were some sins from which I could not seem to get free.

It was these sins which I had to confess over and over again. Father Joe was the priest that God used to impart His forgiveness and absolution for me in a warm and affirming way. No matter how many times I went to confession with the same sins, I always felt the goodness of God in this sacrament.

It was not that Father Joe had extremely profound and awe-inspiring thoughts or words, but he was very intuitive, and his comments were thought provoking, helpful and practical. It was as if Jesus were present in the confessional with me.

Father Joe showed a genuine love for God's people and made me feel very secure. I knew that Father had tons of things to do, as he was the only priest for five parishes in that rural area; but he was never hurried, or made me feel as if I were taking up his time needlessly. It became a joy to go to confession.

One day I went into the confessional and told him that since I was always confessing the same sins every time, perhaps I should record my sins and bring in the tape for him to hear. He got a big laugh from that and we joked for a bit, but then he got serious and, in his quiet, intuitive way, told me what he knew I needed.

Father knew of my frustration at not being able to overcome my everyday failings and weaknesses. He understood the struggle that it was causing within my spirit. I remember once getting emotional and my eyes started to tear up. He simply waited patiently until I was ready and then continued to provide the spiritual direction that I needed.

God spoke to me that day and many other times in the confessional. Sometimes we would talk for a short period of time and sometimes for a long time, "Too long," my husband would say, as he always reminded me that there were other people waiting to go to confession. But Father Joe's words were exactly what I needed in my relationship and my walk with the Lord.

The graces and the strength that I continue to receive from the sacrament of penance can never be measured. For me, it is a powerful way to stay in relationship with God.

Dora C. Gallardo   *Uvalde, Texas*

Total Love and Forgiveness

About thirty-five years ago, when I was a young wife and mother of two small children, I went to confession at a different parish. In the course of my confession, the priest called me an extremely offensive word. I was devastated and heartbroken, and knew Jesus would never talk like that to me. After that humiliating experience, I continued going to church out of duty and went to confession once a year, but neither brought me a sense of peace or joy.

A few years later I attended a charismatic conference in New Orleans; before it ended it was announced that priests would be available throughout the building to hear confessions. My friend wanted to go to confession, so I told her I would wait in my seat for her to return. There was no way I was joining her; I didn't need any more pain in my life.

As I sat in my seat with my heart hardening even more, I looked around at all the people talking to priests, unburdening themselves. I dug my heels in deeper, telling myself that I really was okay and that confession was fine for people who had never been hurt during one. Then my gaze stopped on one particular priest and penitent.

41

The priest had his arm around this person's shoulder and their heads were bent forward, almost touching. I stared at that sight and thought about how peaceful they looked. Then God, in His infinite mercy and love, allowed me to no longer see the priest standing there, but the Good Shepherd instead. I could not believe my eyes. All I felt was mercy and love, and I knew with every fiber of my being that I wanted what that person was receiving at that moment—total love and forgiveness.

I am not ashamed to say that I literally ran to the confession line and yes, the prodigal daughter was welcomed home with open arms. I experienced the deep joy and peace that only God can give, and was finally able to forgive the priest who had hurt me years before.

Frances D. Huck   *Picayune, Mississippi*

The Gift of Confession

When I was a child, I attended Holyrood (which means Holy Rod) secondary school in Glasgow, Scotland and went to Holy Cross Church. Every First Friday all the children would walk down the street to our big church for confession. I was never prepared, so I developed a habit of making up sins when it was my turn in the confessional. This became my normal way of confessing until I ran into serious problems later on in life and had to confess my *real* sins.

In 1968, I witnessed many young women burn to death in a former whiskey warehouse that had been converted into an upholstery factory. The iron bars on the windows prevented the victims from escaping the inferno. I was a bus conductress and was able to see the horror from my bus platform.

I took the rest of the day off, and as I sat on the bus on my way home, I thought about the victims of the fire and how death came so unexpectedly for them. Then I spotted the church where I had gone to confession with my classmates every month as a child.

I approached the rectory and knocked on the door. The housekeeper answered, and I told her that I needed to go to confession. She told the resident priest and he invited me into the church and heard my confession. This resulted in my returning to America and joining my ex-husband again. We had been divorced for six months. I tried hard to change my life and live according to the laws of the Church, but the marriage did not succeed any better. I soon found myself separated once more and living outside of the Church's safety net.

I married again and my next crossroad came after the birth of my third child, the first with my new husband. I decided to please my mother by having my daughter baptized. I made all the arrangements and my mother was very happy. However, our plans fell apart when the priest told me he couldn't baptize my child because he found out that I had remarried outside of the Church without having had my first marriage annulled. I was furious.

My anger inspired me to want to expose the *hypocrisy* of a Church that would punish an innocent child for my sins. As I sat next to my sleeping child thinking of which newspaper to write to about this hypocrisy, I had what I can only describe as a conversion experience. I could see myself falling downward and was aware of having to make an account of my life. This made me realize how I had hurt others, and I even felt what they felt as a result of my sins.

I knew I was going to hell, and I knew that was where I belonged. I slid to the floor, sobbing for the way I had wasted my life and for the pain I had caused others, especially my God. I stayed on my knees until morning.

This experience led me to knock on the door of a church to confess my sins. After that, I applied for and received an annulment from my first marriage.

The day before my *Catholic wedding* with my new husband in 1976, I met with Father Vanderloo at St. Joseph's Church in Oneida, Wisconsin. As I sat in his kitchen trying to go over my life since my last good confession, I cried because of how patient God had been with me.

My life finally seemed complete when another crossroad presented itself. My second husband decided that he wanted to marry someone else. I still had four children at home. How would I manage? How could I go on? One of my sons went wild, but before his death at age seventeen he returned to the sacraments. I was blessed to be next in line as he entered the confessional with great remorse and hope.

I will remain forever thankful for the gift of confession where God has met me at so many difficult crossroads in my life.

Rose Mary Danforth   *Jacksonville, Florida*

Dad's Return

In the summer of 1979, I was visiting my mother and father in Long Beach Island, New Jersey. During a conversation with my dad about the changes happening in the Catholic Church, he asked me if the prayers and format of the sacrament of reconciliation were still the same.

My dad had not been to reconciliation in many years. We talked about the different steps: examination of conscience, initial blessing, telling how long it has been since the last confession, confessing our sins, receiving absolution, getting our penance, and making an act of contrition. We practiced the act of contrition several times until he felt comfortable.

Later in the afternoon he announced that he was going to church for a while. I asked if he wanted me to go along with him. He said, "No."

He returned an hour later with a broad smile on his face, saying he was greatly relieved, "Do you know what that lovely priest did? When I was finished, he actually came out of the confessional, put his arms around me, and gave me the warmest hug."

The next day my dad was beaming when he received holy Communion.

Jacqueline D. Henry   *Carolina Shores, North Carolina*

"Conversion is always a response to being loved by God. In fact, the most important part of the conversion process is the experience of being loved and realizing that God's love saves us—we do not save ourselves. Our part in this saving action is to be open to the gift of God's love—to be open to grace."

**The Sacrament of Reconciliation:
Celebrating God's Forgiveness**
by Sandra DeGidio, O.S.M.

see page 71

Thirty-four Million Dollar Loser

In 1998, I found out that I was the biggest loser in the state of Michigan. It happened because my dear mother burned my lottery ticket worth thirty-four million dollars. I knew the ticket was mine because I had played the same numbers since I was sixteen. So, when the numbers of the missing ticket were announced over the radio, I called my mom and told her to stop burning old lottery tickets. "I was a winner!"

It was too late. The ticket had been burned two weeks earlier.

I remember taking the car later that day to pick up my sister Ann. When she got in the car, I told her very solemnly, "Mom is dead." A puzzled look came over her face and she asked me what I was talking about. I told her that I would have to kill mom because she had burned my thirty-four million dollar lottery ticket! I was joking of course, but my sister thought I was being horrible.

I do admit I was *momentarily* mad at my mother, though not seriously. After all, how could I be upset with the person who gave me life? My mother is a strong and loving person. Not only did she give birth to ten children, but she also survived a serious bout with polio. Love never fails; there was no way I could really be mad at my mom.

Still, it was the sacrament of reconciliation that got me through the anger I had about losing an opportunity to assist with a wide variety of charitable projects. More importantly, it helped me heal in my relationship with God. I was mad at God for not letting me collect the money. I had great charities I wanted to assist, and I was not allowed to have the money. Why would God do this to me?

With this sacrament, my spiritual director reminded me that there was a reason that God did not want me to have the money. The thirty-four million was not mine because it would not bring me closer to the kingdom of God. Though I had a hard time believing it in the beginning, I have gradually come to understand God's plan.

After the lost lottery ticket news went around the family, my Uncle Joe called to console me. He told me I should keep trying to win again, recalling that there was a man in Colorado who had won the lottery four times!

Well, I got hooked. I was playing the lottery all the time and spending a lot of money. I would also go to the casino and spend money there. I was preoccupied with getting that thirty-four million back, even though I knew I was not supposed to have it.

This is when the sacrament of reconciliation became even more important to me. One time, I confessed that I had spent five hundred dollars in one hour at the casino. For my penance, I was told to donate that much money to charity. It took me six months to fulfill the penance because I wanted to select good charities. The next time I confessed my gambling problem I was told I had to give up the casinos for Lent. I told my pastor and spiritual director, Father Bill Ashbaugh, that I could not do that because my friends wanted to take me to the casino for my birthday. He calmly but gently told me to offer it up. So I did not go to the casino for all of Lent.

Over a three-year process of confessing my sin of gambling, I finally decided on November 12, 1999, that I could no longer spend my time, energy or money on the lottery. I also vowed to give up the casino, but went one more time on Thanksgiving Day that year.

I am truly thankful that through the sacrament of reconciliation I was able to stop gambling. There are times when I still think about it. Recently, for example, the MegaMillions was up to three hundred and fifty million dollars. I began to think of the good I could do with that kind of money. I even encouraged my mom to get some tickets!

Once when the lottery was worth eighty million, I gave some friends a series of numbers to play, but at Mass that weekend, Father. Bill gave a homily on addictions. After Mass, I confessed the error of my ways. I felt a sense of relief and peace because I knew visiting the confessional would help me to keep saying "no" to my terrible habit.

The sacrament of reconciliation is one of the hidden treasures of the Catholic faith. In my own life this beautiful sacrament has helped me in many difficult times. Growing up, I was always nervous about going into the confessional and telling the priest my sins. However, as I continue to grow in my faith journey, I have experienced how this sacrament has changed my life.

I am not perfect, and I know that the sacrament of reconciliation is a time to practice humility. You have to confess your sins out loud to a priest and this is not easy, but the grace received to continue the faith journey is worth it. I am proof that this sacrament can help people make great strides in their lives. I hope to continue to use the grace from this sacrament to make it to the ultimate prize: heaven.

Lisa A. Stechschulte   *Owosso, Michigan*

My Thoughts...

I think the question on sin is a very good one. Of course anything that qualifies as a mortal sin must be confessed; but if you don't have a mortal sin, the trend that I have experienced in Pittsburgh and Greensburg, Pennsylvania, diocese is that you tell the priest most what is bothering you. They seem to use psychology to help you to figure out the root of the cause. Example: Difficulty in discipline of daily prayer was one of my problems. I talk to Jesus all day, but have trouble with setting time apart to just pray/be.

So, the priest asked me how late I stayed up, how early I got up, how busy my days are, how much stress was I under? Then he tried to give me suggestions on how to handle that stuff.

If I had more sleep and made more time for recreation then maybe I wouldn't be so tired and would be able to find time to pray as well as to pray and not to fall asleep. Basically, what is really bothering you and what is the underlying causes of our faults/sins.

Chris Scholze Zurawski, SFO

Joy and Relief

I was nine years old when I experienced the events that led to the first *major* moral crisis of my life. For a number of weeks, I'd been riding my bike over to a new housing construction site and collecting ceramic tile remnants from the trash piles around the various homes to complete a mosaic table top that I'd been designing. On one of those forays, a security guard for the construction company had stopped to question me and check out what I was doing there. Ordinarily, this would not have seemed very unusual, but unfortunately, as I have come to realize as an adult, this young man was also a pedophile. After engaging me in conversation for some time, he then proceeded on to other things, and ended up using the isolation of the site, as well as the convenience of the empty, fairly completed houses, to molest me on several occasions. Like many children, I did not mention what had happened to my parents, as he had made sure to threaten me with all sorts of dire consequences if I ever told anyone what *we* had done; but I was very troubled by the memories and shame of what had taken place.

The following year, I started fifth grade at a new Catholic school where the Franciscan Friars of the Santa Barbara Province ran the neighboring parish as well as administering to the spiritual needs of the students. It was shortly after Sister had taught our class the Ten Commandments that I began to have turbulent conscience problems about what had happened. I began to suspect that I had surely committed the very serious and grave sin of adultery, since that security guard had told me that he was married and had even shown me pictures of his wife and young toddler daughter.

Every two weeks, the students went to the nearby parish church for confession; so at the very first opportunity after my horrid suspicions arose, I'm afraid I shocked the poor friar priest in the confessional by asking him, point blank, for a detailed definition of the sin of adultery.

There was a moment's pause before Father asked me how old I was. When I replied "ten" he carefully asked me what had made me ask this question, and I replied that I thought that I had committed it!

Once again, Father gently probed and asked me to explain a little further. I told him that I had done some very shameful things with a man who was married, and the way the religious sister had talked about the Sixth Commandment, I was beginning to suspect that maybe that was what had happened, and if so, then I must be in the state of mortal sin.

Father became quite solicitous toward me and after drawing out a few more details about what had actually taken place he became very indignant about the adult involved. He told me that there was absolutely no way that I as a ten-year-old child would have been able to fulfill the conditions necessary for those events to have been a mortal sin, but that the perpetrator, (the one who had done this to/with me) was the one who had done so.

He asked if I had told my parents and encouraged me to do so. He then assured me that I was blameless and innocent in everything that had happened, which finally put my mind and heart at peace. He then heard the rest of my confession, gave me my penance (three Hail Marys) and absolution.

I cannot put into words the joy and relief that I experienced that day, but the compassionate, gentle wisdom, concern, and assurances of that Franciscan priest, and the grace of the sacrament had a very profound effect and impact on facilitating the beginning of healing, for which I have been extremely grateful.

Anonymous   *Los Angeles, California*

Remember Me?

It was January 17, 2006, and I had just left the priest at a Catholic church in a small city in Texas. He had gently and skillfully guided me through my first sacrament of reconciliation in forty-five years.

"Have you felt malice toward others, perhaps wishing them harm because of something they did to you?" he asked.

"Yes," I confessed, "toward two people. One of them has died, but the other is still living. I've asked God to relieve me of my inability to forgive, but I haven't been successful."

After the priest absolved my sins, I left the rectory and then stopped at the grocery store on my way home. As I was crossing the parking lot, someone called out, "Hey Lynn! Remember me?" I looked at him for a moment. I had not seen him for eight years, and he was several pounds heavier, but it was him, one of the men I told the priest I couldn't forgive.

I had worked with him for ten years, much of that time tolerating his bad behavior and the malicious gossip he spread about me and others to fellow employees. At one time I had even thought of bringing a lawsuit against him, but I lacked sufficient evidence.

He was smiling and friendly as we inquired about one another's families and discussed the work place. When we parted company, my malice toward him had completely dissipated. How quickly God had touched me with his healing presence!

In my heart, I had not completely forgiven the man who molested my fourteen-year-old daughter years earlier. When I spoke to my now forty-four-year-old daughter about my experience, she softly told me that she had forgiven Ted. She felt sorry for him and in her heart had forgiven him. He died alone and miserable. I was also finally able to forgive him also.

God has lightened my burden through the sacrament of reconciliation. He brought me peace, joy, healing, and a brighter outlook on life. When I received holy Communion the following Sunday, I shed tears of joy.

Pauline L. Bludau   *Victoria, Texas*

My First Adult Confession

When I was eight years old, I made my first confession. Thirty years later, I made my second.

The second one happened like this. I had just started to participate in a lay apostolate program through Regnum Christi, called Familia (Family Life in America). Through the association, I learned of an audio tape about confession by Fr. Larry Richards. After listening to the tape, the Holy Spirit whapped me upside the head with a two-by-four!

I knew I had to go to confession.

I asked my sister-in-law, "How do you confess thirty years worth of sins?"

Her reply, "Pack a lunch."

I went with the next available time, which happened to be the first Saturday after 9/11. When it was my turn, with my stomach churning, I went in. The priest was startled at first when he realized this was my first confession as an adult but he was incredibly kind and gentle. He carefully guided me through the confession by asking a series of questions. This made it easier to confess the embarrassing sins by answering yes or no.

As I left, he cautioned me, "Don't wait so long to make your third confession."

Jeanne C. McGuire   *Columbus, Ohio*

52

We're On A Mission From God

By Mary Beth Bonacci

Why Bother Going to Confession?

> *In that silence, may inner peace come to you, a peace which can be deepened and more fully possessed through the sacrament of reconciliation. ...I hope you will avail yourselves of the many priests who are here. In the sacrament of penance they are ambassadors to you of Christ's loving forgiveness.*
>
> —John Paul II, Denver, 1993

Have you ever prayed and felt nothing? Stupid question, I know. Everyone who persisted in any kind of prayer life has had times when an encounter with God didn't register on the emotional level. That's normal. Our relationship with God isn't just about emotion. No relationship is. Feelings come and go. They're dependent on how our day is going, how we're feeling, what we ate for breakfast, and various hormonally induced factors. God isn't some feeling factory where we "plug in" and automatically attain peace.

But what's going on when you *constantly* feel empty in God's presence? What's happening when you don't feel connected to Him, or when you feel vaguely uncomfortable around Him? Why is it that sometimes you look for that peace, but it never seems to come?

When this happens, it's time to take a good look at yourself. How important has God been in your life? Are you trying to live a relationship with Him and get all the spiritual benefits (inner peace, etc.) without "picking up the cross." Do you want to have God on your own terms—only when you're in trouble or needing a shot of peaceful easy feeling, while the rest of the time you live by your own rules instead of His?

Is there unrepented sin in your life?

ON A MISSION FROM GOD

When the relationship is off, the peace is off.
You're not comfortable together. That's what
Happens in God's presence when we sin.

Put it in terms of a human relationship. Say you're dating some-one. At first, you feel this wonderful sense of security and bliss when you're together. You love to take long walks, just hold hands and being together. But then this person does something to hurt you—bad. It happens several times. There's never an apology, nev-er any indication that the hurtful behavior will stop. Then suddenly this person wants to take one of those nice long walks. Will there be that same feeling of peace? No way. The relationship has been violated. You're not the same together. The peace wasn't magic—it was a function of the relationship. When the relationship is off, the peace is off. You're not comfortable together.

That's what happens in God's presence when we sin. We're not comfortable with Him any more. We don't want to look at Him too closely, and we certainly don't want Him looking too closely at us. Even if we don't consciously realize that's the problem, it's there.

We can't have peace with God if we plan to keep hurting Him, whether it's by being cruel and uncharitable to people around us or by ignoring His standard for sexuality, or whatever. The relation-ship doesn't work that way.

How do we make it right again? Well, how would it work in the example? The offender would have to come clean and say, "I'm sorry I hurt you, I love you, and I promise to try really hard not to do it again." Then you could talk it out and rebuild trust in each other, so once again you could have those nice, peaceful walks.

It works the same with God. IF we want the peace He gives, the peace the world can't give, we have to walk with Him. All the way. And that walk involves a cross. It's not easy to avoid sin, but it's a part of the bargain, a part of our relationship with Him.

In a human relationship, there are different ways to hurt someone, different levels of violation of friendship. You could say something mean about someone. Or you could murder that person's family.

Obviously the second would be a much bigger violation of the friendship than the first. It would probably rupture your friendship forever.

It's the same in our relationship with God. There are smaller sins and more serious ones. The smaller sins are called venial sins. Most of the sins that people commit frequently—using bad language, telling "little white lies," etc.—are venial sins. Venial sins "chip away" at our relationship with God, but they don't, by themselves, sever it.

Some sins, on the other hand, are big sins. Stealing, murder, destroying someone's life or reputation, sex outside of marriage—those offend God a lot. (Sex? Really? You'll see why soon.) These big sins are called mortal sins. To know something is a mortal sin and freely choose to do it anyway is to cut ourselves off from God. Mortal sins sever our relationship with Him. That's a bad position to be in, especially if you happen to die. Then God is all you have left, and you *don't* want to be cut off from Him. Your eternal life is at stake.

Obviously we need to root all mortal sin from our lives. But we need to get rid of venial sins, too. After all, when you're trying to be a good friend to someone, is it enough not to murder his family? No. You need to strive constantly to be good to him, in the little ways as well as the big. Killing someone's mother will ruin your friendship. But constantly lying to him will eventually do the same thing.

If we want to have the peace Christ gives, we have to root out sin, mortal and venial, from our lives. There's no other way. Sometimes that's not easy. We have to determine if our behavior is sinful—and if it is, we have to stop. We have to respect God's law. We have to be examples of His love. And when we fail to live up to that, which we all do sometimes, we can't run away from our failure. We have to face up to it, repent, and move on.

Have you ever heard someone say, "What I've done is so bad, even God couldn't forgive me." If you murder your friend's family, odds are you'll never get that friendship back, no matter how sincerely you apologize. God, on the other hand, *always* forgives. No matter what we've done, no matter how awful it seems, if we say to Him, "I'm so sorry, I wish I hadn't done it, and I'm committed to trying hard not to do I again," He takes us back.

I want to say that again, because many people miss this point. *No matter what we've done, God always forgives us if we're truly sorry.* We just have to go to Him and ask.

"Going to Him" is a little harder to do than going to a person, because we can't see Him. With friends, we can look at them and hear them and work with them. They hear our apologies, and we hear them forgive. It helps the healing.

God knew we needed that, so He gave us a way. The sacrament of penance. Confession. We can actually go somewhere and hear the voice of someone assigned and called by Christ, who tells us that our sins are forgiven.

Confession restores our relationship with God. If we've committed venial sins, confession repairs the damage. And if we've committed mortal sins, confession reconnects the severed relationship.

The sacrament of penance is the system Christ gave us for the forgiveness of sins. It's the only system He gave us. He told the apostles, "If you forgive the sins of any, they are forgiven them. If you retain them, they are retained" (Jn 20:22–23). In other words, priests have Christ's sacramental power to forgive sins, and they do that in the confessional.

Christ knew what He was doing when He gave us the sacrament of penance. Like all the other sacraments, confession is a physical act. He gave us a place to go, where we can "leave" our sins and take grace in their place. He gave us a place where we have someone to talk to if we have questions—someone who doesn't even necessarily know who we are. God knows that, as human persons, we operate on the physical level. In something as important as forgiveness, He wants it to operate on the tangible level. He wants us to be there, to go to it, to hear it.

I know it's easy to want to avoid the confessional. You're afraid the priest may recognize your voice. It takes effort. It may be a little scary. It's a lot easier just to whisper in the dark, "God, I'm sorry."

Don't be afraid of the confessional. Go regularly. You don't have to go face to face. The priest doesn't have to know who you are. But you don't have to be *afraid* of gong face to face either. You're not going to shock him. He hears this stuff all the time. He, better than anyone, knows that we're all human. And he won't tell anyone. He can't. Even under the threat of death he can't reveal what's been said in the confessional. Your secret is safe with him.

But he will tell *you* something. He'll say, "I absolve you from your sins." You'll know it, because Christ said it was true. That priest isn't just some guy. He's a guy acting for Christ. He's the "ambassador of Christ's loving forgiveness".

And the relationship will be back. The peace will be back. All will be right between you and God.

Nothing is better than that.

Mary Beth Bonacci is the author of We're On A Mission From God *(Ignatius Press) and is a well known speaker and syndicated columnist. She holds a Master's degree in Theology of Marriage and Family from the John Paul II Institute.*

God Did Not Give Up

I am a cradle Catholic who went to Catholic schools, but gradually drew away from God. I became a cafeteria Catholic, picking and choosing what part of my faith I would practice. I went to Mass, but didn't receive the Eucharist because I had married outside the Church. Then, when I went through a horrific divorce, I was brought to my knees in pain, my anger at the Lord was unbelievable. God did not give up on me, though.

At that time, a new friend, Michael, entered my life. Michael had also had a sinful past, but had found peace in his life. One Saturday, Michael and I were going to a movie and he asked if I would mind stopping at a church first so he could go to confession. It was fine with me, so we walked into the church and I sat and waited while he went to confession. There was no pressure on me to go, but I was curious how he found the courage to confess his sins. I asked, and his response was that it had nothing to do with courage and everything to do with knowing it was the right thing to do. He said confession really did make a difference in his life.

The following week when I was at work, I finally picked up the phone and called my parish to schedule an appointment for confession. A priest I didn't know got on the phone and said he could see me that evening. I was surprised that it would be so soon.

When I arrived for my appointment, I met the priest at the rectory and we went into his office. When he asked how long it had been since my last confession, he didn't flinch or show any hint of judgment when I said it had been eighteen years. I confessed what had been keeping me from the Lord, and he showed genuine joy in having me back. He talked about the prodigal son, and said that God was like the father running across the field with open arms, filled with immense love and joy because He had me back. He also said the angels in heaven were throwing a party, and that the celebration is very large when someone has returned to God's arms.

When I left there that afternoon, I drove with tears running down my face. I felt that a huge burden had been lifted from me. I am a regular in the confessional line now, and know the unbelievable peace I have is because of the sacrament of reconciliation.

Catherine A. Nelson   *Gurnee, Illinois*

Plenty of Time

Father Peter Hussey was an old Irish priest who, after his retirement, traveled the diocese in search of people in need of spiritual comfort. He brought holy Communion to the sick and heard their confession. He prayed the rosary with different prayer groups throughout the diocese. He encouraged those who struggled with the faith, and he evangelized those who had lost or never heard of the Church. Although his memory often failed him, the Holy Spirit always seemed to put Father in the right place at the right time.

I remember catching an early supper one day at the downtown Burger King and feeling guilty. I forget why. I was a teenager and my parents' law firm was located across the street. Perhaps I had gotten into an argument with my mom or dad. Perhaps I had started smoking again or perhaps I had been less than truthful about an unfinished homework assignment.

Regardless, some sin typical of teenagers piqued at my conscience. Moreover, it was well past lunchtime if I recall correctly. Thus, I had missed confession at the parish one block over. Where would I find a priest to hear my confession before evening Mass?

Upon finishing the last french-fry, I gathered the empty containers and dumped them into the trash bin by the side door. Something white caught my eye on the other side of the door. It was a Roman collar. Standing on the sidewalk was a silver-haired gentleman dressed in a black suit with a matching fedora.

"Father Hussey," I shouted as the door opened.

"Pierre," he replied, using my French nickname as he always did. "You know, I was just thinking of you." He then paused for a moment and stared at me. "Is something wrong?"

I hesitated for a moment. I was still feeling the shame of my actions and the idea of confession was giving me second thoughts. "I need to go to confession but I missed the priest."

"Well I'm a priest," Father said, "and you don't have to be scared. I've heard many a young lad's confession in my day. Now that I'm retired, I have plenty of time to hear more."

I breathed a sigh of relief. Father had taken control of the situation.

"Come along, Pierre," he continued as he put his arm around me. "There's a church down the street. I'm sure Monsignor won't mind if we borrow his confessional for a few minutes. Here's an extra rosary you can use to say your penance. Let's get that sin off your conscience and your soul right with Christ."

Pete Vere   *Sault Ste. Marie, Ontario, Canada*

You Came Back!

His name was Father Janvren. His history included membership in the diplomatic corp in Washington, D.C. and a stint as a secret agent during the Second World War. By the time he came to us in Victoria, British Columbia, at St. Andrew's Cathedral, he had put his brother through university and cared for his mother till her passing before entering the seminary.

I was a teenager. Like many young people of my age in the early sixties life was full of heady experiences. I found myself with habits and behaviors that I shudder to remember. Guilt finally drove me to confession as we called it in those days. I was sweating as my turned approached, my mind was in turmoil and my heart was racing. "I'm going to get blasted! Boy, I can't imagine the penance I will receive!"

The voice on the other side of the grill was a soft and gentle English one. I poured out my behavior and I heard...*joy*! I can almost quote him: "Well done! Jesus is so proud of you to come back to Him. Keep coming! Don't forget He loves you so very much. Keep praying!"

I came out of confession in a state of euphoria. No wonder the line was so long. Everyone loved this man who was so full of encouragement.

I kept coming back, still battling my demons only to find him full of joy that I was trying to break from my behaviors. He would say to me time and time again, "You came back! This is so good! Keep up your prayer and remember Jesus is with you in this struggle."

I think it was his voice in my ear, telling me of his support and encouragement, which helped me to finally change. Each time I went to confession I was filled with greater courage and determination to do better. I kept coming back as he was full of wisdom and common sense.

Joan Ann Pogson   *Saanichton, British Columbia, Canada*

Penance of Love

I was a deacon in the Baptist Church when I decided to become a Catholic nearly seventeen years ago. I am also a community worker, and most of my colleagues were Catholics who were very supportive during my conversion.

Having done the RCIA program, it came time for my first reconciliation. Because I was well known in the area, the priest knew my background and I think he was about as nervous as me. As a penance he told me to go and kneel in the church for ten minutes and reflect on how lovable I am. That certainly calmed my nerves about confession and I have never been frightened of it again.

Andrea Ellen Bentham   *Logan Central, Queensland, Australia*

Think a Little Harder

Back in 1955 at the Church of the Resurrection in Lansing, Michigan, Sister Marie Padua made sure that our second grade class went to confession every Friday. The best part was that Father John Gabriels, the founder of our church, was always the priest who heard our confessions. Since he frequently walked the streets surrounding the school visiting all the Catholic families, he knew all of *his* children very well.

One time I was in the confessional and felt I hadn't sinned since the last time I had been there. When Father Gabriels told me to begin my confession, I told him that I had been good and didn't have any sins to tell him. He put his face up to the screen and said to me, "Susie Jean, I know you and I can't believe that, so think a little harder." I didn't want him mad at me and surely didn't want Sister Marie Padua mad at me either, so I admitted that I had been mean to my little brother.

Father Gabriels gave me a penance to say and I returned to the pew where I did a double penance for lying to him. Now, when I think of the beauty of reconciliation, I think of that time when the first priest I ever loved knew me so well that he couldn't believe I could be good for a whole week. He knew that just maybe I had been mean to my little brother.

Susan Kay Newberry   *Lansing, Michigan*

"We need to be reasonably convinced that, yes, we are good no matter what. When we make a mistake, it is not the end of the world for us. We may have to make some amends, say we are sorry, and do some repairs, but we are still the good persons God made us to be."

The Sacrament of Reconciliation and Taking Charge of One's Life
by Fr. Alberic Smith, OFM

see page 191

I Want to Come Back

I truly believe that God, in His wisdom, at some time and in some miraculous way, uses each of us as His instruments.

After my younger sister left home and married, she had a very difficult life. She had one son, the light of her life, but lost another son shortly after his birth. She was always strong, keeping her trials inside, but always there for me and our *brood* of six children.

As the years passed and our children grew up, we both decided to move upstate for our retirement years. I had been blessed over the years to continue practicing my faith and attending Mass on a regular basis. My sister, unfortunately, had been away from the sacraments for many years, but she always graciously drove my husband and me to our small parish. She would attend Mass with us, but did not partake of holy Communion. I could see how sad she was and how much it troubled her, but I did not know what to do about it except pray.

A few years ago, on the Monday after Easter Sunday, my sister suggested we drive up to Stockbridge, Massachusetts, to the Divine Mercy Shrine. First, we visited the church and then we walked about the grounds. As we strolled along, enjoying the day and each other's company, suddenly we came upon a giant trailer with big black letters on the side that spelled out one single word: "Confessions"!

My sister stared for a moment and then said, "I'd love to go to confession, but I wouldn't know what to say." God must have leaned close to my ear because I heard myself saying, "Just say, 'I've been away so long. I'm sorry. I want to come back.'" It must have been just what she needed to hear. She nodded, took a breath, and went inside the trailer.

From that moment forward, my sister's faith blossomed until it became even stronger than mine. Two years ago, my sister died, and though

I miss her very much, I am consoled with the knowledge that she has returned to the fold of the Good Shepherd.

Virginia E. Heim   *Copake, New York*

One Bad Apple

I have had many wonderful experiences when going to confession; however, my first time was not great at all.

It happened in the city of Caico, Rio Grande do Norte, Brazil. Padre Deoclides, a priest at the Diocese of Caico, came to the Church of Our Lady of the Rosary to listen to our confessions. While each of us was in the confessional, he touched each of us little girls in a very inappropriate manner. I can never forget that first experience.

It was traumatic, but with God at my side, I continued to pray and went back to confession the following month. I remained a Roman Catholic, faithfully devoted to the Church, except for two years after finishing college in 1964. In 1966, I met my husband, an American, who was in Brazil on duty. I learned that he was a convert Catholic, and with him I started going back to the Church I love.

We were married in the Church and have had a wonderful marriage for forty years. My husband passed away this year, and if it weren't for my faith and the wonderful people in my Church, I don't know what would have happened. All of our children came home for their dad's last days and were amazed at my church community. They saw how fortunate I was to have two wonderful priests and a great nun to support me with love and compassion through those days of grief.

Carmen Creamer   *Jacksonville, North Carolina*

My Sins Were Forgiven

In the 1980s I left the church. I was a new nurse in my thirties who didn't have time to be bothered with it. One day while I was at work, a very handsome doctor came into the emergency room where we were treating an accident victim. I told another nurse that I thought he was so good looking; I just had to have him. She laughed and said he was married. Well, that didn't stop me from going after him. I did end up with him for a while, but felt so guilty about it that I left town.

I started going back to church, mainly to please my parents, but was in no way ready to go to confession. My father died in the meantime and I could feel God pulling me closer and closer to confession. I finally did go, but could not bring myself to tell of the life I had led.

By now I was taking an active roll in caring for my aging mother and my great niece and nephew. Although she had never been baptized, I started taking my niece to church with me when she was about three years old. When she was six years old, she asked her mom if she could be baptized Catholic. There was some discussion about it since her mom had left the Catholic Church when she was about ten years old, and my niece's father is Southern Baptist.

Finally her mom consented and my dear, precious Goddaughter was officially welcomed into the Catholic Church. I had to set a good example for her, so off to confession I went. There was a visiting priest that day, and for the first time there was no partition between us. This in itself was disturbing to me, but as I started my confession, I couldn't contain my sorrow for my sins any longer. This very kind priest told me that I had suffered long enough and that my sins were forgiven. I knew it was true the moment he said it.

I hadn't felt so completely forgiven and clean since I was a child making my first confession. It was my mother's custom to change all the sheets on the beds on Saturdays, and then we would go to confession that evening. There was nothing better in the world than when I would slip into my clean bed that smelled like the fresh outdoors with my clean conscience. I had that same clean feeling after I confessed that terrible sin from long ago.

I didn't get the name of the priest who heard my confession that day, but I have seen him on occasion since then. I have thanked him in person and more often in my prayers. I can't begin to tell you what a change this has made in my life, but I can tell you that God is so very good to have given us this wonderful gift of reconciliation.

Yvonne J. Nihart   *Seale, Alabama*

Grandpa

November of 1963 was a cold month in Greenville, Pennsylvania. An Alberta clipper drew cold arctic air across Lake Erie, burying our town in a foot and a half of snow. I was twelve years old and was not happy that I had to shovel our property before I could make a few dollars clearing the walks of neighbors. The work was good for me though, because it took my mind off my grandfather's illness.

My mother's father was in his late fifties, and as long as I could remember, he had smelled of cigar smoke and ale. He had worked as a welder at the boxcar plant until he got sick that July. My mom and dad would talk and sometimes argue about him until they heard my sister or me coming, when they would suddenly hush. When we asked them what was wrong with Grandpa, they said he was feeling poorly, but getting better. I often heard fragments of sentences with the words "alcoholism", "undertaker", and "hardened liver". My sister and I pieced the truth together from the snatches of conversation and gossip we had overheard.

When I returned home that snowy Saturday to the smell of a sauerkraut and kielbasa dinner, I confronted my mother in the kitchen. "Mom, is Grandpa going to die?" I asked. My mother glibly replied, "Billy, we are going to all die someday but Grandpa is getting better. I don't want you to worry." Something in me snapped and I said, "Mom, he has cirrhosis and will be dead by Christmas." She turned towards me and slapped me across the face. "Who told you that—your father?" she said angrily. I ran sobbing like a young child up to my room.

I was burning with anger against my mother and thought I had sinned in some way that made her hit me. My father came to my room fifteen minutes later and told me to come downstairs to eat. I told him I wasn't hungry, and he told me I was to sit at the table even if I didn't eat because we always had dinner as a family. I was afraid he would beat me, but miraculously he was just cold and neutral, and nothing more was said about Grandpa's disease or my comment.

When we went to Mass the next morning, I did not receive Communion because I was convinced I was not in a state of grace. I worried all week about the sin on my soul and anxiously waited for Saturday so I could go to confession.

That Saturday as we drove up the hill to St. Michael's Church, I prayed that I would get the younger priest in the parish to hear my confession. The Virgin Mary must have been interceding for me because I got Father Ciola, who had been ordained only a few years before.

As I blurted out my fears and my "sin", he listened calmly and said, "Son, you have missed what the actual sin is. I understand your confusion, but you did nothing wrong in asking your mother about your grandfather. Your real sin is your anger against your mother. That will hurt you worse than your mother's slap. What she did was not right, but she is feeling pain and anger at the idea of losing her father."

He continued, "Your grandfather is very sick and may die soon. But Jesus and His mother are waiting in heaven to welcome him if he dies in a state of grace. If he doesn't, he may have to spend some time in purgatory. It sounds like he's a good man with a problem. I feel sure you and your mother will be sad, but you will see him again. I want you to say five Our Fathers as penance, and please say a rosary for your mother, not as penance, but to help her get though her weakness in slapping you."

It then became clear to me that my mother was not perfect. She died in 1983 and when I pray for her on the day of her death each year, I dedicate the first decade of the rosary to Father Ciola who helped me on my way to becoming an adult soul.

William R. Baxter   *Spokane, Washington*

I've Been Healed!

Our former pastor, Father Milt Jordan, who was the chaplain at the Bronx Fire Department, told us this beautiful story about the power of healing in the sacrament of reconciliation.

One day while he and the guys were sitting around the firehouse talking, in walked another fireman. Something major was bothering him. Soon he asked Father Milt to hear his confession, so the two of them went up to the lieutenant's office where they could talk privately.

After Joe received absolution from Father Milt, he went tearing out of the office, almost yanking the doors off their hinges, and yelling at the top of his lungs, "I've been healed!"

Father Milt said, "What have I done?" Joe had confessed things that he thought were seriously sinful. Father said he didn't think they were that bad, but he knew what Joe thought was more important because he was the one involved in the situation.

About six months later, Father was at a Christmas party when an attractive woman came up to him and thanked him. Father appreciated her thanks, but wondered why he was being thanked. She said that he had given her husband back to her and that their children had gotten their father back.

Father told us that Joe's personality completely changed after his confession. He was a "new creation in God."

Nancy H. Cioffi   *Chesapeake Beach, Maryland*

My Decision

The children, the house, the finances, health and the relatives —it was just all getting to me. Some of it was caused by me and some by others, but it was all getting me down. And I mean down.

Since I suffer from depression and anxiety, feeling down is more serious for me than for many others who are feeling blue. I began to think that the only way for me to solve my problems was to remove myself from them. For me, that meant suicide. I thought about it and decided Wednesday would be the best day to do it. This would be after the family retreat we had planned, and the girls would have completed the jobs they were doing to raise money for a trip.

At the family retreat, several priests were available for reconciliation. I took advantage of this, telling my husband that I really needed to go to confession, and asked him to take care of the children for me. Then I stood in a long line with many elderly people, young people, toddlers, and babies. Finally, it was my turn.

I began my confession, telling the priest about my confusion and decision to commit suicide, and as we spoke, I could feel Jesus healing me through this priest. I felt so much better when we were finished talking. The priest and I spoke many more times during the rest of the retreat, and he continued to counsel and help me. Although I am not completely healed, I am feeling significantly better. If it had not been for reconciliation, I would not be here and my children would be without a mother. That Wednesday has come and gone, and I thank God that I am still here.

Anonymous   *College Station, Texas*

The Sacrament of Reconciliation: Celebrating God's Forgiveness

By Sandra DeGidio, O.S.M.

The well-known parable of the prodigal son is perhaps the most strikingly powerful illustration of the human process of reconciliation, and of the theology inherent in the new rite of reconciliation. But many of us find it difficult to believe the story (see Luke 15:11-32). The father welcomes the son back instantly—doesn't even wait for him to get to the house. And he isn't at all interested in the young man's confession, only in celebrating.

This is not the way we Catholics have viewed the sacrament of reconciliation. Even with the new rite, most of us tend to view this sacrament with the attitude of the older son in the story: Forgiveness comes only after you recite your list of sins, agree to suffer a bit for them, do something to make up for your offenses, give some guarantee you won't commit the same sins again, and prove yourself worthy to join the rest of us who haven't been so foolish!

But God really is like the merciful parent in this parable: not out to catch us in our sin but intent on reaching out and hanging on to us in spite of our sin. Reconciliation (and the new rite is careful to point this out) is not just a matter of getting rid of sin. Nor is its dominant concern what we, the penitents, do. The important point is what God does in, with and through us.

A journey home to God

God's reconciling work in us doesn't happen in an instant. Reconciliation is often a long, sometimes painful process. It is a journey not confined to, but completed in, sacramental celebration. It is a round-trip journey away from our home with God and back again that can be summed up in terms of three C's: conversion, confession and celebration—and in that order.

In the past the order was different: Receiving the sacrament meant beginning with a recitation of sins (confession). Then we expressed our sorrow with an act of contrition, agreed to make some satisfaction for our sins by accepting our penance, and resolved to change our ways (conversion). Celebration was seldom, if ever, part of the process.

The parable of the prodigal son can help us understand the stages in our journey to reconciliation—and the order in which they occur. This helps us see why the theology of the new rite of reconciliation suggests a reordering in the pattern that we were familiar with in the past.

The journey for the young man in the parable (and for us) begins with the selfishness of sin. His sin takes him from the home of his parents—as our sin takes us from the shelter of God and the Christian community. His major concern in his new self-centered lifestyle—as is ours in sin—is himself and his personal gratification. None of the relationships he establishes are lasting. When his money runs out, so do his "friends." Eventually he discovers himself alone, mired in the mud of a pigpen, just as he is mired in sin. Then comes this significant phrase in the story: "Coming to his senses at last...." This is the beginning of the journey back, the beginning of conversion.

Conversion: An ongoing process

The conversion process begins with a "coming to one's senses," with a realization that all is not right with our values and style of life. Prompted by a faith response to God's call, conversion initiates a desire for change. Change is the essence of conversion. Shuv, the Old Testament term for conversion, suggests a physical change of direction; metanoia, the term the New Testament uses, suggests an internal turnabout, a change of heart that is revealed in one's conduct.

The Gospel vision of metanoia calls for an interior transformation that comes about when God's Spirit breaks into our lives with the good news that God loves us unconditionally. Conversion is always a response to being loved by God. In fact, the most important part of the conversion process is the experience of being loved and realizing that God's love saves us—we do not save ourselves. Our part in this saving action is to be open to the gift of God's love—to be open to grace.

Moral conversion means making a personal, explicitly responsible decision to turn away from the evil that blinds us to God's love, and to turn toward God who gifts us with love in spite of our sinfulness.

Persons who turn to God in conversion will never be the same again, because conversion implies transforming the way we relate to others, to ourselves, to the world, to the universe and to God. Unless we can see that our values, attitudes and actions are in conflict with Christian ones, we will never see a need to change or desire to be reconciled.

The need for conversion does not extend only to those who have made a radical choice for evil. Most often metanoia means the small efforts all of us must continually make to respond to the call of God.

Conversion is not a once-in-a-lifetime moment but a continuous, ongoing, lifelong process which brings us ever closer to "the holiness and love of God." Each experience of moral conversion prompts us to turn more and more toward God, because each conversion experience reveals God in a new, brighter light.

When we discover in the examination of our values, attitudes and style of life that we are "missing the mark," we experience the next step in the conversion process—contrition. This step moves us to the next leg of our conversion journey: breaking away from our misdirected actions, leaving them behind and making some resolutions for the future.

Let's look again at our story. The young man takes the first step in the conversion process when he "comes to his senses," overcomes his blindness and sees what he must do. "I will break away and return to my father." Before he ever gets out of the pigpen, he admits his sinfulness. And in this acknowledgment of sin he both expresses contrition and determines his own penance. "I will say to

CELEBRATING GOD'S FORGIVENESS

73

him, 'Father, I have sinned against God and against you…Treat me like one of your hired hands."

Contrition means examining our present relationships in the light of the Gospel imperative of love, and taking the necessary steps to repent and repair those relationships with others, ourselves and God. The repentance step in the conversion process is what is commonly called "making satisfaction for our sins," or "doing penance."

For many people in the past penance connoted "making up to God" by punishing ourselves for our sins. But true reparation is not punishment. At its root, reparation is repairing or correcting a sinful lifestyle. In the past we were told to do penance as temporal punishment for our sins. Now, however, we understand that our real "punishment" is the continuing pattern of sin in our lives and the harmful attitudes and actions it creates in us. The purpose of doing penance is to help us change that pattern. Penance is for growth, not for punishment. "Doing penance" means taking steps in the direction of living a changed life; it means making room for something new.

Lillian Hellman provides a wonderful image of this process of reconciliation in her explanation of the word pentimento at the beginning of *Pentimento: A Book of Portraits*: "Old paint on canvas, as it ages, sometimes becomes transparent. When that happens it is possible, in some pictures, to see the original lines: a tree will show through a woman's dress, a child makes way for a dog, a large boat is no longer on an open sea. That is called pentimento because the painter 'repented,' changed his mind. Perhaps it would be as well to say that the old conception, replaced by the later choice, is a way of seeing and then seeing again."

Confession: Externalizing what is within

Confession, one aspect of the sacrament which used to receive the greatest emphasis, is now seen as just one step in the total process. Confession of sin can only be sincere if it is preceded by the process of conversion. It is actually the external expression of the interior transformation that conversion has brought about in us. It is a much less significant aspect of the sacrament than we made it out to be in the past. This does not mean that confession is unimportant—only that it is not the essence of the sacrament.

Look again at the parable. The father, seeing his son in the distance, runs out to meet him with an embrace and a kiss. Through one loving gesture, the father forgives the son—and the son hasn't even made his confession yet! When he does, it seems the father hardly listens. The confession is not the most important thing here; the important thing is that his son has returned. The son need not beg for forgiveness, he has been forgiven. This is the glorious good news: God's forgiveness, like God's love, doesn't stop. In this parable, Jesus reveals to us a loving God who simply cannot not forgive!

Zorba the Greek—that earthy, raucous lover of life created by Nikos Kazantzakis—captures this loving God when he says: "I think of God as being exactly like me. Only bigger, stronger, crazier. And immortal, into the bargain. He's sitting on a pile of soft sheepskins, and his hut's the sky…In his right hand he's holding not a knife or a pair of scales—those damned instruments are meant for butchers and grocers—no, he's holding a large sponge full of water, like a rain cloud. On his right is paradise, on his left hell. Here comes a soul; the poor little thing's quite naked, because it's lost its cloak—its body, I mean—and it's shivering.

"…The naked soul throws itself at God's feet. 'Mercy!' it cries. 'I have sinned.' And away it goes reciting its sins. It recites a whole rigmarole and there's no end to it. God thinks this is too much of a good thing. He yawns. 'For heaven's sake stop!' he shouts. 'I've heard enough of all that!' Flap! Slap! a wipe of the sponge, and he washes out all the sins. 'Away with you, clear out, run off to paradise!' he says to the soul…Because God, you know, is a great lord, and that's what being a lord means: to forgive!"

Our attitude toward the sacrament of reconciliation is intimately related to our image of God. We need to really believe that our God, like Zorba's, is not some big bogeyman waiting to trip us up, but a great lord who is ever ready to reach out in forgiveness.

The rite of reconciliation reflects this image of a God of mercy. Formerly, it was the penitent who began the encounter in confession—"Bless me, Father, for I have sinned"—not unlike the way the sinner of Zorba's imagination approached God, or the way the son in our parable planned to greet his father. But both Zorba's God and the parent in the parable intervened. In the same vein, now in reconciliation it is the confessor who takes the initiative, reaching out, welcoming the penitent and creating a hospitable environment of acceptance and love before there is any mention of sin. Thus, the sacramental moment of confession—just one of the sacramental moments in the whole rite—focuses on God's love rather than our sin.

Of course the new rite does concern itself with the confession of sins. But one's sinfulness is not always the same as one's sins. And, as a sacrament of healing, reconciliation addresses the disease (sinfulness) rather than the symptoms (sins). So, the sacrament calls us to more than prepared speeches or lists of sins. We are challenged to search deep into our heart of hearts to discover the struggles, value conflicts and ambiguities (the disease) which cause the sinful acts (the symptoms) to appear.

A question that often arises is: Why confess my sins? And why confess to a priest? Why not confess directly to God, since God has already forgiven me anyway? From God's point of view, the simple answer is: There is no reason. But from our point of view, the answer is that as human beings who do not live in our minds alone, we need to externalize bodily—with words, signs and gestures—what is in our minds and heart. We need to see, hear and feel forgiveness—not just think about it.

We need other human beings to help us externalize what is within and open our hearts before the Lord, which puts confessors in a new light. They are best seen, not as faceless and impersonal judges, but as guides in our discernment, compassionately helping us experience and proclaim the mercy of God in our lives. As the introduction to the rite puts it, the confessor "fulfills a parental function…reveals the heart of the Father and shows the image of the Good Shepherd." Another of the confessor's roles is to say the prayer of absolution. Contrary to what we may have thought in the past, this prayer, which completes or seals the penitent's change of heart, is not a prayer asking for forgiveness. It is a prayer signifying God's forgiveness of us and our reconciliation with the Church—which is certainly something to celebrate.

Celebration: God always loves us

Celebration is a word we haven't often associated with the sacrament of reconciliation. But in Jesus' parable, it is obviously important and imperative. "Quick!" says the father. "Let us celebrate." And why? Because a sinner has converted, repented, confessed and returned.

Celebration makes sense only when there is really something to celebrate. Each of us has had the experience of going to gatherings with all the trappings of a celebration—people, food, drink, balloons, bands—and yet the festivity was a flop for us. For example, attending an office party can be such an empty gathering for the spouse or friend of an employee. Celebration flows from lived experience or it is meaningless. The need for celebration to follow common lived experiences is especially true of sacramental celebrations. All of the sacraments are communal celebrations of the lived experience of believing Christians.

Perhaps what we need to help us feel more comfortable with the idea of celebration in relation to reconciliation is a conversion from our own rugged individualism. Let's face it—there is something about believing in a bogeyman God from whom we have to earn forgiveness that makes us feel good psychologically. It's harder to feel good about a God who loves and forgives us unconditionally—whether we know it or not, want it or not, like it or not. In the face of such love and forgiveness we feel uncomfortable. It creates a pressure within us that makes us feel we should "do something" to deserve such largess—or at least feel a little bit guilty.

The older brother in our story expresses this same discomfort.

Upon witnessing the festivities, he appeals to fairness and legalism. In a sense, he is hanging on to the courtroom image of the sacrament of reconciliation, suggesting that there is no way everyone can feel good about the return of the younger brother until amends have been made.

But this older son is far too narrow in his understanding of life, of God and of the sacrament. He is too calculating, too quantitative, not unlike the butchers and grocers that Zorba refers to in his description of God. This son finds it difficult to understand that we are never not forgiven. The sacrament of reconciliation does not bring about something that was absent. It proclaims and enables us to own God's love and forgiveness that are already present.

The older brother's problem is a universal human one. It's tough for most of us to say, "I'm sorry." It is even tougher to say, "You're forgiven." And it is most difficult of all to say gracefully, "I accept your forgiveness." To be able to do that we must be able to forgive ourselves. That, too, is what we celebrate in the sacrament of reconciliation.

The community's liturgical celebration of reconciliation places a frame around the picture of our continual journey from sin to reconciliation. Only someone who has never experienced or reflected on that journey will fail to understand the need and value of celebrating the sacrament.

The older son in our story may be such a person. When the father calls for a celebration, everyone else in the household responds. Not only do they celebrate the younger son's return, they celebrate their own experience of forgiveness, mercy and reconciliation as well. They, like us, have been on that journey from which the young man has returned.

So there is something we can do about the unconditional forgiveness we receive from God: forgive as we have been forgiven. Having been forgiven, we are empowered to forgive ourselves and to forgive one another, heal one another and celebrate the fact that together we have come a step closer to the peace, justice and rec-

CELEBRATING GOD'S FORGIVENESS

onciliation that makes us the heralds of Christ's kingdom on earth.

A communal celebration

Sacramental celebrations are communal because sacramental theology is horizontal. Sacraments happen in people who are in relationship with each other and with God. In the area of sin, forgiveness and reconciliation this is particularly evident. Our sinfulness disrupts our relationship in community as well as our relationship with God. And since the sacrament begins with our sinfulness, which affects others, it is only proper that it culminate with a communal expression of love and forgiveness that embodies the love and forgiveness of God.

Unconverted "older sons" will always be out of step with the Christian community. When we celebrate the sacrament, we celebrate with joy and thanksgiving because the forgiveness of the Christian community and of God has brought us to this moment— and that is worth celebrating. There is no room for the attitude that forgiveness comes "only when you have recited your list of sins, agreed to suffer a bit for them and proven yourself worthy to join the rest of us who haven't been so foolish."

Such "older sons" are looking for what theologian Dietrich Bonhoeffer called "cheap grace"—grace without discipleship, without the cross, without faith, without Jesus Christ living and incarnate, and without the conversion necessary to live reconciliation within the Christian community. Such a person is hardly ready to celebrate the sacrament of reconciliation as it is understood today.

Originally Published in Catholic Update by St. Anthony Messenger Press C0386
©1996-2006 www.americancatholic.org

Sister Sandra DeGidio, OSM is an author, speaker, consultant and spiritual guide. She is also development and communications director for her religious congregation. She lives in the Milwaukee, Wisconsin area.

CELEBRATING GOD'S FORGIVENESS

Out of This World

I am forty years old and have been Catholic my whole life. In the early to middle 1970s, when I was about nine or ten years old, I attended Assumption of Mary Catholic School in Missouri. I warmly remember all the kids preparing to go into the church to receive the sacrament of reconciliation for the first time.

Once inside the church, we sat in the pews to examine our conscience before we went into the confessionals. My friend that I was sitting next to told me she didn't know what to say, and that she was a little afraid. I remember very vividly telling her what I was going to say.

I said, "I am just going to tell God the truth about what I have done wrong against Him. I know that if I tell Him the truth and am truly sorry for what I have done, He will forgive me." I also remember telling her that I was not scared at all. For some reason, I really wasn't frightened as I sat in that pew with all those kids, knowing what was about to happen.

I had taken a close look at the previous weeks and months and could recall things I had done that I knew were not pleasing to God. When I thought of those things, I remember feeling very sad knowing that I had hurt someone by what I said or did.

Finally, it was my turn to step inside the confessional. That's when I became a little nervous. When I sat down, I looked the priest right square in the eyes. I knew that it was really God that I was talking to because I knew He uses the priest as an instrument in the confessional.

I explained all my sins with a sorrowful tear running down my face. Then I poured my heart out, telling Him how sorry I was for what I had done. When I finished, the priest helped me say an act of contrition. Then I bowed my head as he laid hands on my head and said the words of absolution.

At that very moment I could feel the healing power of God come upon me and fill my soul with joy and love. In that instant I understood what it was to be reconciled to God. The feeling I had was out of this world! I thought, "Wow! If this is how forgiveness from God feels, I want to be here all the time!"

When I left the confessional I saw the big beautiful church and the pews where the other children were still waiting for their confession. I kid you not, I was afraid to put my arms in the air, which I was feeling compelled to do for some reason. I thought that if I did, I was going to fly way up high to the cathedral ceilings.

I didn't put my arms up and I didn't fly, but in the depths of my soul I knew without a doubt that God was living inside of me. He was with me, He forgave me and He loved me. It was the best experience I can ever remember as a child, and it had a profound effect on me.

To this day, when I receive the sacrament of reconciliation, I go back to that time in my childhood and remember how powerful the love of God is when we turn from our sins and become more and more like Jesus wants us to be.

Lisa M. Coleman   *Lee's Summit, Missouri*

I Love Being Catholic

In the past year I have grown to love and truly appreciate the sacrament of reconciliation. It has taken me years to come to this point. In the past, when I sinned I was filled with guilt and fear which pushed me farther away from God. As a result, I did not go to confession for many years. I thought that if I ignored and denied my sins, maybe God would too.

In September of 2005, I attended a Eucharist centered retreat offered by the Franciscan Friars of the Renewal. They had one of the priests available for confession during the entire retreat. I drummed up the courage to go. During my confession, it became clear that God was present and speaking to me through the priest.

I told the priest about my conversion experience: how I grew up Catholic but had fallen away from the faith for many years. I confessed that several years ago, when I was single, I became pregnant. For the first time in my life, I put my faith and trust in the Lord. I ended up having a miscarriage, but as a result of my pregnancy I started living my faith in a way I never had before.

The priest asked me if I had named the baby, and I said, "No." He suggested that I give the baby a name and then listened to the rest of my confession. I told him about some struggles that I had encountered over the years, and he absolved me of my sins.

After my penance, I started praying. Suddenly the name Agatha came to me. What was interesting was that I wasn't even praying about names. Agatha is not a favorite name of mine, nor do I know anyone named Agatha. I wondered if she were a saint.

On that same day we had Mass, and during the part of the Mass where the priest mentions the name of a saint, he said St. Agatha. There was my answer! Later I found out that she was a saint who was a martyr known for her beauty and her great love of God. She was tortured because she would not give herself up to prostitution.

I continue to go to confession on a regular basis. It's a beautiful thing to sit in front of God, say anything that's in my heart and tell Him I am sorry for my sins. He doesn't look at me in a disapproving manner, judge me, or turn His back on me. He loves me unconditionally and forgives me. What a wonderful sacrament Jesus has given us. I love being Catholic!

Amanda M. Mason   *Jacksonville, Florida*

A Serious Decision

At twenty-eight years old, I was blessed with three children after miscarrying one. I loved being a stay-at-home mom and wanted to have a house filled with kids. I was full of love and energy. My housework was always done early in the morning, before any of the children were awake. All I had to do was tidy up the kitchen after breakfast and make the beds, then off we would go for a full day at the beach. We'd get home in enough time for me to make dinner.

My last pregnancy caused damage to my internal veins from my waist down and I was in a lot of pain. I desperately wanted more babies but the doctors said if I became pregnant again I could die. They said they'd have to perform an abortion to save my life if I did get pregnant, and advised me to get a tubal ligation to permanently prevent future pregnancies.

I said, "No way. It's against my beliefs." They warned me that no other birth control would be safe enough to protect me from another pregnancy.

I didn't know what to do. I was afraid that God would be angry with me for using this form of birth control. At that time in my life I believed that God was watching me, just waiting for me to sin. I grew up with a fire and brimstone atmosphere in my church, and heard about God's wrath so often that I was convinced I would go to hell if I used birth control, even if it was to save my life.

I knew I had a serious decision to make that could affect my relationship with God so I went to confession. However, I went to a different church because I didn't want my own parish priest to know my dilemma.

The priest I confessed to was very understanding and kind. I never experienced a confession like that in my whole life. He compassionately told me that God certainly understood my desire for more children. He also said that sometimes when confronted with a difficult choice like this, we have to choose the lesser of two evils.

We talked for a long time. He said he couldn't tell me what to do, but knew that if I placed my situation in God's hands, I would get my answer. He told me to pray and to trust in God's love for me. When I told him that I often pray to the Blessed Mother and pray the rosary, he told me to pray to her about this situation too.

This priest wanted me to truly believe that God would not send me to hell when I wanted nothing more than to do the right thing. When I left the church, I felt a peace inside me like I had never felt before. I cried in the car before going home and wondered if the priest was telling the truth. Did God really understand my confusion, my pain?

I prayed to God and Mary for two years before I made my decision. I finally knew without a doubt that I had to get a tubal ligation as the doctors recommended in order to keep a healthy marriage and not have to choose between my life and a baby's life. When I went into the operating room, I knew in my heart that if I died during the surgery, God would take me to heaven. I truly believed it.

Because I still wanted more children, I became a foster parent. Our home usually had anywhere from one to three foster children at a time. At one time two little girls who were sisters lived with us for three years. We wanted to adopt them, but when their father remarried, he got custody of them. Fortunately, we were given the opportunity to see them often after they left our home, and being a part of each other's lives was very special for all of us. Now, as an adult, one of them lives near us with her child and we share in many holiday family dinners and special occasions.

Many blessings came out of a difficult situation. Through a compassionate priest in the confessional, I learned of God's mercy and forgiveness, and I will never be afraid of Him again.

Connie A. Andretta   *Denver, North Carolina*

"The sacrament of reconciliation is an invitation to place yourself in God's gentle presence. Because Jesus wishes to heal your broken parts, so that you can be made whole and confident, he offers you God's assurance of acceptance through the words and absolution of a priest who is, like you, aware of his own need for forgiveness."

Preparing for Confession:
Taking Your Spiritual Temperature
by Fr. Thomas M. Casey

see page 111

A Special Dream

I grew up in a devout Catholic family in Ohio and received all the sacraments. As I entered my teen years, I began questioning many Catholic practices—especially the sacrament of reconciliation. I couldn't understand why I had to confess my sins to a priest instead of going directly to God. As a college freshman, I continued learning, reading, and seeking answers to questions about my faith, but still had reservations.

That Lent, in the spring of 2003, a friend and I decided to go to reconciliation. I was still unsure about the sacrament though, and the night before we went, I lay in bed struggling with my doubts. I felt very nervous. In my heart I was not at peace about confessing my sins to a priest despite all of the explanations I had heard. I eventually fell asleep and had a dream, or vision, that forever changed my attitude about the sacrament of reconciliation.

In my dream, I was sitting in an old-fashioned confessional with a grille between the priest and me. From my vantage point in the dream, I could see that the priest was dressed in normal clerical clothing. However, I could tell without a doubt that he was Jesus. I knew that I was confessing my sins directly to my Savior. At my feet was a hole in the screen between Jesus and me that measured about one square foot. As I confessed each sin, I passed planks of wood through the hole to Jesus. At His feet was an incinerator where He slowly fed each plank until they were all completely burned.

At that point, I woke up and the meaning of the dream was clear to me. Each piece of wood was one of my sins, and as Jesus received it, He destroyed it. He never held on to my sins and never held anything against me. As soon as it left my lips, my sin was gone. I also recognized each piece of wood as wood from Jesus' cross. He had been nailed to my sins.

As startling a realization as it was, I felt nothing but love and forgiveness from the man who suffered an agonizing death for my sins.

From that day on I have never been afraid to go to confession. As I prepare to receive the sacrament, I recall my dream and Jesus' presence, love, and forgiveness. Like the wood, my sins are destroyed in the sacrament of reconciliation and peace fills my heart.

Jessica A. Zajac   *Northfield, Ohio*

Since That Moment

When I went on a pilgrimage in France with my husband, I knew that if my ninety-three-year-old mother should die while we were there, I would not be able to return to her funeral. She had been living in a nursing home for seven years and her health had failed on many occasions. It was a chance I took. I thought I was prepared for it.

A week after we left home, the telephone call came from our oldest son telling us Grandma had died. We were in northern France around Lisieux and Omaha Beach, and there was no time to return for the funeral. Our middle son offered to handle the details of flowers and arrangements for us. I knew my six siblings and my children would lovingly supervise a grace-filled funeral for our mother and grandmother.

As the tour continued, I prayed for my mother at every shrine we visited. I was present in spirit at my mother's wake, funeral, and burial, and at the dinner afterwards, but I was still very unhappy.

At Paray le Monial in the Chapel of the Visitation, I went to confession and told my confessor, "I am upset with not being at my mother's funeral and am concerned about my siblings' reactions to my not being there."

His response continues to comfort me to this day. "If Jesus wanted you to be at your mother's funeral, you would have been there. Here we are in the chapel where Jesus appeared to St. Margaret Mary, where He told her about the devotion to His Sacred Heart. If Jesus wanted you at your mother's funeral, you would have been there." Since that moment, I have been very conscious of Jesus' will in my life.

When I was met at the airport, everyone was concerned about me. My nephews had taken many pictures "for Aunt Mariann." I was surrounded by the love of my family. The Sacred Heart of Jesus knows what is best for each of us.

Mariann H. Otto   *Lester Prairie, Minnesota*

Serious Trouble

For a number of years I was away from the Catholic Church thinking I could work out all my issues on my own. When I began going to Mass again in 1997, I began growing in my faith and realized how I had offended God, not only by my sins, but also by the way I had dismissed His Church.

I finally went to confession at St. Ray's Cathedral in Joliet, Illinois. As I stood in line I became convinced that once I confessed my sins I was going to be in serious trouble. I knew my penance would be great.

I confessed all my sins and began to weep uncontrollably. I felt so bad for what I had done. Then the priest told me that Jesus loved me. I cried even more. I felt as if Jesus had just given me a huge hug. Me, a big sinner!

When the priest absolved me of my sins I asked about my penance. He said, "You have suffered enough. From now on, defend the Lord's Church the best way you can. Peace be with you my daughter. Welcome back!"

Anonymous   *Johnstown, Ohio*

I Wanted More in Life

My parents raised me well, but despite that, I became a very rebellious teenager. I hung with the *party-hard* crowd throughout high school and by my senior year I was well known as a star football player and crazy party animal. When I graduated, my life revolved around friends, beer, girls, and popularity. This carried over into college.

After entering Texas A&M University, I found a group of buddies who also loved girls and beer. I was arrogant and confident on the outside, but I did not feel that way on the inside. My grades were poor, I was unhappy, and life wasn't very good. I wanted more in life, but I didn't know where to get it. Then I started talking to some other young men in my dorm whom I found interesting because they always seemed to have a good time without partying. They intrigued me with their lifestyle and joy.

These guys became my closest friends in college, and they still are to this day. They are a mixture of Catholics and Southern Baptists who didn't like me too much at first because I was too drunk and lazy for them. But this didn't keep them from encouraging me to go back to church, which I did once in a while.

At church one Sunday, I heard about a parish mission that was coming up the next week. I wanted to go, but I didn't want to seem too Christian, so I went the last night only. That night, the priest told a story of how he failed to see Christ in an annoying homeless woman on a bus in New York City. After the story, I thought that if I had been the priest in that situation, I would have beaten the woman up. This thought bothered me.

Because the Holy Spirit was kicking me in the pants, and due to the encouragement of my friends, I decided to attend a retreat called Aggie Awakening. I told myself and others that I was going only because a lot of good-looking Catholic women would be there. Of course, I thought about backing out several times, but two of my friends were also going and wouldn't let me. In my heart I knew I needed something, and I was hoping I could get whatever it was from the retreat.

When I got there, I was taken aback by the fervor and zeal of all the *Jesus freaks* and *Bible thumpers*. I had never met Catholics like these before. On Friday night of the retreat there was a talk about confession and the need to repent our sins. I was convinced that I was a sinner, but I decided confession was useless and I wasn't going to go.

After the talk, there was an examination of conscience that took us through the Ten Commandments. It was geared toward college students, and I think I could have checked almost every one of the hundreds of sins covered. This was an eye-opener for me, and for some inexplicable reason I found myself walking to confession. I didn't want to go, and I still don't know why I did. I was scared, angry, and confused.

I stood in line to see a priest I had neither seen before or since. While waiting for my turn, I became even more frightened because I had never before gone to confession with a priest face-to-face. When I finally sat in front of this man of God, whom I truly consider to be my guardian angel from heaven, I immediately started sobbing.

For the first time in my life I talked about all the sins I didn't even want to admit to myself. Confessing them was both painful and amazingly beautiful. After the priest calmed me and told me about God's love for me, my heart opened wide and I had my initial conversion to Christ. This was the moment I was *saved* and allowed Christ to enter my life. After confession, I felt like a new person, and I knelt in the chapel where I truly prayed to God for the first time. I told Him I was now His, and He welcomed me home with open arms.

From that moment on, I have tried to live my life for Jesus. I became involved in my parish community, started to pray daily, and began attending Mass. My spiritual journey began from where I had left off as a child. Of course, the road has had its bumps and problems, but I still find Christ's love and healing when I go to confession.

I now work as the director of campus ministry in a large campus ministry at Texas Tech University where we have the same Aggie Awakening retreat program that changed my life. I am blessed because I am able to be a part of the conversion process of hundreds of young people every year through the sacrament of reconciliation.

Marcel R. LeJeune   *Lubbock, Texas*

Heaven is Warm

I am an alcoholic, and the day I finally turned it over to God, I immediately went to confession for the first time in years. It was at a church I hadn't been attending, with a priest I didn't know.

At that time in my life I was working, going to school, and raising two young children on my own. I was barely scraping by. Before going to confession, I wondered what on earth I could tell the priest that would be just a small amount of information, but enough that he would quickly give me absolution and let me leave.

When I got into the confessional, I forgot the words to the act of contrition and had to be coached through it. I also had my two small children crammed into the booth with me, asking questions as I tried to give as brief but as honest a confession as I could.

As I left the church with my absolution clutched figuratively in my hand, I felt only halfway forgiven. It had nothing to do with the priest; I felt I had made a hasty, halfway confession and was terrified that God wasn't going to accept it. I took my children home to our cold apartment and bundled them into bed, my infant son in his playpen and my toddler daughter with me on a mattress that was on the floor. I covered us with every blanket we had in an attempt to get warm enough to sleep.

I was worried that God wasn't going to accept or forgive me because I'd been way too imperfect, so I lay there in the cold and cried. Moments later, I was above the mattress and seated almost sprawled at the feet of Jesus. I rested my head on His knee and felt the soft billowing of His white robes. I never once looked up; I never felt the need to. I knew who He was. And I was warm, so very warm. No one said anything and I never moved, nor did He.

Eventually I returned to my bed. He was gone and I was once again shivering beneath the blankets. I wrapped my arms around my little girl and pulled her close to me, my heart swollen and aching with the agony of ecstasy. I now know this for certain—Heaven is warm, and the Son accepts our most inept confessions if they come from our hearts.

Jeanne M. McClure   *New Albany, Indiana*

Face-to-Face With Jesus

Because of my ever-increasing hearing loss, celebrating the sacrament of reconciliation face-to-face has become the best way for me to experience a healing encounter with God. Like many hard-of-hearing people, I unconsciously rely on lip-reading and body language for better communication.

When I used the confessional with a screen, I didn't always hear the priest very well and sometimes I left wondering if I had really been forgiven. I also didn't have the feeling of the joy that contact with God brings. Now that I sit face-to-face with the priest, not only do I understand what he is saying, but it is like being face-to-face with Jesus. The friendly smile and gestures, and the very personal blessing make it a truly sacramental experience filled with grace and joy.

Rita F. Prenavo   *Chicago, Illinois*

Confessions of a Catholic Convert

By Elizabeth Ficocelli

> *Once she feared confession. Now she experiences its blessings. From the Catholic family magazine St. Anthony Messenger.*

A few years ago, as I served as a sponsor in our parish's Rite of Christian Initiation of Adults, our class watched a video on the sacrament of reconciliation. Although the piece was interesting in terms of its historical content, I felt it missed a great opportunity. The film reviewed proper procedure and obligation, but not once did it mention what a gift the sacrament of reconciliation can be for Catholics.

As a convert myself, I always thought confession seemed a confusing and intimidating practice of the Catholic faith. What was the purpose of those dark little rooms where you whispered the unthinkable to a total stranger? I didn't even like to think about sin, much less talk about it. It was only through the grace of God—literally—that I finally came to appreciate the beauty and significance of this life-giving sacrament.

Out of a Formal and Routine Past

In the Lutheran church of my youth, confession was handled in a rather tidy manner. The congregation would stand and, together with the pastor, face the altar and read aloud a statement of confession. The pastor would then turn to face the congregation and read a response that essentially told us we were forgiven.

I don't remember feeling heartily sorry for my sins—or heartily forgiven, for that matter—it was just a part of our Sunday worship.

I suppose I must have talked to God privately about my sins growing up, but forgiveness and reconciliation do not hold strong memories for me.

93

CATHOLIC CONVERT CONFESSION

I was a catechumen in 1983 as a young adult preparing for marriage. When our RCIA class broached the subject of confession, the priest arranged to meet with each of us privately. I remember feeling incredibly nervous.

My faith was not yet strong enough to see beyond the man sitting across from me. I couldn't comprehend that it was Jesus and his forgiveness I was encountering in this sacrament. The priest was helpful and patient, taking me through the Ten Commandments one by one.

I squeamishly admitted my faults, looking to him for clues or approval. The next thing I knew, the priest absolved me and sent me on my way. I didn't feel any different and wondered if maybe I hadn't done it right. Puzzled, I decided that this part of Catholicism was going to be a learning process for me.

As I entered the Church formally and began receiving the sacrament of reconciliation on a somewhat regular basis, I still found myself immersed in the "sin" part of the equation. I was focused on how terrible I was, how unforgivable, and completely missed out on the benefit of forgiveness.

I dreaded having to bare my soul to a man who, in my opinion, must be almost sinless (after all, he was a priest, wasn't he?!). I was still concerned about what he would think of me, not only in the confessional, but also every time we crossed paths. It was not uncommon for me, therefore, to go to other parishes when it was time for confession.

At the same time, however, something significant was happening. I was beginning to realize that, once I made a confession, I truly felt better. Forcing myself to verbalize and take responsibility for my offenses and ask pardon for them really did make a difference in how I felt afterward. It was harder than my Lutheran way, but I was starting to see the benefits.

My biggest stumbling block remained not being able to forgive myself. I used to come out of the confessional disappointed by the act of penance—to say an Our Father or something easy like that.

I would have much rather been told to take ten laps around the church property. Still seeing things from a purely human point of view, I was unable to grasp God's ready and complete forgiveness.

Then, I experienced a miracle.

Miracle of Mercy

It occurred during Lent, not long before Easter. I had just read the writings of a young Polish nun, the recently canonized Sister Faustina Kowalska, and I was really excited about her message of God's divine mercy. I was praying the Divine Mercy novena and had planned to go to confession on Divine Mercy Sunday for a complete pardon of sins as promised.

Inspired to share her story with my prayer group, I located a video about Sister Faustina and prepared a little presentation. All in all, things were going quite well. That's when disaster struck, and I committed the most regrettable sin of my life.

A continual string of sleepless nights caring for my newborn was taking a serious toll on my patience level and rational thinking ability. One bleary morning, I lost what was left of my emotional control and raged against my four-year-old in a way that filled me with profound shame and regret. I was devastated and shocked at how such an unbridled outburst could occur during the holiest time of the year.

When I regained my composure, I immediately sought forgiveness from my son and, soon after, from my husband. I knew, however, that most importantly I had to reconcile with God. A part of me wondered if I could be forgiven at all.

The following day was Palm Sunday. As the Church prepared for its most holy celebration, I felt as if I should be counted among the ranks of Judas and Peter. Ashamed and unable to live with myself, I went to my parish to make a confession. My plan was to talk to a retired priest who heard confessions, because I was too embarrassed to talk with my pastor.

When I arrived at church, however, I saw twenty-five people in line for the retired priest and only three waiting to speak with the pastor. Humbled, I joined the shorter line. God wasn't going to make this easy for me.

Inside the confessional, it all came out. Between sobs, I told the pastor the unpleasant details of my crime. He was very understanding and said pretty much what I expected, then he administered absolution. I still felt terrible.

As I was leaving the confessional, however, an amazing thing happened. I experienced an incredible, tangible sensation—as if someone were pouring a bucket of water over my head. I felt washed clean, tingling all the way down to my feet, and feather-light, as if the weight of the world had just been lifted off my shoulders. I had never experienced anything like this before.

I recognized at once that God was giving me a hit over the head, an unmistakably clear sign that I was truly forgiven. He saw how my heart was breaking and how genuinely contrite I was, and he was happy to welcome me back.

His words, as given to Sister Faustina, occurred to me, "Let not even the weak and sinful fear to approach me, even though their sins be as numerous as the sands of the earth, all will vanish in the fathomless pit of my mercy."

If forgiveness from God were always to come as tangibly as I was privileged to experience it that day, I'm sure the lines for confession would be far longer. But I suppose that's where our faith must come into play.

Divine Dimension Holds Sway

God works signs and wonders in our lives according to our needs. Evidently, on that day, I needed something pretty significant to get my attention. From that experience, I was finally able to learn how to let go of my sins and truly forgive myself.

Today, when I receive the sacrament of reconciliation, I no longer drag my feet, focusing only on my sins. Now I look forward to receiving God's mercy. Even though I don't feel it in that same tangible way, I know it's happening just the same. I look forward to being unburdened, and feeling close to Our Lord once again.

Instead of seeking out priests I don't know, I can now go comfortably to any of the clergy in my own parish. Each priest has his own style, but the absolution is always the same because it comes from God.

Through the years, I've developed a special relationship with one of our priests by making him my primary confessor. This way, he's better equipped to help me overcome obstacles in my spiritual growth as I live out my vocation as wife and mother.

For me, an adult convert, the sacrament of reconciliation has become a way of encountering Christ intimately and meaningfully, second only to receiving him in the Eucharist. At last, I experience confession the way I believe God has always intended it: as a great gift. Forgive me, Father, for not recognizing this gift sooner.

Originally Published in Catholic family magazine St. Anthony Messenger.
©1996-2006 www.americancatholic.org

Elizabeth Ficocelli is the author of Shower of Heavenly Roses: Stories of the Intercession of St. Therese of Lisieux *(The Crossroad Publishing Company) and* The Fruits of Medjugorje: Stories of True and Lasting Conversion *(Paulist Press).*

Torn Between Good and Evil

When I was a young girl, I was a very devout Catholic. I spent every morning before school at church, and after school I would return alone to pray. When I became a teenager, I gradually started moving away from the Church. Like most girls, I started spending more time with boys than with God.

Later I married, and after ten years and two children, I began to find my heart yearning to go back to my Catholic faith. My children were attending Catholic school, and my oldest son was in the process of making his first reconciliation when I felt my heart being pulled by Jesus.

My marriage was a wreck. I was working full time and spending many hours away from home. I began to fall into a bad lifestyle, but at the same time, I felt God tugging at my heart. I was extremely torn between good and evil.

One night I fell into a deep sleep, and in my sleep the devil came to me. The appearance of the devil was so grotesque that I cannot put it into words. He fought me. I was engaged in a complete physical altercation with Satan. I looked up for a moment and saw my two guardian angels looking down on me with such sorrow in their faces that I knew this was it. I had to make a decision. Do I go with Satan and continue to live in sin, or do I turn my life over to Jesus?

At that moment I screamed out, "Leave me alone, Satan! I am a child of God!" As I said the words, he slithered away. When I awoke, I was soaking wet from head to toe, and I was shaking. I was so frightened that I had to leave all the lights on in my room.

I now knew the choice I had to make. I knew I could no longer live in perpetual sin. That's when I called my local parish. After being away from the confessional for more than ten years, I wanted to start my life anew.

It was about six o'clock in the evening when I called the church to find out what time confessions were heard. The parish priest answered the phone. I explained that I wanted to know the confession schedule. He told me what it was and then said, "Or upon request." He invited me to drop everything and meet him at the church. He would go over and open the church so I could make my confession immediately.

At seven o'clock that night I entered the confessional for the first time in many years. After examining my conscience, I made a very heartfelt confession. I actually felt the Holy Spirit lift my burdens and knew when I walked out of that confessional that my life was going to be changed forever. It was.

Anonymous   *Twinsburg, Ohio*

Guilt Relieving Machine

People frequently carry a heavy burden of sins and cannot forgive themselves. To make matters worse, there is often someone in their life who is constantly reminding them of what they have done wrong. Fortunately, we Catholics have the best guilt-relieving machine on the planet —the sacrament of reconciliation. Sadly, though, many people in pain don't realize their burden can be lifted through this healing sacrament.

When a person comes to confession with an *unforgivable sin* such as abortion, infidelity, blasphemy, or any other serious sin, a priest can't restore his broken spirit by simply saying that everything is going to be all right, and then sending him on his way. In the confessional, Jesus speaks to the penitent through the priest and brings true healing through Scriptures, the apostles, and through the laying on of hands. He reassures us saying, "Have courage my son or daughter, your sins are forgiven."

When the priest says the powerful words, "I absolve you in the name of the Father and of the Son and of the Holy Spirit," it is actually Jesus forgiving the person, not the priest. These words of absolution literally change lives. I tell penitents who are struggling to forgive themselves that they can completely trust these words of forgiveness, and that there is no doubt that God's judgment of their sins is over. Scripture gives the Church the power to forgive sins, and this can facilitate miraculous inner healings.

As a priest, there are few experiences more gratifying for me than when Jesus works His miracle of healing forgiveness during the sacrament of reconciliation. Christ's incredible gift of mercy is made audibly present to those who take advantage of this divine gift.

Fr. Gary L. Zerr   *Keizer, Oregon*

Touched by a Heavenly Gift

In September of 1997, I went with my mom to visit my cousin in England. On October 2, the three of us flew to Knock, Ireland, because I really wanted to visit a shrine somewhere in Europe.

After we arrived and found accommodations, we drove to Our Lady of Knock Shrine. As we entered the shrine area I wondered, "What do I do first?" Then it occurred to me, "Of course, go to reconciliation!" I walked into the huge confession building and looked around. There were so many confessionals!

"Okay, what do I confess?" I wondered. I decided to confess my pride; I was sure that the Holy Spirit was my inspiration.

To my left there was an open confessional door. So I went in. I saw a priest sitting sideways on his chair with his right arm hanging over the back of the chair. He looked bored.

After I knelt on the kneeler and confessed my pride, he looked at me and said that many people had been confessing their pride lately. I was absolved, and the penance he gave me was to say ten Hail Marys. I thanked him and went to kneel before the altar.

I looked around at the beautiful surroundings and then said my Hail Marys. Leaving the building, I noticed I had to struggle to get my feet to touch the ground. I actually felt as if I were floating and had to put pressure on one foot and then the other to touch the ground so I could walk. I felt joyful, as if I had been touched by a heavenly gift!

When I looked up, I saw my mother and Margaret coming towards me. I wondered if they noticed I was having a hard time walking. I don't think they did because when we met they just told me that Mass was being said in the chapel.

When I left them, I was able to walk normally and went into the chapel in time to take part in the Eucharistic celebration. After Mass, I remained seated so I could look at the life-sized statues. There was humble St. Joseph on the left, and Mary, Our Lady of Knock, smiling as she prayerfully looked up to heaven.

The statue of St. John the Evangelist amazed me because it looked as if he were evangelizing with every fiber of his being. A statue of the Lamb of God was on the altar, and angels encircled the cross and the altar. To the right was the tabernacle. It was an awesome sight to behold and experience.

Suddenly, I smelled roses, and because I felt that Our Lady must be present, I immediately knelt down. I remained there for awhile until it was time for me to meet Mom and Margaret.

As we left the shrine area, I stopped at a shop to buy a small statue of Our Lady of Knock. The lady brought me one, but when I looked at it, I told the lady, "It doesn't look like the one in the chapel." She said, "Yes, it is the same one." I told her that the one in the chapel was smiling and this one wasn't. She smiled and said that happens to some people. The one in the chapel isn't smiling either. I didn't believe her, but when we went back to the shrine, the statue of Our Lady of Knock wasn't smiling!

During my confession, I renounced my pride. I am so glad I did. My pride didn't totally disappear that day, but during the past few years, I have experienced an awareness of the damaging effects of pride.

Frances M. Rychlo, SFO   *St. Albert, Alberta, Canada*

Ten Commandments Song

I am sixty years old and learned the following song when I was in second grade at a Polish Catholic school. After all these years, I still sing it to myself when I'm tempted, and it helps me avoid sin.

First, I must honor God,
Second, honor His name,
Third, honor His day, keep holy,
This will be my aim.
Fourth, I must be obedient,
Fifth, be kind and true,
Sixth, be pure in all I say or sing or hear or do.
Seventh, I must be honest,
Eighth, be truthful in all things I say,
Ninth, be pure in mind and heart,
In all I think and desire each day.
Tenth I must be satisfied,
Not be jealous come what may,
These are God's Ten Commandments,
These I must obey.

Paul J. Gwozdz   *Poestenkill, New York*

"Obviously we need to root all mortal sin from our lives. But we need to get rid of venial sins, too. After all, when you're trying to be a good friend to someone, is it enough not to murder his family? No. You need to strive constantly to be good to him, in the little ways as well as the big. Killing someone's mother will ruin your friendship. But constantly lying to him will eventually do the same thing."

We're On a Mission From God

by Mary Beth Bonacci

see page 53

A New Marriage

In June of 1992, my husband, John, walked out the door. Half of me went with him, and I felt as though my heart had been ripped out and stomped on. My worst nightmare of a divorce was becoming a reality. Little did I know then that through this terrible journey across rough seas, Jesus would lead us to the shelter of His Church and, in time, to the renewal of our marriage.

John and I had met in seminary and were both United Methodist ministers. I left the ministry and went into library science in 1989, and John took a part time pastorate and went full-time back into practicing as an attorney in 1990. Since 1973 I had been reading the lives of the saints of the Catholic Church and now with the divorce, I longed to become Catholic.

The Rite of Christian Initiation of Adults (RCIA) started in October. Mary Corso was the team director of RCIA and Father Richard Engle was our priest at Immaculate Conception in Dennison, Ohio. Mary said we all answered an inner call of God to come to the Catholic Church. I had never before looked at my desire for the Catholic Church as a call of God but I began to see how true that was.

When I came to the Catholic Church in 1992, I was broken and starving for human touch. The emptiness and deep pain within made me realize that a Christ who is only *spiritual* is not enough. The Church, through her members and priests, began to give me the gifts of the Church and I began to receive them. The whole year in RCIA I was crying out to God for mercy for my sins in contributing to the divorce. I began to see John as a human being in much need of the gifts and graces of the Catholic Church as well.

During Lent of 1993, I went to Confession as preparation for first Communion. From this sacrament of reconciliation I learned that if I truly confess my sins there is power in absolution. When I confess alone in prayers, I do not receive the same sense of assurance that I have received God's forgiveness. Through the sacrament of reconciliation I enter the confessional weighed down by my sins but leave free from sin and experience the marvelous grace and love of God.

During the Easter Vigil of 1993, I received the sacrament of confirmation and my first holy Communion, the body and blood of Christ, and was welcomed into the Church. I found a new land of God's presence and love.

In June of 1993, I met John at his parent's house to pick up our children. He asked to talk with me in private. He was a broken man. I confessed to him my sins toward the divorce, and with tears in his eyes he confessed what he had done to lead to our divorce. The walls between us came crashing down. We forgave each other and then embraced, weeping in the love and presence of God.

Father Engle counseled us and guided us back to reconciliation between each other, God and the Church. The following October, John started RCIA classes. Father Engle said we each had to take responsibility for our own sins and not keep blaming the other. Father Engle married us in January 1994. In the spring John went to confession for the first time and received confirmation and holy Communion.

John and I are still deeply in love and have new respect and trust for one another. We are new people and have a new marriage. We have not *arrived*, but the Church is teaching us how to live and love.

Brenda McCloud   *Canton, Georgia*

God's Surprises

Last year the Lord called me to conversion through some amazing experiences. On New Year's Eve of 2004, I read Father Gabriel Amorth's book about exorcism and began to realize that my materialistic, partying, lesbian lifestyle was not only sinful but evil. Father Amorth says that going to confession and Communion are the best ways to remove evil from one's life, so I began to do both.

After two months (the day I put on a blessed St. Benedict medal) I told my live-in partner that she and I would have to stop *sleeping together*. She was reluctant at first, but now she and I attend daily Mass and pray the rosary daily. The Lord and Our Lady have given us the grace to live together in chastity.

After our initial conversion, the Lord had more surprises in store for me. I have a long family history of alcoholism and was drinking heavily. I was concerned about my drinking but never seriously considered giving it up, even though it was affecting my life. My family would complain that I always got "drunk and stupid" at parties and events.

On the day before Passion Sunday last year, I went to confession at my local parish, Assumption of the Blessed Virgin Mary in Pasadena, California. The pastor, Father Gerard O'Brien, was hearing confessions. I confessed that I thought I drank too much. He asked me how old I was (forty-two) and if my family knew about it. I told him they knew. Then he asked me if I were an alcoholic. I said, "I think so."

He proceeded to tell me that I was too old to carry on like that and my penance was to go to Alcoholic's Anonymous. Needless to say I was stunned, but I thought that God was obviously speaking through the sacrament and I was not going to ignore Him. I performed my penance and started going to AA.

After a couple of weeks I realized that I had very little craving for alcohol. I have been sober ever since and do not miss alcohol at all. After that I began to pray and go to daily Mass. I believe that God gave me not only a spiritual healing but healing from my addiction through the sacrament of reconciliation.

I tell my story to people and often get some strange reactions. The people in AA were very impressed by Father Gerard's wisdom and insight. Some of my friends thought it was weird but it was good that I quit drinking.

God has continued to bless me and my family so abundantly that I cannot describe it. He invites me to come to adoration several times each week and Father Gerard even asked me to be a Eucharistic minister. I cannot begin to tell you how much happier and more fulfilled I am as a sober, chaste and faithful Catholic.

Sylvia A. Green   *Pasadena, California*

Airport Confession

I am a Catholic priest, and nearly six years ago I almost died. When the Lord spared my life for me, I decided to return home to California to regain my strength and be enveloped in the loving care of my family.

While waiting for my departure in Chicago's O'Hare Airport, I sat in a corner by myself reading a book about the life of my favorite saint, Therese of Lisieux. I wasn't wearing my clerical clothing because they no longer fit, and I had decided to purchase new ones while I was home with my family.

While I was reading the book, a man cautiously approached me and asked if I were a Catholic priest. Trying to minimize my surprise I said, "I am." He wondered if I might hear his confession, to which I agreed. He explained that long ago he had abandoned his faith, but when he found himself frightened to board a plane, he asked God to forgive his obstinacy and send him a priest. At the conclusion of his prayer he felt compelled to go to gate K-6, which was where I had planted myself. He saw me in the corner and just knew that I was the priest God sent.

He was right. I was in that place at that moment for this man to bare his soul. We spoke for almost an hour, but it seemed like mere minutes. He was a good man at heart who needed his life explained within the context of love and redemption, something I tried my best to do. One of the greatest moments of my priestly life was when I raised my hand to absolve him. If for no other reason, I believe that God spared my life for this man and his need to be forgiven.

Fr. Gary C. Caster   *Washington, Illinois*

Author of Mary, In Her Own Words: The Mother of God in Scripture *by Servant Books—October 2006*

Confession After Abortion

When I was seventeen years old, living at home, I unfortunately became pregnant. I was raised in a very strict home environment and didn't know how I could tell such news to my parents. I knew they would be devastated, so my boyfriend and I decided the best thing to do would be for me to have an abortion. I struggled with the idea, but I was young and scared and just wanted the pregnancy to go away. My boyfriend and I had been dating for about a year and never planned for this to happen, but it did.

I called the local woman's clinic and made an appointment. I remember having a waiting period as well as going through a consultation where they showed me graphic pictures of abortions that had been performed at various stages of pregnancy. I looked at the pictures and mentally blocked the images from my mind. All I could think about was getting rid of the baby so my parents would never find out.

The day I went to have the abortion, I woke up and asked the Lord to please forgive me. I was scared and just wanted to get it over with. My boyfriend picked me up at the corner of my street and we drove to the abortion clinic in silence. We walked in and waited for them to call me back. I have never felt as guilty in my entire life as I did when I knew I was about to kill my unborn child.

I had the abortion and tried to forget about it as I went through life. I later married a wonderful man and had two beautiful children. Despite all this, I carried around the guilt of that day and never got over it. For more than fifteen years I was haunted with thoughts of the child I knew I would have had. I hated myself for going through with the abortion.

As an infant, I was baptized in the Catholic Church and now I wanted my children to be baptized as well. I also wanted to be confirmed since I had never received that sacrament. I worked toward the day that I would be confirmed and my children would be baptized. Unfortunately, the very thought of going to confession for the first time scared me, but I knew this was what I needed to do to get rid of the guilt I had been carrying around.

My very first confession was made to Father Pellegrino from Saints Peter and Paul Church in West Valley City, Utah. I practiced over and over what I needed to tell him, hoping I would not feel like a complete idiot. As I drove to the church that night, I had a knot in my stomach and just wanted to turn around and go home, but something kept telling me that everything would be okay.

The wait in line seemed like an eternity as the events of my past abortion flashed over and over in my mind. Father Pellegrino called me in and listened to my confession as I cried and poured my heart out to him. I asked for the Lord's forgiveness and felt a feeling of peace as Father prayed over me. As I left to go home, the dark cloud that had been following me around for the last fifteen years finally disappeared.

Pauline M. Wilson   *Stansbury Park, Utah*

My Thoughts...

I will always remember the words a priest at Westminster Cathedral told me during confession. I was disheartened and disillusioned by my awfulness.

He told me quite simply, "Christ adores you."

Audrey Lynn Newbury   South Harrow, Middlesex, England

Tomorrow

In 1942, I was baptized as an infant in the Presbyterian Church. Since my family was faithful and active in that church, there was no question as to where I would attend Sunday school and church services each week.

In 1972, I married my husband, Al, who was a lifelong Catholic, and relocated to where he was living. After I moved, I attended the Presbyterian Church a few times, but the Catholic Church, which had fascinated me since my childhood, drew me closer and closer. I began attending Mass, and the more I learned about the faith, the more I was convinced that the Catholic Church was where I belonged.

One day I was talking to the pastor of the Catholic parish, and although I hadn't planned to, I heard myself telling him that I wanted to become Catholic. My first question to him was, "When may I go to confession?" "Tomorrow," he replied. I was thrilled and went home to search my soul and to prepare to confess all my transgressions. I never experienced the least bit of apprehension, but only joyful anticipation.

My first confession lasted a rather long time, but after I received absolution, I was filled with an unbelievable sense of God's love and peace. What a reassurance of God's forgiveness! To this day, each time I receive the sacrament I feel great happiness and peace, and the overwhelming need and desire to praise and thank my God.

Virginia Schmuck   *Portales, New Mexico*

Preparing for Confession: Taking Your Spiritual Temperature

by Fr. Thomas M. Casey

Have you ever heard the question, "Why should I confess my sins to a priest, when I can go directly to God?"

One answer is that we can talk directly to God and ask forgiveness for the sins or faults that weigh on us. There is allowance made for this approach in the penitential rite at the beginning of Mass, and surveys indicate that many Catholics use this opportunity to examine their conscience or take their spiritual temperature and ask forgiveness. The Church has always taught that God's love and acceptance are available whenever anyone is truly sorry for harmful words, deeds or attitudes.

Most of you probably find yourselves talking to God at some point during the week, perhaps even daily. You may ask God to help you do well on a test, to make a sports team or just to be liked by your classmates.

Other times you may be uncertain about a decision that you have to make and you feel the need to pray over it. Maybe a close friend has asked you to lie to his or her parents about being with you when the friend was really with someone the parents disapprove of. At times like this, talking to God will help you sort out your feelings and be honest to your conscience.

At other times you find that you need to ask someone else for advice, simply to get a second opinion about some concern. You might ask an older brother or sister: "What should I say when my friends pressure me to drink or try drugs?"

A Sacrament for Seeing the Truth

The priest in his role as confessor in the sacrament of reconciliation can also serve as a kind of sounding board or mirror who helps you see points you may not have thought of.

111

YOUR SPIRITUAL TEMPERATURE

Y
O
U
R

S
P
I
R
I
T
U
A
L

T
E
M
P
E
R
A
T
U
R
E

When you look to others, whether priest, family or friend, it probably isn't because you doubt God. You're checking with those you trust and respect to reassure and inform you. God, after all, speaks to us through those around us. So it is with the sacrament of reconciliation.

You sometimes need feedback from another individual who can help you understand your feelings, examine your motives, analyze your actions and suggest a resolution of your concerns. Catholics believe that God is so close to creation that the divine enters our life in the most personal manner imaginable: God becomes a visible part of our world in the person of Jesus Christ.

This Jesus meets you in the sacraments of the Church in order to give you the gift of his presence through the most common elements of your daily life: water, bread and wine, touch and speech.

Jesus gives you the sacrament of reconciliation as a help because he understands that you often need to hear a voice other than your own to assure you that you are forgiven, that all is well and that you do not need to be haunted by past mistakes.

Some Family History on Reconciliation

If you are ever asked why Catholics believe that Jesus gave us the sacrament of reconciliation, you can simply refer to John 20:22, "After saying this ['As the Father sent me, so I send you'], he breathed on them and said: 'Receive the Holy Spirit. Whose sins you forgive are forgiven them, and whose sins you retain are retained.'"

The early Christians had no doubt that the Lord Jesus had left with his community the power to forgive sins. What was not clear was the form that such forgiveness was to take, and it is clear that the understanding of the sacrament has evolved over centuries.

Scholars tell us that the earliest form of forgiveness of sins was expressed through the sacrament of baptism. When a person was baptized, sins were forgiven at the same time that the person became a member of the Christian community. As time went on, however, the question arose of what to do about sins committed after baptism.

Some strict Christians like Tertullian (who lived from about 160-230 in the Christian era) taught that some sins like murder and adultery could not be forgiven by the Church, but his views were not accepted by the majority of the community.

Tertullian did not prevail, but the early Church nonetheless required a severe penance of a public nature when a Christian confessed, usually to the bishop. This penance might take as long as two years to fulfill, after which time the sinner was reconciled to the community. As you might guess, few persons were willing to undergo the embarrassment of having everyone know that they had done something so serious that they were not allowed to take part in worship. They often had to stand outside the church in rags to symbolize their sinful condition.

As a result of this demanding tradition, which was allowed only once in one's lifetime, most persons who intended to become Christians would wait until they thought they were near death and then ask to be baptized. In this way, they had their sins forgiven. It seems that most Christians did not consider themselves either great saints or great sinners, and they simply avoided the rigors of public penance through the more usual means of prayer, giving alms, fasting and attending the eucharistic liturgy.

In the fifth century, a major change in the form of the sacrament took place in Ireland. Here, the monks would travel the country to hear individual confessions privately. They would then give a penance to be performed, and when they returned, months later, they would pray with the sinner to ask for God's forgiveness. Gradually this practice became popular in Europe, even though it was resisted by some Church leaders as too lenient. By the year 1215, the Church officially adopted this practice of private confession to a priest, but absolution was now given after the confession of sins and before the assigned penance was completed. This remains the common Catholic practice today.

You may have taken part in a communal reconciliation service in your own parish. The community gathers and, after prayers and Scripture readings, the people are urged to reflect upon their personal sins and faults. Afterwards there is the opportunity for personal confession to a priest. In this way, both the private and the communal dimensions of sin are emphasized.

A third form, which is rare, is general absolution. In some instances, usually during wartime or where there are many persons and few priests, individuals are asked to privately express sorrow for their sins and then the priest absolves the entire group at one time.

All these developments are based upon changing circumstances, but each reflects the teaching in John's Gospel.

Be Sorry for What?

When you were younger, it seemed that something was wrong if it caused your parents or teachers to get upset or punish you. You may remember coming home covered with mud and having your mother yell at you; or your teacher may have had you stand in the corner after you kept talking during class. If these adults praised or rewarded you, you felt you were good.

Now that you are older, not only the approval of your parents and teachers counts, but you also need the acceptance of your peers to judge what is good or bad. This is a very confusing stage for many.

In some circles, teenagers are made to feel guilty if they spend time on their studies. In other circles, they may be made to feel guilty if they refuse to try drugs. Much depends on the values your peers hold, values that can reinforce or contradict those that your parents, society or Church have tried to give you.

Some adults seem never to have outgrown this stage of conforming to the group, so morality becomes a matter of loyalty to the group in order to have their approval. Ultimately, however, it must be your conscience that determines what you should be sorry for.

Conscience means "judging with correct knowledge." Conscience is not a "little voice" inside you that automatically tells you when you have done good or bad. Conscience simply means having a sense of yourself when you make choices, knowing that you are actively involved in what you do and say. It is your sense of personhood in moral matters.

Conscience, like speech or your sense of self, has to be developed. It involves listening to the voices of your parents, your community, your family and friends and your Church in order to hear, as best you can, your own voice as you make your choices in life. Conscience is the most sacred space where you seek to be responsible to God and others for who you are and what you do. Within this space, you judge your "spiritual temperature."

Reconciliation, in or out of the sacrament, starts with facing the facts of your behavior and attitudes honestly and humbly. The ancient Greek philosopher Socrates said it well: "The unexamined life is not worth living." For Christians, the unexamined life is incapable of moral growth and development. You would remain a "moral infant" if you never reflected on your actions. This first step in the sacrament of reconciliation is called the examination of conscience.

Following the examination of conscience, where you look clearly and honestly at your life patterns, you reach the second step of sorrow. This step will usually be a mixture of thinking and feeling about your choices. It is one thing to know that you may have done something wrong, but it is just as important to feel remorse for those things that have gone against your conscience. In those actions where you have hurt others, it is feeling that allows you to see things from the viewpoint of those you may have hurt and to feel the pain you may have caused.

This vision will help you to experience regret for violating values and standards that you believe are crucial to living your life in conformity with the life and teaching of Jesus. In the sacrament of reconciliation, the priest can help you to express your sorrow, confess your sins and receive forgiveness in the name of Jesus the healer.

YOUR SPIRITUAL TEMPERATURE

A Double Check for Your Conscience

Catholics have usually reflected upon the Ten Commandments as they prepare for the sacrament of reconciliation. This is a sound tradition and here I merely wish to ask some practical questions based on the commandments and the teachings of Jesus. These questions can help you form your own conscience and prepare to celebrate the sacrament. Even if the questions do not always touch on actual sin, they help us form our conscience by weighing moral values.

This list does not tell your temperature precisely, but it does help you to recognize some symptoms of spiritual or moral "illness." When you read these questions, do you feel unmoved or unaware that such a question touches on your spiritual condition? Do you want to excuse yourself from responsibility for your answers? Do you find yourself thinking of ways to change your attitudes or behaviors so that your answers reflect your deepest beliefs?

If you find yourself resolving to be more loving, you are basically healthy. If you become aware of ways that you treat others as possessions or have deliberately damaged the reputation of others, this is a moment of grace for admitting poor moral "health" and praying for the strength to seek help.

1. Do you worship the "false gods" of status, consumerism or peer approval? Do you ignore or avoid old friends in order to be part of the popular crowd? Do you make unreasonable demands on your parents for clothes or money, or feel no responsibility to save for your college education? Do you give support to your peers when they tell racial or ethnic jokes? Do you show disgust or indifference toward the poor and homeless, thinking them "losers" by social standards? Why do you find it hard to see the value in those who are different from you?

2. Do you use language that you would never speak in front of your grandmother? Is this choice prompted by the violence of the vocabulary, its low opinion of others, its insulting character? Why do you choose such language?

3. Do you skip Mass because few of your friends go to church or because you feel that the gift of God's presence should be as entertaining as MTV? Why do you think Jesus gave us the Eucharist?

4. Do you thank your parents for what they do for you? Do you offer to help around the house or do you see yourself as a guest? If your parents are divorced, separated or widowed, do you try to understand their pain or loneliness? Why do you try to impress others and yet have little sense of the needs of those in your family?

5. Do you value your life and that of others? Do you drink and drive or travel with those who do? Do you fool with drugs and pretend that doing so does not affect your grades, your self-respect or your relationships? Have you ever hit your girlfriend or boyfriend? Why do you feel the need to control or humiliate someone you claim to care about?

6. Do you use other persons for your own selfish pleasure? Do you lie to get sex or force others to act against their values? Do you see sex as a way to be popular or to rebel against your parents? What do you think the casual use of your body or that of another says about your self-worth?

7. Do you cheat on tests or homework assignments? Do you ever shoplift or take things belonging to other students? How do you feel about yourself after you do these things?

8. Do you gossip or pass on rumors that hurt another's reputation? Can you be trusted to keep a confidence after you promise? Do you lie to protect your own ego, even if someone will be hurt? Why are you upset if you are the victim of such actions?

9. Are you envious of others? Do you resent their popularity or success? Do you feel you have to put others down in order to feel better about yourself? How do you feel inside when you do?

10. Do you resent your parents when they tell you that they cannot afford to buy the things that you feel you need to keep up with your friends? Do you ever ask your parents what their financial worries are?

Y
O
U
R

S
P
I
R
I
T
U
A
L

T
E
M
P
E
R
A
T
U
R
E

Forgiveness Is Freeing

One sign of your moral maturity is the ability to see things clearly, to be honest with yourself and to hear the insights and challenges of others in a non-defensive manner. That can be difficult unless you can trust others to respect your attempts to be true to yourself.

The sacrament of reconciliation is an invitation to place yourself in God's gentle presence. Because Jesus wishes to heal your broken parts, so that you can be made whole and confident, he offers you God's assurance of acceptance through the words and absolution of a priest who is, like you, aware of his own need for forgiveness.

Jesus taught that "the truth will set you free" (John 8:32). It is this freedom from self-centeredness and selfishness that is given you when you examine your conscience, express genuine regret and seek divine forgiveness for whatever hinders your relationship to God and to your fellow human beings. A firm purpose of changing those patterns and completing the assigned penance concludes the reception of the sacrament. This experience will make real and immediate the promise of Jesus: "I came so that they might have life and have it more abundantly" (John 10:10).

God is always present and you are always free to speak to God in the quiet places of your heart. Yet there will be times when you may feel the need to take your "spiritual temperature" and seek a more tangible assurance of divine forgiveness through the sacrament of reconciliation.

In both these ways, God seeks to remove your fears and guide you into the future, confident that you are loved and comfortable with the call of living the Christian life.

Thomas M. Casey, O.S.A., is an associate professor of religious studies at Merrimack College, North Andover, Massachusetts. He has also taught high school and was once a teenager himself.

Courage for Confession

I had committed a mortal sin and knew I could not receive holy Communion on Sunday morning if I didn't go to confession first. Thankfully, Father Heinz always hears confessions before every weekend Mass. Unfortunately though, what should have been a simple solution wasn't simple at all. I needed to muster the courage to confess my sin.

Normally, courage is not a problem for me when I go to confession. However, this was a grave sin and I knew I needed help. I don't drive so my dear husband, Mark, took me to Mass. The car ride gave me plenty of time to dwell on my lack of courage.

I thought about how much easier it would be if I went to a different priest, perhaps one who didn't know me. But of course, that wasn't to be since I was already on my way. We drove from our home in Portland, and when we crossed I-7 into town, I began praying to the Holy Spirit to grant me the grace I needed to do what I had to do. I was very afraid that I would be cowardly and skip holy Communion until I got the nerve to go to confession.

The thought of not receiving Jesus was more disturbing than anything else I was feeling. As I continued to pray, the strangest thing happened. To this day I'm not sure if I imagined it or not, but I felt the Virgin Mary's loving arms around me, embracing me. This was very comforting, but all I could think and wonder was, "Why is she here? I was praying to the Holy Spirit, not to her."

As soon as the car stopped in front of the church, I jumped out and hurried inside. Since nobody was in line, I walked quickly into the confessional.

Hours later while pondering what had happened in the car, I remembered that the Holy Spirit is the spouse of the Blessed Virgin Mary. We all know that on earth, a husband and wife become one in the sacrament of holy matrimony. I realized that it must be even more so with Mary and the Holy Spirit.

I still do not fully comprehend what happened on the way to church that day and may never understand it until I get to heaven. It is possible that I imagined it all, but whatever it was, it gave me the strength for which I had prayed.

Judith F. Smedley   *Portland, Ohio*

A Pain-Free Confession

In November of 2004, I went to a *Journey* retreat in Auburn, Maine. This was my second year attending, and I had thoroughly enjoyed it the previous year. My only problem was that they offered confession every day. Mind you, I always knew that confession was important, but I absolutely dreaded it.

At this point in my life I was a freshman in college, ready to turn over a new leaf and try to figure out why people got so excited about the sacrament of reconciliation. After a friend tried talking me into going to confession at the retreat, I finally got up and stood in line. I was extremely nervous and not sure what to make of it, when all of a sudden it was my turn to talk to the priest.

I made it through my confession pain free and left with a smile. I felt so clean, refreshed, and happy. For the first time, I truly understood and found the beauty in confession.

Then I sat back down with my friends and pondered over what had just happened. This thinking continued for upwards of two hours! Finally, I decided that I needed to go back to confession. I didn't know why, but I really wanted to go again.

I made my way over to a different priest and began, "Forgive me Father for I have sinned. It has been two hours since my last confession." He immediately gave me a funny look and asked why I was there. I told him that for the first time I enjoyed confession and I just had to go back.

It turned out not really being a confession. He sent me back to my seat and asked that I pray for those who were having problems with going to confession, as I had previously experienced.

A year and a half later, I still love going to confession. Every opportunity that arises, I am there. It's so amazing that no matter what the degree of your sins, God forgives you and gives you amazing graces.

Danielle M. Sabine   *Greene, Maine*

First Penance Service

About thirteen years ago, I was reluctantly on my way to a penance service at St. Pius X Catholic Church. I didn't believe in this type of service because I was raised in a very strict Orthodox Catholic family and we always went to confession in the traditional way.

Three Redemptorist priests from out of town were finishing a three-day mission at this church, and they did the service. During it, one of them announced that if anyone were not in a state of grace or had committed a mortal sin, he would have to go to confession individually with one of the priests.

At the end of the service, a priest gave us absolution, and I immediately felt that all of my sins had been washed away. I pictured my soul as a car windshield with rain pounding on it. My sins were cleared away like the windshield wiper that washed the window. My soul felt as if it was completely clean, and my whole being was changed. I have never forgotten the grace that our dear Lord gave me the day I opened my mind and went to my very first penance service.

Lou Therese Anthony   *Flint, Michigan*

The Stuff of Great Poetry

The fourth Wednesday of October 2000, was like any other day in the boarding-care home where I lived. At 9:30 that morning, I was preparing to go to morning snack, where I would tiptoe carefully past the activity room door where the monthly Catholic Communion service was going to be held. I had been away from the Church for nine bitter, angry years and away from the sacrament of reconciliation for almost twenty. I had no intention of rejoining the flock.

But then came a knock at my door. I opened it, and the only thing I saw for several seconds was a clerical collar at the level of my eyes. The mouth above the collar said, "You're thinking of closing the door in my face." I was, actually, but I have too much respect for the priesthood to do that. Then I took in the rest of the tall figure: black shirt, grey suit, and black tooled-leather cowboy boots, topped by a smiling face with collar-length white hair and a walrus mustache.

"May I come in?" he asked. "Sister Karen said you need to see me." Sister was the extraordinary minister of communion at the facility.

I thought to myself, "Sister Karen should keep her mouth shut." I was still standing in the doorway.

He said, "I'm Father Ed Molumby, and if you slam the door in my face, I'll only come back next month." He became serious: "Are you a Catholic?"

"Yes."

"Been baptized?"

"Yes."

"Confirmed?"

"Uh-huh."

"Good. Then I'm here to hear your confession and bring you home." He pushed gently past my bulk (still in the doorway) and, taking the only

122

chair, indicated that I should sit opposite him on the foot of the unused bed.

I needed some coaching to get through the ritual, and I'm not sure I heard the words that follow "God, the Father of mercies, through the death and resurrection of his Son…" but a granite boulder had been lifted off my spirit. I was home.

Some weeks later, I told this story in a letter to a former English professor. Her response was, "That is the stuff of great poetry, and you, my dear, are the poem."

Angela Schweig, SFO   *Spokane, Washington*

My Thoughts…

I think we should pray for help to the Holy Spirit before examining our conscience in preparation for confession. Then as we think through the Commandments and our duties in our present circumstances, I think it would be good to confess recurring faults like unkindness to others, unfaithfulness to duties that puts work and burdens on others, lack of forgiveness.

I think certain attitudes like a subtle feeling of superiority should be confessed, because those thoughts prompt actions that could be mean and hateful.

Concentrating on faults that hurt others and accepting my guilt with sorrow and resolve to overcome seems important to me.

I do believe God rewards our effort to be truthful and honest in our accusations with the strength and grace to overcome bad habits.

Also, how about asking the priest hearing our confession for help with doubts or problems?

Sr. Mary Caritas Quinn

Filled With Grace

Standing in line to go to confession was a weekly Saturday morning ritual during the early 1960s. Because I lived on a farm near Hays, Kansas, and attended a country school, my parents drove my sisters and me ten miles to town each Saturday morning for catechism class. We would have a two-hour session with the nuns from the St. Agnes Convent who taught us our faith from the Baltimore Catechism.

Usually one of the Franciscan priests from St. Joseph's Church would stop by the classroom for about thirty minutes and give us a mini-sermon on some aspect of our lesson. Immediately following class, we would walk from the school to the church for confession and morning Mass.

I remember my first encounter with what *sin* on my soul really looked like. One of the pages in my first grade catechism showed three milk bottles. One was filled with white milk (my soul in the state of grace), one had spots in the milk (my soul with venial sins), and one had black milk, or maybe the bottle was empty (my soul with mortal sins and no grace). I readily grasped the idea that I didn't want my soul to look like that third bottle. Thus we were encouraged to go to confession each week to ensure that our souls stayed pure and white.

Those first years of going to confession meant standing in line for what seemed like hours, although I'm sure it was really just a few minutes, while fifteen grade school kids took their turn ahead of me. My turn would finally come and I would open the door of the confessional, walk in, and try to find the kneeler in total darkness. Then the little door in front of me would open, and I would see the shadowy figure of the priest.

"Bless me, Father," I would begin, and then I would tell him all of the terrible sins of a seven year old, most of them having to do with hitting my sisters or lying to my mother. After the priest gave me my penance, I would walk to the pew and say the prayers he had assigned. I knew that if I died in the night, I would go straight to heaven just as the nuns had told me.

Over the next few years, I attended junior high and a Catholic high school in town. Confession still remained a weekly practice as part of our religion classes. Of course, by now the sacrament was referred to as the sacrament of reconciliation, but I still called it "confession."

I remember one of the nuns telling us that going to confession was like cleaning house before a very important guest came to visit. She described it as a room that has been swept clean and the light is off until the guest arrives in the Eucharist. I always imagined the light suddenly coming on immediately upon my receiving Christ's body in holy Communion.

When I started college, I still managed to receive this sacrament about once a month and always looked forward to the feeling of having *my slate wiped clean* so I could once again try to do better.

In the mid seventies, I moved to southwest Kansas where I eventually married and had a family. I made it a point to get both of my daughters to confession frequently because I wanted them to get into the same habit of receiving this sacrament.

A few years later, one of our priests gave a sermon during a Lenten season retreat about how much grace God gave us in the sacrament of reconciliation. For the first time, I seemed to view going to confession a bit differently. I felt as if instead of just having my sins *wiped away*, now I was having my soul *filled back up* with grace; a grace that would fill me with the Holy Spirit who would help me to do better.

As I left the confessional this time, I knelt in the pew and fixed my eyes on Jesus hanging on the crucifix. I suddenly knew how much He loved me. His arms were spread wide there on the cross as if to say, "This is how much I love you."

I thought back to the game I had played with my children when they were small. I would hold onto their small hands and spread their arms apart as I asked them, "How much do I love you? This much!" My heavenly Father was repeating those words to me. Suddenly the sacrament of reconciliation had taken on a whole new meaning.

Annette Sosa   *Hugoton, Kansas*

"All my unhappiness can be traced back to something I want and can't have. It's all related to desire. I have expectations for myself, for others around me, and even for God. I want to be able to control things: I want the sun to shine; I want my car to start; I want to be on time; I want people to like me—in short, I want things to follow my script."

O Happy Fault:
A Confession of Hidden Sin

by Vinny Flynn

see page 133

A Successful Mission

I was sent to preach a parish mission in a small parish church. There was a family who was helping the pastor prepare for the mission. They were very devoted to Our Lady of Fatima. For six months before the mission, this family and two other families gave up their Saturday mornings to come to the church and pray the rosary for the success of the mission. This was especially difficult for the children, but they believed their prayers would help.

On the opening day of the mission only thirty-five people came. The pastor, the three families, and I were all were very disappointed. After the first service I went with the pastor to the confessionals.

The first person who entered my confessional began by saying, "Father, it has been forty years since my last confession."

The second person who came in began with, "Father, it has been twenty-five years since my last confession."

I was overwhelmed. The third person who came in said, "Father, I don't know how long it has been since my last confession."

One after the other, with a few exceptions, had been away from the sacrament for a long, long time.

I came out of the confessional thinking I was the last one in the church, only to find the pastor coming out of his confessional. We met in the center aisle, and before I could tell him of the wonderful experience I had, he excitedly told me: "I have never heard confessions like that in all my priesthood. People who have been away for years and years came."

I then shared my experience with him and we both looked to the tabernacle and gave thanks to the Lord and Our Lady.

The next day we shared with the three families what had happened and how their prayers during those six months helped so many people find the courage to approach the sacrament.

We all agreed that the mission was successful, not because of the number who attended, but because of those who found new life through the sacrament of reconciliation.

Fr. Edward R. Wolanski, CP   *Shelter Island Heights, New York*

Healing Love

In August 2000, I spent the summer in a small mountain town an hour east of San Diego. It is a beautiful location, thought holy by the Native Americans. I had been praying frequently to St. Joseph without any specific, personal intention but I know that the story which follows is due to the loving intercession of this wonderful saint.

In this town, a family offered a weekly rosary night, which was followed by the use of their pool and a small barbeque dinner of hot dogs and hamburgers. It was a time of much laughter and fun for several families.

The people seemed to be the epitome of love and natural, Christian prayerfulness. This impression, however, changed one night when a woman began talking about abortion. I had long ago abandoned *women's rights* views on this subject, but her views seemed rigid and uncompassionate to me.

Wanting her to understand why some women would take this extreme step, I responded with stories of women who had abortions. Eyebrows were raised as the discussion got heated and more people entered into the conversation. I began to feel misunderstood, confused and hurt, which did nothing to improve the situation. Finally, feeling backed into a corner, I admitted that not only did I know women who had had abortions, but that I had had one. They were shocked! Questioning ensued. I felt horrible.

My friends could not accept what I had done or why.

Admittedly, the phrasing I had used about my abortion had a lot to do with the response I received. My feelings over the next few days were of confusion, frustration, guilt, fear, hurt and anger.

A few days later, I went to confession. I was surprised to find a young priest there named Father Tony. Father was from our area but had since become a missionary in South America. He was now back in the States because of a health issue, and although he burned with a strong desire to return to his mission work, his superiors had ordered him to stay in our area while he underwent treatment and regained his health. He was helping out from time to time at our church.

Feeling defensive, I explained to him that I had already confessed the sin of abortion some years earlier, but that the excited discussion had so confused me that I wasn't sure what to do with all the emotions I was having. Experiencing so much turmoil and agitation made me feel that some sin must be attached.

Father Tony surprised me by commiserating with my situation. He understood how loaded the issue had become, and how personally devastating it felt to me. Then he said something which surprised me even more. He asked me if I'd ever had a Mass said for the child. I had no idea how to respond. I wasn't sure how to have Mass said for anyone. I asked him, "Don't you need a name to have a Mass said for someone?" Rather tentatively, he suggested I name the child. But how did I know if it was a boy or a girl?

I left with the question unanswered, but the conversation stayed with me all week. Finally, it dawned on me that there are children's names which can be used for either sex. I thought Frances would be a good one because of Saint Francis of Assisi, and because I had warm, personal memories associated with that name.

The following week we celebrated the Assumption of Our Lady into Heaven, a day which was very special to me. It was also my year anniversary since leaving the East Coast to move to the West Coast. Unexpectedly, Father Tony was again at the church to offer Mass for this special feast. A minor miracle in itself was that I was actually early enough to speak to him before he entered the church. I hastily scribbled "Frances" on a piece of paper and put it and twenty dollars in an envelope and handed it to him before he walked up the aisle.

That Mass will forever remain in my memory as a spiritual blessing and a time of cleansing, healing and renewal. I cried as I had never cried before. The tears came down in buckets. A pain I hadn't been aware of seemed to wrack my body. Then, as suddenly as it appeared, it left. Holy energy poured down upon me as a shower beats water upon one's body.

By the time the Mass ended, I was full of peace, joy and great love. My hurt, pain, confusion and anger had disappeared.

Anonymous   *Bedford, Massachusetts*

My Thoughts...

In the six years that I was a director of religious education (DRE) I wanted those entering the church to understand the awesome grace of the sacrament without falling into the trap of becoming overly scrupulous in their examination of conscience.

I shared a lot in our discussions about a nightly check in with God, as part of their daily prayers. If one makes a daily examen then they would be less likely to fall into a pattern of sinfulness and more likely to know when they needed to avail themselves of the sacrament.

The one thing that I tell the catechumens and candidates about what they need to confess is anything that gets in the way of their authentic relationship with God. I usually don't use the distinctions between mortal and venial sin, but rather those habits and actions that damage the relationship that I have with God and with other people.

Maggie Geene

Nothing Changed—Everything Changed

My community of faith, All Saints Catholic Church, is located in Manassas, Virginia, at the site of the famous Civil War battlefield. However, in April 2001, the battlefield that concerned me had nothing to do with the Civil War. I was dealing with an emotional battlefield of my own. As an adult, I was grappling with memories of the terror of childhood abuse and wondering how I could ever be ready for the joy of Easter.

Since our parish has 18,000 members, neighboring parishes lend their priests for our Lenten penance services. Lines were long and formed early for the twenty-five priests who come to administer the sacrament of reconciliation. I paid little attention to which line I joined, knowing only that I needed God's divine help with this very heavy burden, and that I didn't even know how to pray.

My confessor was Father Mike Bazan. I explained the terror and anxiety that I'd been experiencing for the past three months remembering what had happened to me when I was four years old. He told me that I needed to invite God into that situation. I didn't understand. I said, "But God is with me every moment." "That isn't what I meant," he said, and explained that I needed to ask God to come directly into the turmoil, the fear, and the pain I had from the abuse. He said I was holding on to the experience like a security blanket because it was familiar. "God wants to be your security; you can't erase what happened or throw it away. Without your past personal history there would be a big hole, but it doesn't have to define who you are."

I was startled. It seemed so obvious.

For my penance, I had to give it to God and invite Him into my pain and turmoil. As I knelt near the altar I thought, "This is going to be so hard!" I prayed, asking God to come into that experience. With tears streaming down my cheeks, I offered it to Him for healing and peace.

Nothing changed. Then everything changed.

Driving home afterwards, I realized that whenever I felt disappointed or unhappy I blamed others. I recognized that it was time to take responsibility for myself, to make choices and live with the consequences. I needed to learn from my mistakes and make positive changes in my life.

Janet L. Smith   *Gainesville, Virginia*

No Sin Too Big

In 1980, I made a very bad choice and committed a grave and serious sin. Afterwards I was torn by immense guilt and sorrow. After going to many different priests to confess this sin and having it absolved, I still didn't feel forgiven. Finally, I confessed this sin to a priest whose response made a big difference in how I view God's mercy.

He was a priest helping out at a Cursillo Renewal Weekend at St. Basil's Seminary in Methuen, Massachusetts. When I confessed my grave sin to him and told him how often I had already confessed it, he told me that my biggest sin was pride. He said that pride caused me to believe that I could commit a sin so grave and so big that God could not forgive it. I was very humbled by his words, and I truly came to know God's great love and mercy.

Bonnie E. Doherty   *Haverhill, Massachusetts*

O Happy Fault:
A Confession of Hidden Sin

By Vinny Flynn

I have a confession to make. A real confession. Of real sin. I have a great sin that has lain hidden in me for a long time, unrecognized, unconfessed, unrepented.

It's not your common, everyday brand of sin—not included in the usual list: pride, greed, jealousy, immorality, drunkenness, stealing, etc. These are easier to recognize, easier to fight against. This sin is different. It's like a traitor within me, lying in wait to jump out and trip me up, over and over again.

It has become like a cancer, living and growing inside me, dragging me down, away from God, and dragging others with me. So I need to expose it, to confess it publicly to all who will listen. And I'm not afraid to confess it to you, because you have sinned in the same way.

The sin is this: I have been unhappy! Repeatedly—at the slightest provocation—unhappy!

"Oh, come on now," you say, "It's not a sin to be unhappy! Everybody gets unhappy." Yes. Everybody gets unhappy. And it is sin. Dangerous sin, because it's habit-forming, extremely contagious, and seldom diagnosed as sin. It's usually viewed as something like a cold—it just happens to us, and we have to endure it until it goes away. We don't really have any control over it.

But that's a lie. Part of the Great Lie. We *do* have control over it. My unhappiness is *not caused* by something that happens to me. It is caused by my response to something that happens, a response generated by my attitude, my way of looking at things. Is my glass half full? Or is it half empty? It's a matter of perception, and the way I choose to perceive things determines my emotional response to them.

Let me give you an example: *Two men looked out from prison bars. One saw mud; one saw stars.*

Several years ago, I came upon this old verse as I was reading a book by Fr. John Powell, SJ, and it has stuck with me ever since. Powell's book is entitled *Fully Human, Fully Alive*. Its basic premise is that our happiness is not determined by our situations, but by our personal perceptions of these situations. The two men in the verse share a common experience. It's their way of viewing the experience that shapes it meaning.

I think we can safely assume that neither man is overjoyed about being in prison. But one looked beyond the confines of his im-mediate situation and finds something to rejoice about. The other allows the pain of his situation to color his view of everything and thus remains a prisoner in spirit as well as in body. To the pain of his unavoidable suffering, he adds the unnecessary pain of being unhappy about it. (If this doesn't make sense yet, don't give up. There's more.)

I used to think of sin in a very narrow, punitive way. Sin was simply an offense against God, something "mortal" or "venial," something wrong for which I needed to be punished. And I had neat little lists of these offenses categorized in my mind.

I'm not saying this view was all bad. As a matter of fact, today's world might benefit from a greater awareness of sin.

What I *am* saying is that my view of sin was *incomplete*. I tended to try to avoid the mortal sins, the serious offenses against God, and I didn't worry too much about the venial ones.

I never realized that sin is also an offense against *myself*. I never saw my sin in the larger sense of *"sinfulness"*—a state of being that carries with it its own punishment, that cripples me and pre-vents me from being who I could become—that makes me see mud when I could see stars.

Why is my unhappiness a sin? Because, like all sin, it is a turning away from God to focus on myself, my desires, my problems, my pain. And, like all sin, it's a form of rebellion.

All my unhappiness can be traced back to something I want and can't have. It's all related to desire. I have expectations for myself, for others around me, and even for God. I want to be able to control things: I want the sun to shine; I want my car to start; I want to be on time; I want people to like me—in short, I want things to follow my script. From moment to moment. It's all *self*. No wonder St. Therese said, "I forgot myself, and henceforth I was happy."

Part of my problem has been that I thought suffering and sadness were the same, but they're not. Suffering is *unavoidable*. We all have it—a lot of it. Some things just hurt! And there's nothing I can do about it—or almost nothing. The one thing I can do is decide not to make it worse by being unhappy about it.

But most times I don't do this, because the only way to keep from being unhappy about suffering is to accept it, and I don't want to do that. Herein lies my sin. When things don't follow my script, I rebel against them. I don't want to suffer, so I refuse to accept suffering, and as a result I'm miserable. I'm not only in pain; I'm *unhappy* about being in pain.

I remember a scene from Herman Hesse's book *Siddhartha* that suggests very powerfully that, though suffering is unavoidable, unhappiness is not.

Siddhartha has just gone through a period of deep suffering but, through his acceptance of it, he has grown and is able to retain an inner peace, even in the midst of a very painful grief. His wise friend looks at him and says, "You have suffered…yet I see that sadness has not entered your heart."

This is what it really means to be a Christian—to have joy in our hearts, trusting that, no matter how bad things seem, God can turn all things to good for those who love Him. St. Paul admonishes us to "rejoice in the Lord always and in all things give thanks" (1 Thes 5:16-18).What a powerful teaching! Rejoice always. Give thanks in all things, not just the good things, but the bad as well— even pain, suffering, failure, tragedy.

What this teaches us is that happiness isn't a feeling. It's a chosen attitude, an inner peace that comes from trust.

Joy isn't the absence of sorrow. It's the presence of God. And if we allow the presence of God to penetrate deeply into us, even in the midst of great pain, we will be happy.

But can we really do this? Or is this just an unrealistic, pious theory? In his book, *Man's Search for Meaning*, Victor Frankl shares the conclusions he came to as he observed himself and his fellow inmates of the death camp at Auschwitz. He noticed that, under the same basic circumstances, some of the prisoners became animals, others retained their human dignity, and still others became willing martyrs. "We who lived in concentration camps," he writes, "can remember the men who walked through the huts comforting others, giving away their last piece of bread. They may have been few in number, but they offer sufficient proof that everything can be taken from a man but one thing: the last of the human freedoms—to choose one's attitude in any given set of circumstances, to choose one's own way."

So this is my confession, and my resolve: Yes, I have sinned, but I'm not going to be unhappy about it. Trusting God, no matter how dark it seems, I'm going to look out and begin to see the stars.

A Confession of Hidden Sin © *Congregation of Marians of the Immaculate Conception, Stockbridge, MA 01263. www.marian.org. Used with permission.*

Just For Me

My early duty was more out of obligation to my parents and grand-parents than to any real conviction of my own. I went through the usual route of attending CCD and weekly Mass until I was confirmed but then drifted away from even going to Mass.

As an adult I felt pulled back into my faith when I became pregnant with my first child. My husband and I had tried to conceive a baby for more than a year, and we were very discouraged. Finally, God's grace shone on us and we became pregnant. I knew my child was a gift from God, and I desired to faithfully practice my Catholic religion. It was not only for my salvation but so that I would be a good parent and raise our child properly in His ways.

During my pregnancy, I felt a strong desire to attend Mass each week and pray the rosary daily. It was truly a gift from God. The last piece of the puzzle was to return to confession since I had not gone since I was confirmed nearly twenty years earlier.

I was petrified, not only because I had twenty years worth of sins to atone for but also because I was afraid the priest would scold me and tell me I was a terrible person. I knew I couldn't confess to my parish priest. What would he think of me?

The need to confess my sins was constantly on my mind, but I couldn't get past my fear. Finally, after a couple of months of this, I saw an ad-vertisement for a local Eucharistic Congress that was offering adoration and confession. I knew that this was my chance to reconcile with God since the priests hearing confessions were from across the diocese, and I wouldn't know any of them. I bought a confession guide and spent time praying over my confession and identifying my sins. There were so many that I wrote them out on a piece of paper.

I went to the Eucharistic Congress and headed for the adoration room, which was also where confessions were being heard. I waited a couple of minutes and randomly picked an empty confessional. The priest looked up from his book, smiled, and welcomed me. My heart sank. I hadn't realized that this would be a face-to-face confession! Not only did I have to confess all my sins, I had to look at the priest while doing it. Could I do this?

I smiled nervously and knelt down. I told the priest that I hadn't done this in twenty years and that I was rusty and nervous. He smiled kindly and said we'd get through it together. I unfolded my long list of sins and quietly and earnestly confessed them.

I started crying, perhaps from relief that I was finally coming clean. The priest was so sweet to me. He congratulated me for returning and said I had great humility. Then he absolved me of my sins and gave me my penance. I was done! I had done it! I had returned to God and He had absolved me of my sins! I felt an amazing weight removed from me.

As I gathered my things to leave, the priest told me that he had volunteered to hear confessions that day but had sat reading most of the day. Then as he looked me in the eyes, he smiled and said, "I was brought here today for you."

Melissa Shaw   *Millbury, Massachusetts*

The Long List

In the summer of 2005, a retired priest filled in for a month at the northern Arizona parish where I was living. That same week I received an e-mail from someone in my Medjugorje prayer group which spoke about confession and gave a very long list of common (and often grave) sins.

Reading that list, I recognized a large number that I had committed as a teen or young adult. Some, while knowing they weren't the best things to do, I hadn't really thought of as sins, such as partying or drinking to excess; but others were just plain embarrassing to admit to. I knew it was unlikely that I'd confessed them before. It nagged at me that there were so many unconfessed big sins in my life. The problem, however, was recognizing what had or had not been confessed.

So, just to be on the safe side, I brought the whole list with me, unaware that the new priest had already arrived and was handling confession that night. I was dismayed, how does one explain such things to someone who has no past experience or connection with me?

The desire to chicken out was strong. It would have been very easy to make a simple confession of the usual sins, yet something held me to my resolve. I chose to be honest and explain my intention, and why this was important to me. I asked if he had the time that night to hear this confession as it was a long list. He looked a little nervous, but agreed to hear the whole thing.

While difficult and embarrassing, I was surprised to discover in this priest a wonderful spiritual advisor. During the time he was there, my spiritual life blossomed. Thinking about the change, I believe it was due to Father hearing my complete confession.

Anonymous   *Bedford, Massachusetts*

Changed Attitude

For years I was challenged by the sacrament of reconciliation. I believed it was a necessary sacrament, but I didn't want to take the time to go. Confession was easy to avoid because I knew no one was keeping track of how often I went, plus I thought it was enough to privately tell God how terribly sorry I was for my sins. When I wanted to raise my children Catholic and was forced to face this faith issue, my attitude changed.

I began going to confession at least twice a year, and I felt myself drawing closer to the sacrament. When a Catholic friend of mine told me she didn't go to confession, I found myself defending the sacrament to her. Hearing my own words made me realize the full power and beauty of reconciliation. It became clear to me that when we take our sins to a priest, we connect with Jesus personally. Reconciliation is His gift to us that keeps us grounded in our faith and to Him.

Wonderful experiences with the sacrament of reconciliation continue to happen over and over for me. Someone called this "the journey toward the face of God." Through my growth, I have learned that confession doesn't just lead the penitent closer to God. The peace in our families, our communities, and in the world rests on our ability to reconcile ourselves with each other and with God.

Toni I. Leach   *Oak Hill, Virginia*

Stuffed Scarves in Her Mouth

I grew up in a little town in Alberta/Saskatchewan, Canada. Our town's main street is the border between the two provinces. Although my dad and his construction crew built our church, St. Anthony of Padua, our whole family of seven kids proudly took credit for the work.

During the 1950s and 1960s our parish was blessed to have Father Bernie Gorman as our pastor. He was a most gentle and loving man, and a great friend to my parents. He often came to our house for dinner and was a regular at their Saturday night card games. Everyone went to him with their problems; no matter how busy he was, he always had time for everyone. He was loved.

For a ten-year-old child to go to confession and admit imperfection to a great man like Father Gorman was a real chore. Because he was the sweetest, nicest person and a *man of God,* it was very difficult for me to think for one moment that he wouldn't somehow think less of me when he saw me again at—horror of horrors—my parent's home!

So, after worrying about this for an entire week, I came to the conclusion that the thing to do was to devise some sort of scheme wherein the holy man of God wouldn't recognize me in the confessional.

Although it was our routine to receive the sacrament of reconciliation on Friday evenings, I waited until Saturday afternoon to go to confession that week. This was part one of my deception plan.

As the little sliding partition opened in the tiny confessional and the familiar silhouette of our dear pastor came into view, I put my mouth to the several silk scarves I had nabbed from my older sister's dresser. This was part two of the plan. I disguised my voice in the very best way possible, and carried on with my confession.

Looking back on the scenario, I remember that the sins I had committed were things like sneaking a piece of candy during Lent and thinking bad things about my brothers. Through it all I coughed violently and tried to talk in a very sophisticated, albeit hoarse whisper, through the layers of scarves that were stuffed in my mouth.

Father Gorman was his usual kind and loving self as he listened intently. He said a few words of encouragement and gave me my small penance. After he had said the words of absolution, he added, "By the way, Denise, if you don't mind, would you tell your dad I'll be ready to go fishing around four o'clock?" I swallowed, coughed, and choked, "Okay, Father!"

Mortified, I slunk into the darkness of the church to say my penance, wondering if hiding behind silk scarves while having a coughing fit in the confessional could possibly be yet another sin.

Denise R. Buckley   *Comox, British Columbia, Canada*

"We need to look deeper, asking the Holy Spirit, 'Come in. Probe my heart. Reveal to me what the real problems are. What are the things that lead to sin? What are the attitudes? Where do I need mercy most? Where do I need healing? What are the things in me at a deeper level that need to be healed?'"

A Spiritual Maintenance Agreement

by Vinny Flynn

see page 13

Catholic Treasure

I was a cradle Catholic, and in my younger years, I was very devout. I found much joy and life through my faith. However, during my young adulthood, my faith was tested and I fell away from the Church.

In my late thirties, I felt a strong yearning to totally commit myself to God, and to a specific faith. After months of prayer and discernment, I returned home joyfully to where I started: the Catholic Church. I had tried some Protestant denominations, yet the calling of the Holy Eucharist always burned inside of me, and I knew I could never live fully without it.

Much to my surprise, once I totally recommitted myself to the Catholic faith, I found that the Eucharist was not the only treasure God was to give me through the Church.

It was Lent 2003 and it had been years since I had been to confession. I knew I needed to go, but I was not looking forward to it. Finally, on a cold, rainy day in March, I made up my mind and headed to St. Charles Church near my home in Spokane, Washington. I confessed my sins with remorse and prayed earnestly for forgiveness. Immediately I could sense God's presence in the confessional. It was difficult to get through the confession without breaking into tears.

I was offering all my sins from those confusing, lost years to God, though I could only verbalize a tiny fraction of them to the priest. Somehow I knew that God heard them all, even those I did not remember. After I did my penance, I felt a lightness within myself and a profound sense of God's mercy and love. But the blessings were not over yet.

That night I fell into an extremely deep sleep and had a very vivid dream. In my dream, it was Christmas and my family and I were around the tree opening presents. There was a really special gift wrapped in a box with a huge bow. I don't know how I knew it was special, but I did. I also knew without a doubt that it was specifically and personally for me.

Surrounded by my loved ones, I opened the gift. Inside, in a way I cannot put into words, was the gift of the sacrament of reconciliation. God knew me inside and out, and when I opened the gift I felt better known than I have ever even known myself, and more loved than I can ever express. Light, goodness, and healing shone from within that box, and they were now shining inside my being.

When I woke up the next morning, the gift was inside me, and that dream felt more real than any waking experience I've ever had. When times are hard and faith is tested, I return to that dream and know that the gifts I receive from the sacrament of reconciliation are always there for me whenever I need them.

Julia M. Becker   *Spokane, Washington*

Courage to Change

I was in my first parish in Yuma, Arizona, when one day a young man came to the rectory and asked to talk to a priest. He had broken up with his live-in girlfriend in San Diego and had just arrived in Yuma. He was thinking about going back to her but something told him to stop at the church first.

We talked for quite a while. He knew that he wasn't living the kind of life that the Lord wanted but confessed that the fear of the unknown was worse than the fear of the known. He wanted to go back to her, but something kept telling him to seek advice first.

We talked about life goals and about having the courage to make positive changes even when the future is in doubt. He ended up going to confession and decided to go to his hometown instead of back to California.

About a month later, I got a letter from the young man. He was very much at peace with his decision not to go back to San Diego. He felt new and forgiven and that God was going to lead him through the rest of his life. He was grateful that I was there for him and that I had taken the time that was needed for him to become reconciled with God.

Fr. James W. Modeen   *Tucson, Arizona*

Dance With Joy!

I am a thirty-five-year-old Catholic woman who, at one time in my life, preached with the anti-abortionists at school and was a right-to-lifer. I was judgmental and self-righteous and was the virgin who had it all together. Then, when I was twenty-one years old, I became pregnant from a boyfriend whom I did not intend to marry. I flew into a panic; confusion and torment filled my waking hours as well as my dreams at night.

To cover up the devastation and shame I felt after the abortion, I began drinking and partying and justifying why women have abortions. I hated myself and tried to numb the pain by sleeping with my boyfriend and living a life of earthly pleasure. Once again, I became pregnant when I was twenty-three. This time I really wanted to keep the baby.

I fought with my boyfriend and pleaded with him for us to keep the baby. He told me, "No way", and once again I was the *single mum* facing a fragile, chaotic future. I had just graduated from teachers college and faced many unsure things in my life. I had many unresolved issues to work on before I had a baby. And so, regrettably, I had another abortion.

The pain and shame were too great to describe in words. My work and relationships suffered greatly, and I went from being a bubbly, happy, successful girl to a depressed, troubled, sinful woman with a dark past. How I longed to be freed and to be able to just turn back the clock and right all my wrongs. The biggest wrong was that I had ever had sex before marriage at all.

The following year, when I was twenty-four, a mate said she was going overseas. I wanted a change in my life and thought traveling would get me away from all the memories of what I had done, so I decided to go too. It was a four-month trip, and it was a most wonderful, adventurous, refreshing time for me.

We went to World Youth Day and met great people with whom we shared accommodations and laughs. But the whole time I had this pain deep in my heart, and my soul longed for forgiveness and healing.

When we were in Croatia we intended to go to Medjugorie, but many things almost prevented us from actually going—sickness, buses, lethargy and laziness—and especially my attempt to keep running away from God, not wanting to confess my sins or be seen as the sinner I was.

We did go, however, and it was the most peaceful, prayerful place I have ever been to. My heart and soul were lifted up and I felt myself slowly recovering. I prayed in the church and saw some miracles, but what I remember the most was my four-hour confession. That I really remember! I confessed and cried and cried and cried. The priest absolved me and I felt like a new person.

People still condemn me to this day for having the abortions, and I keep reminding myself that I have been forgiven and am a new creation in Christ Jesus. This experience has made me a more compassionate, humble and gentle person. I still remain opposed to abortion, and I advise women when I can. I advocate abstinence and saving sex for marriage, but I do not judge.

I receive great comfort from the sacrament of reconciliation and sometimes go to confession for a *soul-check*! The bubbly girl is gone, but the depth is there. I'm a child of Jesus married to a wonderful Catholic man who loves me with the eyes of God. We have a beautiful baby girl, with more to come, God willing.

I am blessed, and I praise God that He forgave me, and that I cried out and He heard my cries, dragging me out of the gutter and into the light. Nothing will ever take away the pain and regret I have from the abortions, but I know that I am forgiven and have a right to be in heaven one day to see my children and dance for joy!

Rachael S. Williams   *Melbourne, Victoria, Australia*

A Final Gift

In fifth grade, I took violin lessons from a man in our parish who was a family acquaintance. He had divorced his wife and was living with his two unmarried sisters. Although he had stopped practicing his faith after his divorce, Joseph always drove his sisters to church on Sunday and then sat in the car reading the newspaper until Mass ended.

Years passed. Then one day, about two years after I had been ordained a priest, I went to Columbus to visit my mother and she told me that Joseph was very ill. She suggested I visit him, when I arrived at his home his sister Mary showed me upstairs to his room where he was confined to a bed. When I went back downstairs, Mary was eager to know if her brother had gone to confession. I said, "Mary, he's known me since I was little boy. He wouldn't go to confession to me." But Mary said, "He's been out of the Church for thirty years. We can't let him die without getting him back in the Church."

I told Mary I would go back upstairs and asked her to kneel and pray the rosary in the dining room while I spoke with him. When I got to his room, I asked Joseph if he would like to receive holy Communion and he said, "Yes." I asked if he would like to go to confession, and again he said, "Yes."

I heard his confession and then phoned the pastor of his parish to arrange to have holy Communion brought to him the next morning. I can't tell you how happy I was as I drove back to my parish in Lancaster that day. I spent the rest of the day walking on clouds; I was so happy! By the grace of God, Joseph's funeral Mass was offered the following week in the parish church.

Fr. Charles Foeller   *Mt. Gilead, Ohio*

Warned to Keep it Secret

When I was a small girl, an older person to whom I had looked up and admired molested me. I was too young to fully understand what was going on, but old enough to know that it wasn't OK because I was warned to keep it secret and not tell my parents.

Although I was sinned against more than I was guilty of the sin, it left an ugly residue and I felt horribly unclean by the part I played. The fact that I should tell my parents but couldn't bring myself to do so made the pain worse. In addition (this is difficult to verbalize even forty years later), although I was ashamed and loathed being molested, I submitted to and even, more oddly, appreciated the attention paid to me because this person usually snubbed and treated me unkindly in public.

By the merciful grace of God and before many such incidents, I was able to stand up to this person and refuse to be alone with him anymore.

Fast-forward several years. It was time for our eighth grade confirmation retreat. I had been to confession over the years but had never been able to reveal my dark secret to anyone. Thinking of confessing would start my stomach turning into knots and my heart pounding, and I would be awash in feelings of self-loathing and fear.

By the grace of God, I decided I couldn't continue living like that and would make my first full and complete confession in years. Fr. John McGrann, our priest at St. Patrick Parish in Spokane, Washington, was kind and patient, and then I heard the blessed, miraculous words, "I absolve you…"

Confession washed me clean and healed the wounds. I knew that I was forgiven and was able in turn to forgive the person who injured me. I was so happy, relieved and at peace, I could have flown out of the confessional! It was as if I had been rotting from a painful, crippling disease for years and was suddenly healthy, whole, and dancing in the sunlight.

Anonymous   *Seattle, Washington*

Welcome Home

"Is anyone there?" the deep masculine voice asked from the other side of the screen. I knelt in the dark confessional, speechless and trembling with fear. I knew that I had been a bad little girl and was expected to confess some sins, but the truth was that I didn't know how to go about it. I had never done this before. If there had been a practice session in class, I had missed it, probably when I had been home sick with the flu.

While I was desperately trying to figure out what to say, the confessional door opened. There stood my first grade teacher—a strict, serious nun in her black habit and veil—and the priest. Both were staring at me. I don't remember the conversation that took place, but I do remember feeling very embarrassed and thinking, "Why do these things always happen to me?"

Fortunately, I wasn't scolded as I expected. Sister left and the priest gently helped me say the proper words. Then he prompted me to recall my sins. I was glad and relieved when it was all over.

I went to confession weekly with my family on Saturday afternoons. Every time I approached the confessional, I was nervous and afraid that the priest might recognize me. I prepared myself well beforehand, confessed my sins promptly to avoid a repeat of that first embarrassing experience, and spoke in a low voice—just barely above a whisper.

Later in my life, I left the Church. I was away for fifteen years. When I decided to return in 1987, I knew that I would have to confess my sins. I was definitely not looking forward to it.

I had never enjoyed going to confession nor fully understood its purpose, and after so many years had elapsed, I had no idea what to say. Things had changed in the Church after Vatican II, and now people were going to confession face-to-face. What was I supposed to confess? I had lost my understanding of what sin was. I knew that I had not murdered anyone or robbed a bank, but what was the definition of a sin? I knew that the Church had certain rules, and there were the Ten Commandments, but I couldn't recall all of them.

Finally, I made up my mind to do it. I went to church on a Saturday and sat near an older woman. I kept asking God to give me the courage to do this. Once again, I was trembling with fear, but thought that since I had made it this far, I would let God take me the rest of the way.

I couldn't remember the lighting system for the confessionals. If the light was on, did that mean the confessional was occupied, or did it mean that it was available? When I whispered to the woman seated near me, she spoke in a voice so loud that the entire church could hear. "What? What did you say?" Then I noticed the hearing aid in her ear and waved my hand saying, "Nothing, that's okay." I decided to watch for a while and figure it out on my own.

When I entered the confessional, which turned out to be face-to-face, I simply told the priest how long it had been since my last confession and that I didn't know what to say. He carefully guided me along. I confessed what I could remember and what I thought at that time was a sin. When it was over, he smiled and said, "Welcome home!" Afterwards, I felt a peace that I had never felt before, and I knew that I was back where I belonged.

Jean M. Heimann   *Wichita, Kansas*

The Other Side of the Confessional

By Fr. Christopher Walsh

Alec Guinness, the renowned British actor, once was filming a movie in a village in Burgundy. During a break from the shooting, he headed off the set, still in full clerical attire, to return to his room in the little hotel. As he was walking down the *rue*, a young boy came running up to him, calling out, *"Mon père!"* Guinness recounts in his memoir, *Blessings in Disguise*:

> My hand was seized by a boy of seven or eight, who clutched it tightly, swung it and kept up a non-stop prattle. He was full of excitement, hops, skips and jumps, but never let go of me. I didn't dare speak in case my excruciating French should scare him. Although I was a total stranger he obviously took me for a priest and so to be trusted. Suddenly with a *"Bon soir, mon père,"* and a hurried sideways sort of bow, he disappeared through a hole in a hedge. He had had a happy, reassuring walk home, and I was left with an odd calm sense of elation.

Guinness recalls being struck at that moment by the mystery and power of the Catholic priesthood: that a young boy would feel such immediate trust and affection for him, a stranger and foreigner, simply because he believed him to be a priest. A year later Guinness entered the Catholic Church.

Of course, in recounting his impressions, Alec Guinness was sharing simply what he felt while playing the role of a priest. But what are the thoughts and feelings of actual priests when they are sitting in a confessional, listening to sinners' heartfelt confessions, offering them counsel and absolving them of even the gravest sins?

It was interesting to me how many lay persons, when I told them about the project of this book, were most intrigued by that question. Are priests bothered by penitents' sometimes tedious recitation of their sins? Do they get bored hearing confessions? Are priests saddened that Catholics are not living more faithfully the moral standards of their faith? What is it really like to be on the other side of the confessional?

A Demanding Ministry

Pope John Paul described the role of confessor in the sacrament of penance as "undoubtedly the most difficult and sensitive, the most exhausting and demanding ministry of the priest, but also one of the most beautiful and consoling." I would certainly say for myself that, compared with almost any other pastoral situation, hearing confessions requires the greatest attentiveness and concentration, the most care and prudence in how I respond. And after a few hours in the confessional without a break, yes, it can even at times become physically demanding. One particularly busy Holy Week I developed a crick in my neck from continuously bending my right ear toward the confessional screen; so I turned my chair around and leaned over with my left ear instead.

But like the pope, I have found my ministry in the sacrament of penance to be one of the most fulfilling and moving parts of my priesthood. I think and hope it is true that, except for situations where I had to leave to say Mass for a waiting congregation, I have never turned down a request by a penitent to go to confession.

There is nothing special about that. In the vast majority of cases in my life, both before and after I was ordained, I have never encountered a moment's hesitation by any priest whom I have asked to hear my own confession, no matter the time or the place. Indeed, a ninety-year-old priest once told me categorically: "In sixty-five years as a priest, I have never turned down a request to go to confession!"

Church law obliges a priest who is entrusted by his office with the "care of souls" (*cura animarum*) to provide for the hearing of confessions for the members of his flock "when they reasonably ask to be heard." And in case of "urgent necessity," canon law states, any confessor is obliged to hear the confessions of the Christian faithful.

I believe we priests intuitively feel that administering this sacrament is, like celebrating the Eucharist, one of the most sacred privileges and important duties that we perform for our people. It is revealing, I think, that for all the abuses and faults that priests have been charged with throughout the long history of the church, I am not aware of any historical period when a major complaint against the clergy was that they violated the absolute confidentiality of the sacrament of penance. On the contrary, just as they have given their lives to celebrate and preserve the Eucharist, so too priests have gone to their deaths rather than reveal to demanding kings or imperious judges the secrets of a soul that they learned under the seal of the confessional.

Given the governmental animus toward religion in general and Christianity in particular in secular Western societies, it is conceivable that priests will again be called to witness to the inviolable sanctity of sacramental confession at the price of their own personal suffering. In some states, for instance, clergy are now included as "mandated reporters" of specific crimes such as child abuse, without any exemption for the absolute confidentiality of the priest/penitent relationship in the sacrament of penance.

Several years ago we even witnessed a state prosecutor secretly taping a prison confession made by a prison inmate suspected of murder. The confessor, a local pastor, knew nothing of the clandestine recording. The Oregon prosecutor only refrained from introducing the tape as evidence in court because of the strong condemnation by Bishop Kenneth Steiner of the Portland archdiocese and the ensuing public outcry.

To begin to answer the question "What is it like to be on the other side of the confessional?" Think of all the different sorts of people whom the priest encounters in the sacrament. The stressed-out mother feeling guilty about losing her temper with her husband and children. The high school student who has begun experimenting with alcohol or drugs or sex. The bachelor in his twenties or thirties, who has not been to the sacraments in years but, perhaps at a wedding rehearsal, suddenly feels the need to go to confession. The middle-aged executive forced to reflect on all his adult moral

OTHER SIDE OF CONFESSIONAL

decisions as he lies in a hospital bed the night before a serious surgery. The woman in her forties, crying over her abortion twenty years before, who desperately wants to hear that God—and her baby—forgive her. The elderly widows and widowers struggling with loneliness and jealousy and despair, who need to know that God has not forgotten them. Yes, even the little boy who expects to be taken very seriously as he solemnly relates how he disobeys his parents and fights with his siblings and teases his cat.

To the confessor there is some undefined trait that all these penitents share when they enter that sacred space, be it a confessional box or a reconciliation room or just the cubicle of a hospital bed. In that awesome meeting of a human being's freedom in admitting guilt and God's love poured out in forgiving grace, every Christian, young and old, comes to resemble the "little children" to whom the gospel promises the kingdom of heaven (Matthew 19:14).

Monsignor Lorenzo Albacete, a theologian and priest of the Archdiocese of Washington, made that point in a column about hearing confessions in *The New York Times Magazine*.

Confession is not therapy, nor is it moral accounting. At its best, it is the affirmation that the ultimate truth of our interior life is our absolute poverty, our radical dependence, our unquenchable thirst, our desperate need to be loved...

Confessing even the most dramatic struggles, I have found, people reach for the simplest language, that of a child before a world too confusing to understand. Silent wonder is the most natural response to a revelation that surpasses all words.

Fr. Christopher Walsh is the author of The Untapped Power of the Sacrament of Penance *and is a pastor of St. Joseph Church in Shelton, Connecticut, and adjunct professor of dogmatic theology at St. Joseph Seminary (Dunwoodie) in Yonkers, New York. For thirteen years he worked in the formation of future priests as vocations director of the Diocese of Bridgeport and spiritual director at St. John Fisher Seminary, Stamford, Connecticut.*

Setting A Good Example

I was born in 1954 and was raised in the Catholic faith, but like so many of my generation who were teenagers in the sixties, I rebelled against the Church and fell away from practicing my faith.

When my husband and I had children, we registered at our local parish, Curé of Ars Church in Merrick, New York, and began going to Mass on Sundays. I felt it was the right thing to do, but I was never quite there in my heart.

In 1998, as my daughter prepared for her first holy Communion, I attended a meeting for parents to prepare for our children's first reconciliation. Our pastor spoke to us about the sacrament and suggested that we, as parents, might wish to set a good example and go to confession regularly ourselves.

Our pastor's words jogged my conscience, and I realized that this was something I needed to do. It had been nearly thirty years since I had gone to confession. I sought counseling from one of our parish priests, Father Robert Romeo, and began to prepare myself by examining my conscience. It was not easy; a lot had happened in thirty years!

Father Bob suggested that an individual appointment in his office would be best for me. The morning for my confession came, and I was a nervous wreck, but I knew this was something I had to do. Father was extremely patient and helpful, and he guided me through the process. When he spoke the words of absolution, I felt that a tremendous weight had been lifted off my shoulders. I was stunned by the enormity of that moment.

I went to the church to pray my penance, and as I knelt, I was overwhelmed with God's love and grace in my heart. I wept tears of joy. Finally, I knew that Jesus loved and forgave me. He was no longer just an abstract idea, but a real presence in my heart.

My religion is no longer a duty grudgingly performed; my faith is a deeply personal relationship with my Lord and Savior. Celebrating the sacrament of reconciliation after so many years was the beginning of a joyful journey back home to the Church. Today, my husband and I are very much involved in our parish, and I celebrate the wonderful sacrament of reconciliation regularly.

Catherine M. Zubrovich   *Freeport, New York*

A Weekly Remedy

I was seventeen and confused. As a cradle Catholic, I went to Mass only because I had to while I was living under my dad's roof. I was told to go to church every week but never knew why it was so important. I despised going to Mass and felt that since I wasn't even sure if God really existed, it was just a big waste of time.

My first reconciliation also made me angry. Pride told me that I didn't need confession. I convinced myself that if I didn't feel guilty about my sins, then going to confession was also just a big waste of time.

Not only was I angry from being forced to practice Catholicism against my will, but also because I didn't know who I was or what I was going to do after high school. The anger built up inside of me causing me to make some poor decisions. I found myself in a pit of misery, which was quite opposite from my great childhood years.

When I was a child, my inner joy caused me to make good decisions and to love everyone I met. I enjoyed my family, even though my parents were divorced when I was three and a half years old. As I bounced between grandparents, aunts, uncles, and my mom and dad, I felt as if I were a complete person. I told myself that if I ever lost that happiness I would just revert back to the faith.

However, in my pit of misery, the last thing I wanted to do was return to the faith. Yet, I thirsted for the wellspring of happiness that I had as a child. I tried many of my old routines, but they all led to dead ends. Finally, I was forced to face my true self and admit that I had been wrong. I had no other option but to return to the Church.

I knew I had turned myself 180 degrees away from God, but now I realized that if there really were a God, then He alone could help me. I attended Mass with a different attitude this time, one of actually paying attention to what was going on for once. I wanted to get something out of the Mass and maybe practice our faith right for a change. After all, what did I have to lose?

Well, I found out that what I had to lose were my sins. You see, I was guilty and I knew it. I prayed to God for forgiveness in private, but that resulted in my receiving more of a lessening of guilt than a removal of guilt. I knew I had to go to confession. I was very afraid and embarrassed just thinking of the sins I had committed. How could I tell another person, especially someone this holy, about the things I had done?

I was very ashamed, but I knew that God was asking me to take this huge and very personal step. I had trusted in Jesus the previous few weeks and I needed to trust Him here.

I consulted a Catholic friend who I thought set the best example for me and who frequented the confessional. I relearned how to go to confession because I hadn't gone since my first reconciliation and wasn't sure how to do it. I got the information I needed and was in a state of complete shame as I entered that confessional.

To my relief, the priest was very understanding. He was very easy on me and was also very sensitive to my embarrassment. Through him, the wounds to my heart and soul finally received the treatment they needed. Remnants of my sins remained like scars, but they eventually faded with time.

After going to confession, I continued to commit a couple of mortal sins because they were addictions. Yet, through time and weekly confession, they have now also been cured. I heard my priest tell someone one time that confession is like an antibiotic. Some sins can't be fixed by one time in confession; they may take several confessions. In my case, it took going to confession once a week for seven years.

Now I continue to receive the sacrament of reconciliation once a week, even if no mortal sin has been committed. A knife that is dull is useless. A knife can be sharpened, but how much harder it is to sharpen that dull knife in order to get it back to new. Why not sharpen it after each use? That way it is always ready for duty.

Confession has been the pivotal sacrament for all of my faith. The soil had finally become moist and soft enough for a seed of faith to grow. It is the seed that God planted in my heart so long ago, and from which a whole garden has grown. Through the sacrament of reconciliation, I once again enjoy the rays of sanctifying grace that I had always relied on as a child.

Joseph M. McDonald   *Colfax, Washington*

Why Bother?

It took the death of my mom to get me back to church and the sacrament of reconciliation. I had not attended Mass very many times for thirty years because I couldn't receive the sacraments due to a divorce and remarriage. Like many other divorced Catholics, I felt that if I couldn't receive the sacraments, why bother to go to church? How wrong I was.

Being unable to receive the Eucharist at my mom's funeral Mass added to my sorrow that day in August of 1992. As soon as I returned home to South Carolina, I made an appointment with Father Joseph Hanley of St. Michael Church in Garden City. After weeks of counseling and him conferring with the bishop to grant me a dispensation, I was ready to make my confession.

I was very nervous knowing I had to confess thirty years of sins as I sat face-to-face with Father Hanley. I was afraid that I would forget to confess something.

The priest was very helpful and patient with me. As I sat there, I wished I had written all my sins down so I could just read them off to him. I had butterflies in my stomach and my hands were shaking even though I had them folded. But as I began my confession, there were no words to describe the feeling that came over me.

I can only say that my tears were of sadness for my sins and joy for being forgiven from them. I truly felt the Holy Spirit dwelling within me, and at last I knew the true meaning of our merciful God. He gave me a second chance through the death of my mom.

Five years ago on Easter, my husband joined our faith. For the past three and a half years he has suffered from kidney failure, amputations of both legs, and numerous other illnesses. He has been close to death at least six times. Each time he was anointed we knew that if God chose to end his life, his sins were forgiven through the sacrament of reconciliation. How fortunate we are to be Catholic and to be able to receive this sacrament. Thank you, Jesus!

Katherine P. Hoff   *Marion, Ohio*

A Difficult Hurdle

As a Lutheran convert to Catholicism, the sacrament of reconciliation was definitely a difficult hurdle for me to overcome. Yet, leap it I did, and now I can't imagine life without it. There is a peace and contentment that comes with this sacrament. I can recall an incident in the confessional over my past decade as a Catholic that was truly memorable.

About five years ago, after I had made my confession, the young priest asked some questions and counseled me. When it came time for him to give my penance, he began saying something, but then suddenly stopped, paused, and said something else. He asked me to pray, "Jesus Christ, Son of God, give me your strength," ten times. I was as touched by the penance as I was by the manner with which it seemed to come to him. It seemed very much as if the Holy Spirit had whispered to him, thereby changing my penance. I returned to my pew refreshed and eager to respond to God's grace.

Tim A. Drake   *St. Joseph, Minnesota*

My Thoughts...

The tips I have learned along the way, from sixteen years of Catholic schooling and different catholic parishes are:

Review each and all of the Ten Commandments and think of how you did not fulfill them to the fullest.

Confess anything that separates you from God (sin).

Confess your issues with intense emotions, for example, anger, jealousy, frustration, impatience....

Review the seven deadly sins, although they are extreme, they are apparent in all shades and we can all see some guilt in those areas...especially pride:

Greed

Gluttony

Envy

Sloth

Pride

Lust

Wrath

Jacqueline Leithauser

"The best way to keep a child regularly receiving this precious sacrament is by our example. If we, as adults, do not make frequent use of this sacrament, we cannot realistically expect our children to do so."

Teaching Children the Gift of Confession

by Christi Gareis

see page 215

Keeping Our Souls Clean

"This kitchen stinks!" I complained to myself more than once. Yet no matter how hard I scrubbed, sprayed, washed, wiped, or scoured, a foul odor lingered. One day, in sheer exasperation, I literally followed my nose through every nook and cranny of the kitchen. Finally, I bird-dogged it to the vent over the cook top. "This is it," I announced as proudly as a pointer that had spotted its prey. I knew I was onto something.

Very carefully, I removed the filter which I supposed was in need of a good soaking. As I took a closer look, I shrieked in horror. There, on the filter screen, were two very dead, very dried up mice. I ran hysterically to the back door with the foul cargo and dumped them on the grass. When I regained my composure, I realized that somehow the two little culprits had found their way through the attic, down the stove pipe and onto the screen. There they had breathed their last and had begun to add their own distinctive bouquet to my kitchen below.

The next day, I had a new vent, a screened in stove pipe to prevent future invasions by unwanted critters, and a fresher smelling kitchen. As I settled down for my morning prayer, however, the thought of that putrid little pair kept coming back to me. That's when it happened. The good Lord *spoke* to me about a great spiritual truth within the framework of my recent experience. "Bonnie," He began, impressing upon my mind the following analogy: "Sin is a lot like those two smelly mice on that filter. It is a dead weight on the soul that sends up a stench into the nostrils of the Almighty. But it doesn't have to remain. The soul can evict it, throw it out, and come to the Master for cleansing. Unfortunately, in today's world, many have lived with the foulness for so long that they've lost their sensitivity and can no longer even detect its presence. They live on, oblivious of the fact that there is a cleaner, purer, fresher way. Remember that. Keep sniffing sin out of your life through regular examination of conscience and confession. Ongoing reconciliation is the healthy way to grow closer and closer to heaven."

Several weeks later, in my high school English classroom, the topic of sin came up as we read a literary selection. I related to the students the story I'd recently experienced on that subject. One boy said, "Mrs. Barry, I don't have dead mice on the screen of my soul. I have a dead buffalo!" The class roared.

"Toss it out," I told him, as we moved on to another subject, all of us well aware that although we'd had a good laugh, we had some pretty serious stuff to think about.

As the day continued, I repeated the mouse story to my other classes. Finally, sixth period arrived, and as the student body proceeded to the auditorium for a benefit auction held by the track team, I made my way to the computer writing lab to work on the school newspaper. Just as the staff members and I were really making progress, one of my English students popped in to tell me that an adorable angel figurine was being auctioned. She wondered if I wanted to bid on it.

"Ten dollars maximum," I told her, as she sailed out hoping to secure the item for me. Moments later she was back—with the angel and a little book of picture postcards that had been thrown in for *lagniappe* (extra surprise).

"Thanks, Heather," I told her as I took a closer look at my purchases. "The angel's darling," I commented, while at the same time flipping through the picture postcard book. Suddenly, I gasped quite audibly. For there, in that lagniappe purchase, was a postcard with a photo of—two dead mice! It seemed too coincidental to be real. "Look, Heather," I told my student whose eyes widened in disbelief. There was no denying what we were seeing. It was definitely two very dead, very dried up mice, just like the ones I had pitched out on the lawn.

The good Lord was at it again. Not only had He taught me a very graphic lesson about sin, but He had repeated the message, like all good teachers do, and had sent me a visual aid to keep as a constant reminder of its importance. To this day, I still carry that book of postcards wherever I go.

Later that week, a story about the track team's auction appeared in the newspaper. Along with the story was a photo of the track coach holding up two items that were up for bid—an angel and a picture postcard book. To the general public, it was a great shot of the coach, but to me it was a photographic record of the buy of the day!

But the story doesn't end here. Later in the week, as I headed to Mass on a cold Sunday in February, I noticed a family, all decked out in church attire piling into their vehicle. Among them was a beautiful little girl, resplendent in first Communion finery.

The scene brought back to mind an issue that was sometimes the subject of controversy between traditional and more progressive thinkers—is it really appropriate to pull out all the stops and dress little girls like brides for first Communion? Doesn't it smack of pomp and pageantry and miss the mark of true reverence?

It had been years since my daughter had participated in her first Eucharist, so I hadn't given much thought to the idea in a long time; however, the sight of that child on this Sunday morning brought it all back in an instant. I turned it into a prayer. "Lord," I asked as I approached the interstate on my way to church, "is the bridal garb overdoing it?"

"No, it is not," an answer popped into my mind. "The white dress and veil symbolize the virginal heart, pure and innocent, for the Lord. Everyone should approach the Communion table as a spotless bride. Today, before Mass, go to confession; follow that child's witness of purity."

Fortunately, I arrived at the church in plenty of time to go to confession, but I was surprised by what I met as I waited my turn in line. A young man just ahead of me turned and smiled as I approached. "Hi, Mrs. Barry," he whispered.

When he saw I had no idea who he was, he quietly explained, "I was in Miss Fuller's class last week when you told us that story about keeping our souls as clean as our bodies. You know the one about how sin in our souls is like the stench of dead mice? Well, I want you to know I'm here in this line because of that story. I figured I needed to throw out those stinking mice, just like you said we should!"

"I'm glad the talk made an impression on you," I told him. "I'm here to toss out a few *dead mice* too."

As we lapsed into silence and examination of conscience, it occurred to me that the first Communion girl also had done her work! Had it not been for seeing her, I probably would not have gone to confession on that particular day; I would not have heard the young man's testimony; I would not have known that my story had found such a hearty recipient. More importantly, I would not have pondered anew how, when we put on our Sunday best, we should also consider the conditions of our hearts, making sure they are in tip-top shape to meet the Master.

Bonnie Taylor Barry   *Sunset, Louisiana*

My Thoughts...

No matter when I look back over a day, a week, a month, or longer, I have three questions to ask myself.

1. What did I think, say, do, or refrain from doing today that has marred my relationship with God, others, or myself?

2. Why did I do what I did?

3. What am I going to do about it?

This probably sounds simplistic but it gets to the root of the offense and forces me, the sinner, to take responsibility for the unloving choices I have made. This in turn leads to my making amends and seeking reconciliation in light of the consequences of my irresponsible choices.

Anita Kalyan

Honest Conversation With God

I grew up in an era when we went to confession every Saturday, like clockwork. As a child, this was unfortunately a very mundane experience. I did not have the kind of joyful preparation that many of today's children receive from theologically informed and spiritually gifted educators.

I was not told in CCD that a sin was something you did wrong, that you knew was wrong, and that you knew you shouldn't do, but you deliberately did or failed to do. I didn't understand how the Ten Commandments applied to my life, except perhaps the one "Thou Shalt Not Steal," because that was pretty straightforward, even for kids.

Not to belabor the point, but this uninspired foundation of my childhood translated into fairly rote confessions. Rather than make genuine, thoughtful confessions, I resorted to reciting a litany of credible sins, from disobedience of parents to lying, and assigning arbitrary numbers to these in an effort to sound believable and contrite. "I lied five times; I disobeyed my parents three times, etc..."

While I did, in fact, deeply regret my basic sinfulness, it was on a generic level and did not remove from me the general dread of going in week after week with my catalogue of sins that I may or may not have committed for the sake of having something to report and repent.

The Church has made many attempts in recent times to make confession more user-friendly and more in keeping with the spirit of the sacrament, but the old training I received ingrained the practice so staunchly that I still find myself falling into the pattern of formulaic confession. This makes for a completely unsatisfying experience and is, no doubt, as stultifying for the priest as it is for me. It also is probably largely responsible for the fact I simply use this sacrament as a semi-annual event, which I continue to dread.

At one point though, in an effort to embrace the new spirit of reconciliation, I examined my conscience against the enlightened standards. I found I had plenty of material to confess without having to invent a thing or resort to fictional accounts and measures.

This new examination of conscience prepared me for confession as to what it should have been all along: a deeply personal and painfully honest conversation with the Lord. I now recognized clearly my shortcomings and failings and knew I needed both pardon for them and assistance in overcoming the tendencies for which I was responsible.

I still do not go to reconciliation frequently. I still agonize over giving accounts of sins I'd rather not expose to priests. But I now understand the peace that is available through this beautiful sacrament and have an entirely different attitude about its meaning and value than that which I had held for most of my life.

Anonymous   *Derwood, Maryland*

A Warm Golden Light

My grandfather suffered a heart attack while returning from his Christmas Eve confession. Grampy died as he hit the sidewalk walking home to our house in the snow. Neighbors carried him in.

I was twelve, and I was devastated. This can't be, I raged. How could God let him die on a cold, lonely sidewalk all alone?

Despite his eighty-four years, I thought my grandfather would be with us forever. He was a widower, a gentleman who always wore a tie to dinner, and a gentle man who lived his faith quietly and well.

Grampy's presents were all wrapped under the tree. His pipe and newspaper were still where he had left them. It was a sad, confusing Christmas. A week later, however, I realized that I had underestimated God's generosity toward my grandfather.

A parishioner called. She told my mother, "I saw your dad at church on Christmas Eve. I didn't put it all together until I read his death notice, but then I had to call and tell you."

The woman had seen an elderly man leave the confessional and approach the manger by the altar rail. He knelt in prayer, gazing at the statues of Mary and Joseph and the still empty crib.

"There was a warm, golden light that encircled both the manger and your dad," said the caller. "My friend next to me saw it, too. And oh, when he turned there was such a beautiful expression on his face, full of peace and joy. His face was radiant."

Grampy had died minutes later.

The caller's story helped me to realize that God had not let this good and faithful servant die alone. No, God had been there to hear his last whispered confession. From the tabernacle, God had seen him gazing with love at the crèche. And I was sure God had welcomed Grampy home as he was born into new life that snowy Christmas Eve.

Gail M. Besse   *Hull, Massachusetts*

New Meaning in Life

I am a male citizen of Kenya in East Africa, hailing from the small village of Mang'u in the Central Province. As I write this story I am twenty-three years old, and I value the sacrament of reconciliation in a special way. I believe that it is the principle sign of God's mercy towards mankind.

For me, a poor sinner, confession is the one source of hope for salvation. I share my story in the hope that someone who is in the same situation as I was may take courage and receive this wonderful sacrament with a sincere heart.

My story happened when I was about nineteen years old and living at home in Mang'u. I had been going to confession about two or three times a year, trying to obey the Church's command to receive the sacrament of reconciliation at least once a year. Throughout the year, I would sin, even mortally, and continue receiving the Eucharist. The problem was that I always rationalized my sins, convincing myself that they were merely venial. I never mentioned the mortal sins in confession because of the shame I felt. Then the dreams started.

I dreamt that while receiving the Eucharist, the sacred Host would stick to the roof of my mouth. When I tried to swallow it, it stuck to my throat. Other times I dreamt I was walking in darkness, and then I would see a priest in the confessional looking at me with a mixture of compassion and exasperation. I would wake up in profound terror and sadness.

These dreams inspired fear in me, and I started examining my conscience. Within me I experienced a great unwillingness to confess those *big sins*. However, a voice within always told me that if I died in this state, hell would be my eternal resting place. I prayed in repentance, but then the same voice would point out that my way of repentance as a Catholic was clear—confession!

To make matters worse, or better, people around me started talking about confession more frequently. I remember a friend who told me of a person who had lived a consecrated life, died with only one unconfessed mortal sin on his soul, and went to hell. Homilies on the sacrament of reconciliation filled me with dread, and I lived with this inner terror for about two years.

Then I joined Strathmore University, which is sponsored by the Prelature of Opus Dei. In the year 2003, I attended a retreat offered by the Prelature of Opus Dei at a place called Tigoni, also in Central Province, where a priest named Father Anthony was presiding. There I learned the value of the sacrament of reconciliation, and I made a good general confession. I learned that there are no *unconfessable sins*.

From then on the terrible dreams ceased, and I felt that a new lease on life had been granted to me by Our Lord. My reception of holy Communion had new meaning and life, and I became more sincere and frequent in receiving the sacrament of reconciliation.

I now strive to go to confession at least fortnightly (once every two weeks), and whenever I forget, a glance at the past sends me back to the confessional. I am still a sinner and a struggler, but the sacrament of reconciliation makes me an entirely new person.

Bernard M. Kago   *Thika, Central Province, Kenya*

A Little Bit Better

During my first year as a Catholic, I approached the sacrament of reconciliation with trepidation. I was unsure of what to do and not totally convinced that confession really did anything. I went because I had come to believe almost everything the Church teaches. I decided I would accept the rest, so off I went to bare my soul.

As I recited the act of contrition, confession began to take on a new meaning. I was often a little fearful because of my sins, but as I said the words, "Most of all because they have offended You, my God," it became clear to me why I was there. I had offended the one who created me.

The priest listened quietly and then began to speak. The only words I heard were, "I absolve you of all your sins." As he said those words, I felt a warm glow in my breast. Afterwards, I went to kneel before the holy tabernacle to reflect on my sins, as the priest had asked. I had done this many times before, but this time I felt something was different.

I knew I would continue to sin, but it would not be the same. Each time I received the sacrament of reconciliation, I would be, as a different priest had suggested, a little bit better. Now I am eager to go to confession because every time I do, I become just a little bit better.

Robert J. Decker   *Maryville, Illinois*

Lessons for Confession

By Father Pat Umberger

It's not easy

The sacrament of reconciliation is a difficult one for most of us. We need think no further than the story of Adam and Eve in the garden. Rather than admit wrongdoing, it was so much easier for them to put the blame somewhere else. We can feel too, that God loves us more when we're doing good. We can even try to make ourselves believe God doesn't know about our wrongdoing.

God loves you

God love us! God knows what the challenges of human life are all about. We can think about the story of the Prodigal Son, the great insult and hurt the son inflicted on the father, and how the father welcomed him back, without even waiting for an apology. I've had occasion to meet many people who were hurt very badly by family members and friends. When I ask the question, "Would you ever be able to forgive them?" the answer is usually, "Yes." If we as humans can be so forgiving, how much more is God willing to forgive us!

God waits

He waits for our return. "But I haven't been to Confession for fifty years!" The response is simply…"Welcome back! How good it is that you are here!"

How do I know if I'm ready?

If you've read this far, chances are you're serious about getting ready. Sometimes we are reluctant to go to reconciliation because we're not sure what to do or what to say. How do we know that we're ready. According to *The Catechism of the Catholic Church*, three things are necessary…

CONTRITION

Contrition is sorrow of the soul and detestation for the sin committed, together with the resolution not to sin again. The reception of this sacrament ought to be prepared for by an examination of conscience made in the light of the Word of God. See appendix A for one version based on the Ten Commandments.

CONFESSION OF SINS

The confession (or disclosure) of sins, even from a simply human point of view, frees us and facilitates our reconciliation with others. Through such an admission we squarely look at the sins we are responsible for, take responsibility for them, and therefore open ourselves again to God and to the communion of the Church in order to make a new future possible. Confession to a priest is an essential part of the sacrament of penance. "All mortal sins of which penitents after a diligent self-examination are conscious must be recounted by them in confession. According to the Church's command, "after having attained the age of discretion, each of the faithful is bound by an obligation faithfully to confess serious sins at least once a year."

SATISFACTION

Many sins wrong our neighbor. One must do what is possible in order to repair the harm (e.g. return stolen goods, restore the reputation of someone slandered, pay compensation for injuries). Simple justice requires as much. Raised up from sin, the sinner must still recover full spiritual health by doing something more to make amends for the sin. The person must "make satisfaction for" or "expiate" sins. This satisfaction is called "penance." It can consist of prayer, an offering, works of mercy, service of neighbor, voluntary self-denial or sacrifices.

What to say.

The priest will greet you in the reconciliation room or confessional. If you choose to meet him face-to-face, simply exchange a normal greeting—good morning—and shake his hand. He'll help you begin. You'll make the sign of the cross together. In the name of the Father, and of the Son, and of the Holy Spirit. Amen.

Don't worry. The priest is there to help you! He may invite you to have trust in God—by saying these or similar words: "May God, who has enlightened every heart, help you to know your sins and trust in his mercy." You could respond with "Amen," if you'd like.

The priest may also read a short passage from Scripture. Simply listen!

Confess your sins.

It could be that after the sign of the cross, the priest will simply be silent. Then you could confess your sins. You might mention how long it has been since your last confession. Many of us are used to beginning by saying, "Bless me, Father, for I have sinned. My last Confession was ____ ago. These are my sins." If you're stumped by this time, chances are the priest will simply ask, "What are your sins."

Then tell him what your sins are. Remember, it is important to confess all serious sins. Reconciliation means that we're ready to let go of all sins too. It's the ones we hold back that sometimes make things more difficult for us. So, no matter how difficult it seems, mention them all.

Penance and Act of Contrition

The priest may then speak to you. He may try to help you to see the source of your sinful actions. Usually, we're sinful because we're selfish. He'll also assure you of God's love for you. He will then propose an act of penance which you accept to make satisfaction for sin and to amend your life.

He may then ask you to pray an act of contrition—or of sorrow for your sin. It is just fine to pray a spontaneous prayer—eg. "God, I'm sorry for my sins. Give me the strength I'll need to leave them behind and live a new kind of life." We may wish to pray the act of contrition we learned as a child. An example:

My God, I am sorry for my sins with all my heart.
In choosing to do wrong and failing to do good

173

L
E
S
S
O
N
S

F
O
R

C
O
N
F
E
S
S
I
O
N

I have sinned against you whom I should love above all things.
I firmly intend, with your help, to do penance, to sin no more,
and to avoid whatever leads me to sin.
Our Savior Jesus Christ suffered and died for us.
In his name, my God, have mercy.

(Another example)
O my God, I have sinned through my own fault
In choosing to sin and failing to do good
I have sinned against you, whom I should love above all things.
I firmly intend, with the help of your Son, to make up for my sins
and to love as I should. Amen.

Absolution

The priest will extend his hand toward you, or perhaps lay his hands on your head as he prays the Church's prayer of absolution:

God, the Father of mercies,
through the death and resurrection of his Son
has reconciled the world to himself
and sent the Holy Spirit among us
for the forgiveness of sins;
through the ministry of the Church
may God give you pardon and peace,
and I absolve you from your sins
in the name of the Father, and of the Son, +
and of the Holy Spirit.
R/. Amen.

Dismissal

The priest may pray a short closing prayer with you. He may also simply say, go in peace to love and serve the Lord. Your response can be very natural—a simple amen, or thank you—have a good day. Then go to spend some time considering your penance.

The Bottom Line

But isn't there something I can take along, so I won't feel like I'm forgetting something? Certainly! My Credit Card to Heaven, the size of a credit card, with all the information you'll need to celebrate the sacrament of reconciliation. You can get a free download from http://frpat.com/reconcard.htm

> In the Name of the Father, and of the Son
> and of the Holy Spirit. Amen.

> Bless me Father for I have sinned, my
> last Confession was _____ ago. These
> are my sins. [Confess sins here]

Act of Contrition

> O my God, I am heartily sorry
> for having offended thee,
> and I detest all my sins
> because of thy just punishment,
> but most of all because they
> offend thee, my God
> who art all good and deserving
> of all my love. I firmly resolve
> with the help of thy grace
> to sin no more and to
> avoid the near occasion of sin.
> Amen.

175

Communal Reconciliation

Sometimes a parish will schedule a communal reconciliation service, usually during the season of Advent or Lent. The first part of the service will consist of songs, Scripture readings, a homily and an examination of conscience. The priest may give all present a common penance, and even have them pray an act of contrition together. There should then be an opportunity for those present to come forward for private confession. Just follow the directions given at the service, and all will be well.

Father Pat Umberger is a pioneer in using the Internet for faith-based purposes. He is pastor of St. Patrick Parish in Onalaska, Wisconcin, and a Fourth Degree member of the Knights of Columbus. Father Pat has a popular and extensive web ministry offering easy to understand information to deepen your walk with the Lord. You can visit him on the web at www.frpat.com.

I Was in Trouble

About six years ago, a number of illnesses and deaths happened in my family. This was very upsetting to me and so in an effort to understand what was happening, I started reading all kinds of near-death-experience literature. It was intriguing, but it didn't answer my questions, so I continued searching.

About that time, my church needed a CCD teacher for the second grade, and I reluctantly volunteered for the position. I began to read a lot of Catholic material and felt something happening inside me, but I couldn't quite put my finger on what it was. Being a *need-to-know* kind of person, I pressed forward in my pursuit to understand spirituality at an even deeper level.

As I was preparing the children to receive the sacrament of reconciliation, I began reading about the Ten Commandments and was totally fascinated by them. I researched them more and more until I finally realized that I was in trouble. You see, although I was a cradle Catholic, I was not practicing our faith the way I should have been. If a belief didn't suit my lifestyle, I ignored it. I did what I wanted, when I wanted, and how I wanted. Church was a place to go on Sundays and that was it.

I began to wonder how I was going to teach the children something that I was not following myself. I was not obeying God's laws and knew I had to do something about it, but didn't know what. When I told a friend about what was unfolding in my life, she said that as long as I was open to God, good and enlightening things would happen. She suggested that I speak with a certain priest in our town, so I reluctantly scheduled an appointment with him.

The priest was very understanding and compassionate, and he assisted me in making the most glorious confession of my entire life. Like my friend, he told me that as long as I kept my heart open to God, I could expect many wonderful things to happen. He was so right. This special priest became my spiritual director for a period of time, and I picked his brain on faith matters until I was completely satisfied.

As my spiritual journey continues, my heart fills with joy when I remember the wonderful day I opened my heart to God and received the sacrament of reconciliation from that holy priest.

Carol Ann Matz   *Hazleton, Pennsylvania*

You Are Missing the Point

A few years ago, I began attending Mass again at St. Anthony Church in Tigard, Oregon. I had been away from the Church for years, and I knew that before I could receive Communion I had to go to confession.

It had been more than twenty years since my last confession and I barely remembered the prayers. My biggest concern was that confessions were now being heard face-to-face. How could I sit and face the priest while going down my long list of sins? It was much too shameful, so I put it off for another three years.

Every time I thought about going to confession, I would start to cry. For the longest time I could not figure out why, but now I believe that it must have been the Holy Spirit grieving inside of me. I had gone to God on my knees and repented, but I was terrified of a face-to-face encounter with a real person. I was too embarrassed and ashamed to confess twenty-five years of sins.

When I mentally walked through the confession, I would ultimately be asking the priest to realize how old I was when I committed this sin or that. At times I am sure the Holy Spirit just sighed, whispering, "You are missing the point."

The first tiny step towards my reconciliation was to log onto the internet and find out when confessions were heard. No commitment, just fact finding. Safe enough. So now I knew when I could go.

Then I e-mailed the priest and explained that it had been years since I had been to confession. What happens there these days? He assured me that I could choose to sit face-to-face or side by side with a partition between us. This sounded so much better to me as I warmed up to the idea.

Weeks went by, and then one Saturday, out of the blue, I decided I would just do it. I wanted to receive Communion that Sunday.

Mercifully, there was no one else in the church that afternoon. I was the only person waiting for the priest. I had arrived early, and I used the time to pray to God to give me courage to go into the confessional. I waited, and then suddenly I got up and went in.

Surprisingly, I sat face-to-face with the priest and blurted out that I had not received the sacrament of reconciliation for over twenty-five years and could not fully even remember the prayers. I was already crying. As the priest listened, he smiled and told me that I could repeat the prayers after him if I needed to.

I began, "Bless me, Father, for I have sinned. It has been twenty-five years since my last confession and these are my sins." Then my mind went blank! I could not remember my sins. He gently suggested that I start with the most recent and go from there.

The floodgates opened and out they came like ugly clumps of disease and filth. I was in there for a long time as I searched my memory. Finally, I said that was all and he helped me recite the act of contrition. Before I left, the priest reminded me of the parable of the prodigal son and said the angels and saints in heaven were cheering for me. That's when it finally hit me what this sacrament is all about.

I had been so caught up in the confession itself and in the shame of my sins that I had forgotten the part about reconciliation. Or maybe the Evil One did not want me to remember it.

I had repented privately of my sins, but going to the priest and being held accountable for them before the Lord was the most liberating thing I have ever done. It was like standing in the presence of Jesus and admitting that I was responsible for His death and suffering. And then the joy of His forgiveness! To go from sorrow and shame to complete joy is inexpressible.

When I was young, I believed the world when it told me that when I was old I would regret not having experienced life to the fullest and that I would smile when I remembered my sins. But that is the big lie.

I have found that the memories I smile about are those when I was honest, faithful, chaste, loving and kind to others. My sins do not comfort me as I grow older. They are painful reminders of my rebellion against God. God forgives them but they do have consequences and leave scars. The sacrament of reconciliation is God's gift to His Church so that we can continue the battle knowing that Christ has already won it for us with His own blood and life.

Maureen Paloma   *Tigard, Oregon*

Struggle to Forgive

True forgiveness can be a very difficult thing.

For years I struggled to forgive my deceased father and deceased ex-husband for all the pain they had caused me. Then one weekend in 1991, I went to a Christ Renews His Parish Retreat at St. Susanna Catholic Church in Mason, Ohio, and things began to change.

During confession at the retreat, I talked with Father Harry Meyer about my situation. He asked me if I ever prayed for my father and ex-husband. When I said I didn't, he advised me to pray for them every morning. He said it's impossible to pray for a person who has hurt us and not experience the healing that Jesus desires.

That was fifteen years ago, and I am still praying for my deceased father and deceased ex-husband. Forgiveness eventually did come, and the hurt I was living with melted away. I have added names to my prayer list over the years, and I pray that they have added my name to their lists. True forgiveness is like the fresh scent of a beautiful flower.

Molly N. O'Connell   *Mason, Ohio*

I Am Not Going to Confession

I was home visiting my mom in Pennsylvania. She had never learned to drive, so when I asked her what she would like to do that Saturday, she said, "Oh Mary, if you could take me to confession in Ebensburg that would be great."

Being a dutiful daughter, I wholeheartedly agreed to drive her, but I myself would not be going to confession. See, I had *outgrown that*. That was part of the *old way*. I was a modern Catholic, picking and choosing the parts of the faith I liked.

The drive took us about fifteen minutes. Although we were talking about all kinds of things on the way there, internally I was having this conversation with myself. It went something like this: "I am not going to confession. I am a grown up now and mom can't make me." Not that mom even asked if I were going; it was my own internal dialogue going on.

We arrived about ten minutes before confession began, and I sat quietly in the pew with my mother. All the while I was stubbornly thinking, "Nope, I am not going." Mom got up and went into the confessional. Then, without missing a beat, when she came out I found myself standing and walking into the dreaded box!

It had changed since I had been there last. There was the familiar kneeler, but there was also a chair around the corner. I quickly knelt, not wanting Father Little to see me. I began softly and quietly. "Bless me, Father, for I have sinned. It has been (deep breath) six years since my last confession." There, I had said it.

As I waited for the yelling and the scolding to begin, I braced myself. Thoughts of "What am I doing in here?" raced through my mind. Then, gently and joyfully, I heard Father respond, "Welcome back!" I melted and my eyes filled with tears. Choking the sobs back I said, "Thank you, Father. Can I come and sit in the chair now and confess my sins?"

My eyes still fill with tears as I think of the awesome welcome that the Lord had for me through Father Little that day. A few years later I thanked my mom for asking me to take her to confession that day, for it was the beginning of a real and total conversion for me.

Mary Kay Soyka   *Salem, Ohio*

My Thoughts...

There are those sins, that as Catholic Christians, we know are sins. Just follow the Ten Commandments. Right there you will see if you committed a serious sin.

Other times, when I am not sure if I've committed a sin, or just a human error, I ask the Holy Spirit in prayer. When I ask in sincerity, at least for me, I either have a "feeling" of calmness, or I get a deep gut sensation, that something is not right. I can not get it out of my mind. I keep wondering. I am bothered by it. That is when I take it to confession.

Now, there are times, that it is not so clear to me. If I still am not sure, I take it to confession and let the priest decide. When in doubt, take it to confession.

Maryann Kolod

"Are priests bothered by penitents' sometimes tedious recitation of sins? Do they get bored hearing confessions? Are priests saddened that Catholics are not living more faithfully the moral standards of their faith? What is it really like to be on the other side of the confessional?"

The Other Side of the Confessional
by Fr. Christopher J. Walsh
The Untapped Power of the Sacrament of Penance–
A Priest's View

see page 151

Lapse of Judgement

The sacrament of reconciliation can be intimidating to many, but it is also a sacrament that is one of my favorites. This is a love that was acquired with the assistance of some truly amazing priests. Over the years, I have confessed common sins like fighting with my siblings, swearing, anger and other matters. But there was one habit—actually an addiction—that was changed by the sacrament of reconciliation, and it saved my life from a world of hurt. I was addicted to gambling. Bingo, lottery, euchre, and casinos were all taking me away from my family, education, work, and faith life.

The addiction began at a young age. As a teen, I began a common habit that involves even more teens now then when I was young—card playing. Today, teens play Texas hold 'em and other poker games for much higher stakes then I ever did but my euchre playing turned into lottery tickets and then a casino was built in my college town.

When I was twenty-one, I was pretty accustomed to getting in line on a Saturday to seek absolution for my gambling. It had become a major sin for me because I continued to want more and more money. I was becoming very greedy and needed to stop. It was then that I knew I had a problem.

God blessed me with the ability to quit gambling cold turkey (it was a penance). I was told I could no longer go to the casinos and gamble. I accepted the penance and received absolution. This was in 1999. Several years later, our state voted a pro-choice Catholic politician into office as our governor. The day after the election, my sister Ellen invited me to go to the nearby casino. She had hurt her shoulder and was unable to drive but wanted to have some fun. She said if I took no money into the casino, I would not be gambling—I could just go for the drive and take my mind off the election.

There is not a great deal to do in my hometown, so I decided to go with Ellen. I drove, and the whole way, I kept saying that I felt like I was breaking my penance as I was going to a casino, but since I would not be taking any money—there would be no gambling. No harm—no foul—I could never have been so wrong!

Once we got into the casino, I got an adrenaline rush. I did not have any money with me and there was no way to get money, or so I thought. Once I realized I could not put money into the machines, I got very quiet and sad. I repeatedly said, "This is so stupid. Why did I drive one hour one way to come here when I can't play?" My sister felt bad for me and she began winning. The next thing I knew, she was giving me money and saying, "Here is some money. You can play that machine for me!" Before I knew it, I was grinning from ear to ear and winning. I was back in my element and the devil loved it! Within an hour, we lost all the money my sister had won and also the money she had brought with her. To make matters worse, I saw some people from my hometown and they were stunned to see me. One actually said, "What are you doing here? You quit gambling!" I wanted to crawl in a hole!

On the way home, I thought I was going to flood the car with tears, as I felt so bad. I had fought so hard to quit gambling and now it was back in my life!

The next morning I called St. Joseph Parish looking for Father Bill, my spiritual director, forgetting it was his day off. I asked for Father John, and thankfully, he was available. I asked if I could make an appointment to see him that day for reconciliation. He laughed and said I was just here for confession on Saturday what could I have possibly done? He knew about my gambling and I told him about the casino so he agreed to meet me after I was done with my parish work as a youth minister.

When I met Father John for confession, I felt so relieved to confess the error of my ways! I had no business being in the casino when I knew that I used to go there daily after work. I feared that this setback would cause me to return to the old habit of hitting the casino on a frequent basis.

Once I was in the confessional, I admitted that I had truly thought I was not erring because I had brought no money, and then my sister gave me money and before I knew it, I was thrilled to be winning money once more. I confessed that I was wrong to step foot in the casino as I knew it is a place I can not visit, much like an alcoholic cannot allow himself to be tempted by visiting a bar.

During our time together, Fr. John reminded me that I had learned a very important lesson. I had fallen by going into the casino, but now, he explained, I could start fresh by not returning! Also, he made me realize that I have no business going near the gaming establishments because they are definitely a near occasion of sin for me. If I am not at a casino, I will not gamble in that manner.

I mentioned to Father John that I saw a woman from St. Paul, my home parish, at the casino. For my penance, I was to apologize to her for being at the casino the next time I saw her. I remember when I made the apology and she thought it was unnecessary. For me, it was the conclusion of an error, so it felt very good.

I felt so much better after I was able to confess my lapse of judgment and was able to get back on my spiritual journey where the ultimate prize is eternal life: a reward better than any jackpot offered from any gambling establishment or lottery jackpot.

Lisa Stechschulte   *Owosso, Michigan*

Fear of Confession

Six years ago, just before my husband and I had our marriage blessed (after twenty-three years), I went to the sacrament of reconciliation for the first time in almost thirty years.

I prepared for confession for a month trying to get everything right. I tried to remember how I did it when I was a kid though I knew things had changed since then. Now, I was an adult with many sins behind me. I went over and over what I would say. I was so embarrassed about so many things I had done in the past and did not know how to describe them to the priest (a man).

I was so scared that I almost turned around several times while standing in line. I finally went in and pretty much stuttered, hyperventilated and cried the whole time. The priest was very gentle and seemed very happy that I chose him to help me back to the Church and our Lord.

I do go to the sacrament now, but I still have this sick feeling in my stomach, and I go over and over what I will say for hours and hours and sometimes days. I only go when I feel I have a mortal sin to confess but I want to go more often because I do feel clean and very close to God after I have been absolved.

I always thought I was the only one who felt this way but I guess there are many people who have the same apprehensions as I do. I never thought to ask anyone how they felt, and no one ever seemed to be dying to tell me. The fear and embarrassment stayed in my head where the devil continued to make me so embarrassed to tell my sins out loud in confession that for thirty years, I didn't.

The fact that my husband and I were going to have our marriage blessed gave me the courage to go to the sacrament. Father Michael was the catalyst that made me realize that the feeling of closeness to the Lord I felt after confession was wonderful.

Mary Grisaffi   *Gretna, Louisiana*

It Is Never Too Late

After many years of general prison ministry, in 1998 I was asked to begin ministry cell-to-cell on Florida's death row and solitary confinement. Florida has the third largest death row in the U.S., with over 370 men, and has over 2,000 men in long-term solitary confinement in the two prisons at which I serve as a Catholic lay chaplain. On behalf of the Catholic Church, the bishops of Florida, and under the pastoral supervision of my priest and bishop, I go cell-to-cell in ministry to the men inside.

Also, I serve as a spiritual advisor for executions. The family of the condemned is not allowed to be present then. My wife ministers to the families during the execution. We also make ourselves available to minister together to the families of murder victims. We do these things as volunteers on behalf of our church. We support our family and ourselves through our separate work.

Although I can bring Communion to the Catholics, our priest and bishop come frequently in order to offer the sacrament of confession, the anointing of the sick and, in case of executions, the last rites. For those who are only just coming into the Church, baptism and confirmation are also made available. In eight years, my wife and I have god-parented or sponsored ten death row inmates into the Church.

When I am on death row, there are ten steel barred doors, a quarter mile of electrified fences and razor wire, and a mountain of steel and concrete between me and the front door of the prison. The death house, which houses the execution chamber and to which a man is moved when his death warrant is signed by the governor, is at the end of the hall. His cell in the death house is less than twenty feet from the execution room.

One with eyes only for this world might ask: Of what use are the sacraments to a man in such a fix? And, in particular, what is the point of confession in his predicament?

I can testify to you that the power of the sacrament of confession and of the Holy Spirit is greater than the darkness of death row, even of the death house.

There was a man who desired to become Catholic because of the influence of Pope John Paul II. After a year of preparation for entry into the Catholic Church, he was suddenly scheduled for execution. His execution date turned out to be just days after the death of John Paul II. Our Catholic governor even considered delaying the execution out of respect for the pontiff.

The morning before his execution, the bishop came to the death house to administer his first confession, his first Communion and his confirmation. This was done with him standing in a narrow cage called a holding cell, with shackles upon his ankles and chains on his wrists.

When the bishop pronounced the words of absolution and then of confirmation, his whole body jerked as though he had been jolted by electricity. He even began to fall back against the rear of the cage, in a manner called resting in the spirit. The guards who were watching were astonished. They said that for a moment he became luminous.

The next day, during his last hours in the death house, he told me that John Paul II had visited him during that moment and told him that Jesus would come for him at the moment of his death. Nothing anyone could say could dissuade him from this belief.

A few hours before the execution, the warden came down to his cell with a message from the mother of the victim of the crime. She had asked the warden to inform the condemned man that she forgave him and bore him no ill will. The reconciliation offered by the sacrament of confession had been actualized on this side of the great divide between the temporal and the eternal.

He died in peace, at one with God.

My testimony is this. Nothing—absolutely nothing that any man can say, build or do as an obstacle or a barrier—not even the mountain of concrete, steel and despair that is death row—is able to prevent the power of the sacraments and the Holy Spirit from entering and remaining in the willing human heart.

Dale S. Recinella   *Macclenny, Florida*

Completely Clean

The year is 1945. It's Saturday in a household of eight children with mom and dad. Mom is known to keep (or try her best) to keep a very clean house. This means that every Saturday each of us is appointed a specific chore. This can be anything from scrubbing the linoleum floors, sweeping, dusting or cleaning out the buffet cabinets and drawers.

Then, because tomorrow we must prepare for Church and our *big* Sunday dinner, we will also be helping mom bake pies, her famous potato dumplings (big job—old German recipe), and so on.

It is also important that each of us be ready for Mass the next morning. This includes our Saturday afternoon baths, setting out clothes, and of course polishing our shoes. How good it feels to have the house all in order and our bodies clean and awaiting the joys of Sunday.

But wait, we haven't yet finished our cleaning! I never feel really clean until I make the long walk to St. Rose Church for confession. After this, I know my soul is clean and I am ready for the Sunday celebration of Mass and the Eucharist. Oh, how wonderful to be completely clean, body and especially soul.

Lois M. Bruce   *Maumee, Ohio*

My Thoughts...

I will tell you and the writer what a SSND teacher of mine told me eons ago.

"Peggy, at the end of the day when you are saying your night prayers think about your day. Start from the moment you get out of bed and everything you did that day and everyone you encountered, and then think of all the things you did and didn't do, all the things you said and shouldn't have. Then ask yourself if all of this would be pleasing to God."

I know it sounds simple and it is simple...it has worked for me for fifty years.

Peggy Murphy

The Sacrament of Reconciliation and Taking Charge of One's Life

by Fr. Alberic Smith, OFM

The sacrament of reconciliation is a special ceremony that Roman Catholics have the privilege to experience. In it, Jesus comes to us in the person of the priest and encourages us to confess our sins with sorrow to obtain forgiveness. Naturally, whenever we approach God with sorrow for our misdeeds, we will be forgiven. In this Sacrament, we bring our sins so Jesus can give us assurance that the sins are forgiven, and at the same time He gives us particular graces to help us avoid the sins in the future. There is a special advantage in speaking to another human being about our sins so we can receive encouragement to take up anew the direction of our lives along the way of the wishes of our beloved God. It is, indeed, a great blessing to receive the encouragement of another sympathetic human being to help us take charge of our lives. Hopefully the Sacrament brings peace, affirmation, and new power to take charge of our lives, own up to our wrongdoings, and move ahead, and use our personal goodness on this earth as Jesus would.

Reconciliation helps us *take charge* of our lives. What does this mean? We all know people who *take charge*. Sometimes they are welcome because they know what they are about, and they act unselfishly to bring about something good for as many people as possible. Other people take charge, and we find ourselves trying to get out of their way, lest we get steamrollered into some favorite project of theirs. Or maybe we just feel they are trying to control us. This makes us wary of becoming people who take control. We don't want to be like that.

We really don't have to "be like that." In fact, when we take charge we don't have to go outside of ourselves at all. We can do very well just taking charge of our own lives. That will give us plenty to do and the satisfaction of knowing that we won't be stepping on somebody's toes. We may step on our own toes. We just need to be sure those toes don't get into our mouths. As I mentioned above,

191

the Roman Catholic tradition has offered the Sacrament of Reconciliation for centuries as an important way to help people take charge of their lives.

In order to take charge of our lives, we need to be convinced that we can really do this. Hopefully, our life experiences have shown us that we have been able to go to school and learn a lot there, learn how to get along with people different from us, adjust to the preferences of others and let them know our preferences, and be able to work out some middle ground where all are fairly comfortable. We learn this not from books but from watching how other people do this, especially our parents and elder siblings, and eventually our personal friends.

Being able to feel good about ourselves is another key for our being able to exercise control over our personal lives. On the emotional level we need to feel good about who we are. We need to be reasonably convinced that, yes, we are good no matter what. When we make a mistake, it is not the end of the world for us. We may have to make some amends, say we are sorry, and do some repairs, but we are still the good persons God made us to be. Young people, as they grow into young adulthood, have relatively little experience with human interactions. Sometimes a humiliating mistake can leave some long lasting scars that will hopefully heal by means of future positive human interactions. All of us had to learn that if we fall on our faces, we can just get up again and watch a little more closely lest we repeat the calamity. An atmosphere of love and acceptance at home, and good friends who stick with us through thick and thin, all help this process of knowing that deep down we are good no matter what.

In the practical view of our lives, many of us do have issues that tag along with us. Parents are not perfect, even the great ones. We may have some experiences from them that haunt us and tend to make us doubt our real worth from time to time. This happens when we are tired, or just feeling down, or when someone does something towards us that reminds us of a less than happy event of our significant past. We do learn not to let these relics of the past influence us too much. After all, we did survive, and we did cope.

192

Why not now? Maybe we need to dialogue with our feelings so we can reassure them and also let them know that we are in charge, so they don't really have to worry so much.

It may also happen that when we look inside we find we have an area where our inner freedom is fenced in. Freedom just can't reign there. No matter what we do, we can't seem to establish our ruling power over that part of us, or over those feelings or impulses. This tends to make us feel powerless and less than worthwhile. This, indeed, is a real obstacle to our taking charge of our lives. We have to know that we can control all aspects of our inner life even if we cannot control the people and the world around us. When emotions get in the way of our basic freedom, we could seek the help of a specialist in human feelings. This person is a psychologist, and he or she is well trained in helping us to achieve true and lasting freedom in our inner life with the consequent control over feelings, impulses, and desires. With this help our actions come closer and closer to being truly free human acts, and they are under our personal control.

Ever meet a person who had troubles and difficulties and tended to blame all manner of forces and persons outside of themselves for the troubles? There you have a person who is not well trained in taking charge of his or her life. If we have charge of our inner life, we can see where we may have made a mistake or where we have done well, and we can assess where responsibility lies for the events that come into our experience. Here the Sacrament of Reconciliation keeps us on track to acknowledge fearlessly our failings and our triumphs, and we see where other people or events have given rise to the things that happen to us as well. Our inner autonomy gets reinforcement to remain intact, and we are able, with the grace of Jesus, to act in the world as we see we should, and we take responsibility for our actions. We are whole persons who can manage the complexity of our lives. We may suffer in the process, but we know who we are in our suffering just as we know who we are in our happy and joyous moments.

We see that in Christians the process of taking charge of our lives finds another great help in the example of Jesus. He made it His care to follow the will of God in His human nature. This is the God Who dwelt within Him and Who dwells at the center of our being. For Jesus it was a relationship of deepest love, and it is to be so for us. It is a matter of continuing to choose what we did at our baptism when we said "yes" to God's invitation to share in God's very life of love. This love of God given to us and returned to God with all our heart, mind and strength, is the essential spiritual basis for our taking charge of our inner lives. With this power to love we accept the power to direct all of our actions according to love so that all of our life is centered on this Beloved God. We have such an incentive to struggle to take charge of our lives, to bring the ship of our person into a course leading as surely as we can make it, into the harbor of conformity with the will of our Beloved God.

An athlete works for years to come to the peak of the sport that means so much to his or her life. In much the same way we work, struggle, and sacrifice to bring our inner person to become a finely honed instrument of goodness. We can find such help for this in the Sacrament of Reconciliation used every month or two, or more frequently if we need. This gift of Reconciliation reinforces a goodness that we rejoice to see in ourselves, a goodness we can reflect back to God our Beloved, and a goodness we can share powerfully with our fellow human beings. When we have taken charge of our lives, there is no limit to what God can do through us when we consistently live from the motive of love, and place our "controlled" lives into God's hands.

Fr. Alberic Smith, OFM, is a Franciscan of the Santa Barbara Province. He has spent his life as a friar priest in teaching high school level science, pastoral ministry, administration, and in the moments in between, writing. He now lives at St. Francis of Assisi Parish in Spokane, Washington, where he is chaplain to the Poor Clare monastery nearby. Father Alberic is also the author of questions 32-42 in the Q & A section in Appendix C.

Take My Hand

I never liked going to confession. In fact, I never went. Something about going into a small room with a guy scared me. I had a good reason, sort of. Doesn't really matter, I had it rationalized to a very good excuse for not going and I didn't.

A couple of times a year, I flew to Alaska to visit my family. My grandmother lives close to the local parish in Palmer, St. Michael's. When I am looking for some stillness, I walk to the church in search of peace. Normally, the warm space is very inviting for quiet prayer.

About two years ago, I was on such a visit. One day I walked to the church, slipped through the door, and slid into a pew. Something was different. Grandma had told me that the regular priest was on vacation and a visiting one was in, but still…it was, different. Then I noticed it: the reconciliation room was open. Uh-oh. Then that little inner voice. "No way." Invisible push. "Oh-no."

Jumping out of the pew, I paced. There was no way I could go in there. Panic took hold. I couldn't run away, I couldn't move forward either. Fear. I had spent years living with abuse. I took it from my father, who wished I had never been born. I took it from my mom's alcoholic boyfriend. I took it from my stepfather, who introduced us to the world of domestic violence. For over twenty years I lived in constant fear. A fear caused by men. And I was expected to go into a small room with one? That scared me. And tell him things about me? That terrified me. Alone, with a guy, in a small space, talking about me? Not happening. Period.

I know what I was taught; I could talk others through it, but me? I couldn't believe it. Fear. Panic was at full throttle. I had promised myself that I would not allow fear to control me; I would control fear. Pacing, I tried to talk myself down.

Movement, from the corner. The priest. He asked if I wanted to come in. Heck, no! With a silent nod, I went back to pacing.

Breathe in…breathe out…breathe in…breathe out. Somebody needs to hold this wall up. Eyes closed, looking down, holding the wall up, I asked God to help me calm down. "We could just sit in a pew if you prefer." That is not what I meant. Turning to the priest, I tried to say, "No thanks," but nothing came.

"Do you *want* to talk?" Shaking, I continued to hold that wall up. How could I tell him, yes I want to but I'm not going to? I remained silent. He said, in almost a whisper, "Why this fear?"

I looked at him; he repeated the question, "Why this fear?"

A very direct, specific, and extracting question. Now I can speak. Thanks, God. I stumbled through a short answer about being confined to a small space with a guy talking about what I don't want to think about.

I waited for him to tell me that my fear was irrational, so I could tell him why it was rational. Instead he asked another question, "Do you want to go for a walk?"

Outside, walking around the church, we talked. I told him about my past; he listened. "How many times did you call out to God, and hear, 'I am over here'?"

I thought about it. "And how many times did you hear 'I am here'?" I had to think on that. He went on to explain that we never have to search God out. He won't make us climb mountains or jump canyons to get to Him. He is always with us. He said that anytime I need to feel closer, especially when I am afraid; to hold out my hand. Don't stick it in a pocket or tuck it under an arm, but hold it out and ask Jesus to take my hand. A simple prayer, said in a short breath: "Jesus take my hand." Then feel His hand.

Still circling the church, I let Jesus take my hand. Father and I talked for a little while longer, about nothing. Soon, that nothing turned into something. We stopped. For the first time, Father looked right at me, I looked at him. It was not a man that stood before me. I received absolution and felt the hand in mine give a gentle squeeze. I returned to my grandma's place feeling a bit overwhelmed.

The next day, I returned to the church. After I been in the pew for a few moments, the priest came over, "Do you want to go for a walk?" Outside, circling the church, Jesus' hand in mine, I took the journey a little deeper into myself. Once again, when we stopped, it was not a man that looked at me. What I had emptied of myself, God filled me with something much better. This time I skipped back to grandma's home.

After I returned to my home, I made an appointment with my parish priest. Before going into his office, I asked Jesus to take my hand. "Do you want to go for a walk?"

Lisa A. Wehrman   *Tacoma, Washington*

Life in the Fast Lane

While I was growing up Catholic, there was one sacrament that bothered me—the sacrament of reconciliation. As a kid, I went to confession because I had to, but as I grew older, I decided it was too uncomfortable to tell my sins. I reasoned that the priests were human too, and I thought they would judge me.

After graduating from high school, I moved from a small town in Wyoming to Beverly Hills, California, to be with my friends. There I worked at Saks Fifth Avenue and also did some modeling. I felt I had accomplished a lot for someone my age, especially when my sister bought a poster with my picture on it from our hometown poster shop. I thought I was on the road to greatness.

Even though I went to Mass every Sunday, I started to feel empty. It was strange, because I was on a fast track to fame and had no reason to feel that way. The tugging at my heart told me that there was something more to life that I needed to know about.

I started to realize that I had high expectations for people, and when they fell short, I felt cheated. It was then that I decided to go to confession. It had been about ten years since I had gone, and guilt was setting in. I tried talking myself out of it but it didn't work, so I made an appointment to see a priest.

When I arrived, the priest and I sat down and got acquainted. I could tell he was a very kind and gentle person, and although I felt more at ease, I was still a little guarded. Finally, I let loose and brought my last ten years of baggage out in the open. At times during my confession, I noticed the priest trying to hold back a look of surprise, but he remained calm and kind. After he absolved me of my sins, I left there a different person. I can't describe the joy I felt, nor the sorrow for hurting my Lord by living such a sinful lifestyle.

After that, I quit my job and moved back to Wyoming to be close to my loving family and to go to college. That was twenty years ago, and I have never forgotten the genuine kindness and compassion of that priest. He gave me the strength to seek Our Lord and not the things of this world. I remain eternally grateful for him and often wonder if he was sent from heaven just to hear my sins, to absolve me of them, and to send me on my way.

Kelly M. Westover   *Centennial, Colorado*

Kitchen Table Confession

Does it ever seem to you that time after time, in the confessional, you continually acknowledge the same sin? Without going into detail, let me explain that mine has to do with how I handle people who injure me in deed or word. My usual response is to bring my tale of woe home to my husband where I begin by relating the incident word for word. Then I follow up with a litany of faults that paint the person in a very bad light. As soon as the words come from my mouth I feel miserable, and now I have included my spouse in my sinful deed as well. How can I stop my pattern? Through the patience and direction of several kindly priests, I have learned, though far from perfected, to undo my thought process and turn this destructive trait into a moment of intercession and grace.

My husband and I are extremely privileged to know a Carmelite priest, Father Louis P. Rogge, from Joliet, Illinois, whose father built a summer lake cottage directly across from our home in the 1930s. On the wall of the cabin, you can glimpse a faded photo of a chubby faced youngster holding a huge stringer of sunfish. That is the future priest, who is now a dear and devoted friend of over twenty years. At the end of every summer season, when days are slow-paced and the sun is still warm and inviting, Father Louis and a boyhood friend, Brad, will drive up from Illinois for a week of fishing, relaxing and visiting. Over a pot of venison stew and a freshly baked pie (my contribution), we will all catch up on our busy lives. Father Louis has spent time in Rome working on his Carmelite's publications, editing and writing articles and books. In the soft glow of the fireplace flames, we would listen as he shared memories of the Eternal City, where he had concelebrated Mass with Pope John Paul II.

On one such visit, I greeted Father Louis at our back door and invited him in for a cup of morning coffee. We sat at the kitchen table and looked out at the glistening sun on the lake. It was natural for us to spend time thanking God for His beautiful creation. After a moment of shared silence, I told Father about my pattern of unforgiveness toward others. He gave me a wonderful and profound answer. He said that we can be hurt daily by others. He went on to say that when we share the incident with someone else, we must always end with interceding for the person and continue to forgive him.

It sounded so simple, yet so powerful. Then, right at my kitchen table, along with the salt and pepper and napkins, Father Louis asked if I would like to receive the sacrament of reconciliation. I agreed, and soon we were bowing our heads into the mystery of a most beautiful sacrament, instituted by Jesus. I felt lighter and happier then ever. After my penance of prayer, we celebrated with a piece of pie, a double blessing for both of us.

My parish priest, Father George Zeck, answered another piece of my puzzle. He has been our pastor at St. Alice Church in Pequot Lakes,

Minnesota, since 1998. Father George has shared several solutions with me for unforgiveness. When someone wounds you by words or actions, immediately forgive him in your heart. His next directive is to intercede, intercede, and intercede. If we fill our hearts with acts of prayer and intercession, soon there will be no room for enmity. Through reconciliation we will receive the grace to eventually forgive and even forget. Father George has also given my husband and me another prescription for grace-filled confessions. He said, "Resolve to be faithful to the sacrament of reconciliation."

Mary Jo McCarthy   *Pequot Lakes, Minnesota*

A Boy at Peace

Our family lives in New London, Wisconsin, and we attend Most Precious Blood Catholic Church. Father David Lewis is an amazing parish priest who has been a tremendous guide and model for all our eight kids, especially TJ.

TJ has autism but, praise Jesus, autism doesn't have him. As his parents, we have always known God is taking care of him while providing us all with graces to deal with the daily challenges associated with TJ.

The sacrament of reconciliation has been a tool of unbelievable comfort. We have no clue what TJ confesses, nor do we know what any of his penances have been. What we do know is that each time he goes in he comes out a different boy. A boy at peace, a boy a little less confused, and, for a while, a boy with improved behavior. He is still human, so he falters, but we don't let the discouragement take control anymore. We just head for the confessional instead!

One of the inspiring actions TJ displays is a bit off the cuff but has become routine. When TJ departs the confessional he walks into church where we are awaiting his excited exclamation, "I have been absolved of my sins!" accompanied by a double high ten slap!

At first I was mortified, but I quickly found myself crying tears of joy at seeing this *developmentally delayed* child rejoicing and celebrating as we all should and shouting it from the rooftops. Even though it is unconventional to react the way he does, so what! We can't help but rejoice with him, and rightfully so. After all, we are taught and we believe that heaven rejoices over each repenting sinner. In the end, the sacrament of reconciliation makes us a family at peace, a family a little less confused, and a family humbled by God's love for us.

Maureen E. Ozminkowski   *New London, Wisconsin*

My Thoughts...

I am the RCIA coordinator in my church. We suggest that our candidates look at their lives and ask them what is causing a break in our relationships with God and with other people. This usually can get to the root of what needs reconciliation.

Another question we suggest is: "What is weighing on me most?" Often everything else is about that.

Finally, after confession, let go of the guilt. God has forgiven, so we must forgive ourselves.

Sheri Wilson

"I dreaded having to bare my soul to a man who, in my opinion, must be almost sinless (after all, he was a priest, wasn't he?!). I was still concerned about what he would think of me, not only in the confessional, but also every time we crossed paths. It was not uncommon for me, therefore, to go to other parishes when it was time for confession."

Confessions of a Catholic Convert
by Elizabeth Ficocelli

see page 93

Clarity of Thinking

Protestant friends shudder at the thought of telling their sins to another person, and as a young child, I guess I felt the same way. Why submit myself to that kind of fear? Back then, I wondered how to answer them. Now as a mature adult, I know that the graces I have received in the sacrament of reconciliation have shaped my spiritual development and strengthened me in my search for the heart of Jesus. Where would I be without the continual *returning* to Christ that this sacrament affords me?

I still have friends who ask, "Why don't you just confess your sins to God and leave it at that?" It is hard to explain to them that the forgiveness and the subsequent sense of elation I receive in this sacrament far surpasses anything I could obtain simply by making an act of contrition.

It is a mystery for me—beyond words. How can this grace be so tangible and yet so abstract as to elude words? When I speak to other Catholics, they too share this same gratitude for the perceived lightness of spirit, freedom, joy, and acceptance by God—lasting qualities of love and being loved that they feel after making a good confession.

Having being trained in the study of psychology, I am constantly amazed at the phenomenal clarity in my thinking after receiving the sacrament of reconciliation.

At certain points in my life, I vacillated back and forth. Now hot, now cold, toward the spiritual practices of my faith, prayer, etc. After awhile, I noticed a certain lackadaisical attitude and dullness overtake my mind. It got to the point that nothing seemed important or relevant, despite having a loving family and children, except my plans for the future. The present took on a sort of numbness and irritation, as though it were getting in the way of satisfying my real needs and goals.

What ensued was a certain vague anxiety, impatience with my family, friends, coworkers, and certainly the less fortunate who came along my path. I could recognize the lack of grace but was helpless to remedy it. Then I went to confession. Immediately, afterwards I could feel myself smiling! The joy was boundless. The clarity of my thinking was a shock. My performance at home and work improved. I even passed Calculus I and II with grades of A+ and A, respectively, classes I had initially failed earlier as a younger student.

What an immeasurably huge gift Jesus gives me through the absolution by the priest! The spin-offs of His grace are unfathomable.

I have come to realize that as a sinner, sin appears attractive to me; but then I realize through the conviction of the Holy Spirit that sin makes a fool of me each and every time I commit one. I fall, but Jesus picks me up again and again.

I, for one, desperately need this wonderful sacrament of reconciliation where Christ heals my mind, heart and soul.

Dale T. Bisanti   *Bramalea, Ontario, Canada*

A Sacred Moment

The Catechism of the Catholic Church in 1548 states, "The priest, by virtue of the sacrament of holy orders, acts in persona Christi Capitis."

I cannot name the exact date, but I remember the experience as if it were yesterday. It was in the late 1970s or early 1980s when our parish, St. Helena's, in Ellendale, a small town in rural North Dakota, was having a communal penance service followed by individual confessions. There was a large crowd, and there were probably four or five visiting priests to help our parish priest hear confessions and grant absolution.

After the communal portion of the service, the lines quickly formed for each of the stations where a priest was waiting. However, hardly anyone lined up for Father Felix, a Polish priest serving in a parish about sixty miles away. Some people complained about Polish priests serving in our diocese because their English was sometimes difficult to understand. I felt sad that Father Felix had made such a sacrifice to drive that far on a winter's eve and would end up hearing so few confessions. My compassion moved me to the last place in his line of three penitents.

In other lines people came and went quickly but I waited patiently in Father Felix's line. When my turn came, I sat down in a chair in front of him, rather than choose the anonymity of the screen. As I began talking about my transgressions, a silent tear or two trickled down my cheeks. Father gently placed a fingertip on one of those tears and very reverently said, "Offer that one up for Father Felix."

To this day, I still get tears in my eyes as I recall that sacred moment, when I truly believe I was touched by the hand of Christ on that winter evening so long ago.

Sandra L. Nicolai   *New Rockford, North Dakota*

Chats With Jesus

I must admit that the sacrament of reconciliation, or confession, as it was known in my earlier years, was often scary to me as a child. Even though I attended weekly catechism classes, I never fully understood what going to confession was all about or what it would or could accomplish.

All I knew was that it was scary and unpleasant, and I did not like going into a dark room to discuss all the bad things I'd done with a priest I could not see. On the positive side, though, at least Father would not know who was telling him all these awful things!

In 1980, I married a divorced non-Catholic who had every intention of getting his first marriage annulled. Unfortunately, after three attempts at trying to get the annulment started, he became discouraged and gave up. I became discouraged as well and left the Church. I wrote a story about this which appeared in *101 Inspirational Stories of the Rosary* entitled "A Sign of Love".

Even though I walked away from the Church, I still prayed and had my *chats* with Jesus and His beloved Mother, and I always felt their presence in my life. I was rather ashamed at not being with the Church, but more ashamed of my predicament and not being able to receive absolution for my sins.

In the summer of 1999, I attended Australian healer Alan Ames' healing Mass and lecture in Omaha, Nebraska. Alan gave a very strong and urgent appeal and lecture for everyone present to go and receive the sacrament of reconciliation after his healing service concluded. Many priests were on hand for this.

I felt very strongly that I should go to reconciliation and discuss my predicament with a priest. I stood in line for an eternity it seemed; however, I did not feel in the least bit nervous.

Finally, it was my turn, and I told the priest about my situation. He told me that he couldn't absolve me of my sins because it was against the rules, but that we could talk and pray together. So, we did talk, and I told him about some personal issues. Then he asked, "Did you sit though this entire healing Mass and lecture?" I replied that I had indeed, and he exclaimed, "You are such a holy woman!"

Up to that point, I had not shed a tear. At his exclamation I thought, "Here I am, full of sin, being told I can't be absolved of my sins. Ouch! And now this wonderful priest has just told me what a holy woman I am. How can I be a holy woman if I can't be absolved of my sins?"

I began to cry, and the priest was very nice and very comforting. He gave me advice on what I could do and who I could talk to about annulment information. We prayed together and then I thanked him, walking away still in tears.

I finally persuaded my husband to try to do the annulment again and I spoke with a pastor of a church I felt called to. Then the annulment process began.

One night, I decided that before I drifted off to sleep, I would take inventory of my day. If I had sinned, I would kneel on the floor in my room and wholeheartedly ask Jesus for forgiveness of each sin. To my amazement, I felt a wonderful warm and tingly sensation and immense peace and love. So, I kept up this practice.

In 2002, during Lent, my pastor at the time, Father Steve at St. Columbkille Parish in Papillion, Nebraska, was talking about what our Lenten practices could be, and the subject of the sacrament of reconciliation came up. He addressed the fact that sometimes we don't feel comfortable in reconciliation and suggested something we could do that would make us feel more at ease.

He said that at the end of the week he wanted each of us to kneel in our rooms before we went to sleep and ask the Holy Spirit to reveal any wrongs we'd committed during the week. Then we were to sincerely pray to Jesus for forgiveness of each wrongdoing. He said, "Then you should feel a warm, tingly sensation and much peace and love coming from Jesus." He said this was not meant to replace reconciliation but to help prepare us for it.

I was pleasantly surprised by this and knew then that I was being divinely guided.

Finally, on November 23, 2002, after the annulment was granted and we were married in the Church, I could go to reconciliation. I was very excited and wasn't nervous at all.

Before I went, I asked the beloved Holy Spirit to reveal to my conscious mind all of my sins that I had committed in the last twenty-two years. I'm happy to say that this really works! But I'm sad to say just how many sins the Holy Spirit revealed to me! I wrote them all down on paper so I would not get flustered and forget any of them. And I thought, "Poor Father Steve; I'm going to be in the confessional for at least an hour!"

When the time came, I tearfully confessed all of my sins. Father Steve was very kind, gentle, and understanding. When I heard him absolve me of all my sins, I wept out of pure joy and felt the heaviness of all those sins being washed away. I was truly healed!

Now when I go to reconciliation, I still rejoice in being absolved of my sins. It always feels so cleansing. My wish is that everyone could understand how wonderful this feels and not be afraid to receive this wonderful sacrament.

Theresa Carol Pettis   *Casa Grande, Arizona*

My Thoughts…

Going to confession and confessing that I had been angry got a quick response from the priest! He told me that human emotions are not sin. It is what we do or how we respond to them that may or may not be sinful. When angry, do we lash out with hurtful words? Saying those hurtful words is then the sin. Since I've learned this, it has guided me in making a good examination of my conscience.

Louise A. Haydon

My Own Disbelief

A few years ago our parish held a Lenten Mission. I was not planning to go, but a friend didn't want to go alone, so I went to accompany her. I think God used her to get me to go!

The Passionist priest giving the mission was very fervent and very much in love with the Lord. I drank in every word he said and thrilled to the truth of it.

It had been awhile since I'd gone to confession because I felt very unworthy. I had feelings that God loved everyone else more than he loved me. Sometimes I would imagine that God was impatient with me for repeating the same sins over and over.

At one point during the mission, the priest pointed to the crucifix. He said to us in a firm and solemn voice, "If you don't think this is enough to forgive what you've done, then there's no way you can be forgiven."

It hit me like a ton of bricks! My feelings of unworthiness could prevent Our Blessed Lord from forgiving my sins? Not because Jesus was unwilling, but because of my own disbelief! I was stunned. Could I actually prevent God from forgiving me?

I approach the sacrament of reconciliation very differently now. It's still not easy. It's still humiliating to admit my faults and deliberate actions, but knowing that there is an ocean of mercy that I can throw those sins into fills me with deep gratitude.

Now I know that God's loving heart is always there to lean on and whisper my sorrows to. I haven't yet been able to live up to my desire to live the perfect life out of love for Him, but I know that this is where I receive the grace to keep trying.

Anne B. Caron   *Newington, Connecticut*

Spirit and Soul Cleanser

In my secondary school, Cornelia Connelly College in Nigeria, a priest came every two weeks to hear our confessions and I celebrated the sacrament regularly. Then, in 1986 or 1987, I realized that I wasn't celebrating the sacrament of reconciliation often anymore, and I knew something was wrong.

One day I decided to pray to God, asking Him to help me frequent this great sacrament once again. He answered my prayer by removing the fears I was having towards going to confession and making me always long for it. Father Ryan, a missionary priest, heard my confessions when I returned to the sacrament of reconciliation.

Great things started happening in my life when I began going to confession regularly again. I soon found that every time I made my confession, I experienced an inner joy that I had never felt before. It gave me spiritual and physical encouragement, and fear left me completely. Since then I have made it my duty to go to confession every fortnight.

I have become a lover of this great sacrament that was given to us freely by God. It has helped me to easily reconcile with myself and my friends. I love this sacrament! To me, the sacrament of reconciliation is a spirit and soul cleanser, and if you experience it you are blessed.

Margaret J. Akpan   *Akwa Ibom, Calabar, Nigeria*

I Am Here for You

Nauseous from feelings of fear, depression, loneliness, and betrayal, I sat alone in the church 300 miles from where I used to call home. How did I reach this point at the age of fifty-five? I was now divorced for the second time, and I had moved to be near my daughter, leaving behind my family and long time friends. I felt so alone. I had been betrayed, and that left a pit in my stomach and a pain in my heart. I wondered if I would ever be free of the ache.

I was early for Mass, sitting in a back pew seeing nothing but darkness and shadows. Slowly the lights illuminated the church as time for Mass was approaching. The church was now bright and I looked up, my eyes going straight to the image of the risen Christ on the cross behind the altar.

Suddenly, I felt Jesus say to me, "Let me hold you in my arms, I am here for you, it will be okay." His outstretched, welcoming arms beckoned me; He was there for me, and I was not alone. My heart stopped aching, but I was still unsure of what to do next with my life and not sure what could be salvaged. I went through the motions of Mass with my eyes fixed on the risen Christ image.

My answer came during the Our Father. As I prayed, "Forgive us our trespasses as we forgive those who trespass against us," I heard the words deep in my soul. I knew I needed to go to confession and that I needed the sacrament of reconciliation to renew my life. As I left Mass, I felt this was something I could actually do to help the way I was feeling and to get back on the right track in life.

Throughout the next week, I planned and prayed as I prepared to receive the sacrament of reconciliation the following Saturday afternoon. I asked myself several questions. What would I say? Could I get through the confession with no tears? Would the priest think I was the failure I knew I was?

It had been a few years since I had been to confession, and I was not sure of the procedure in my new parish. Plus, I was not comfortable with face-to-face confession. As a cradle Catholic, I preferred the anonymity of the way it was when I first celebrated the sacrament of penance

Saturday arrived and I sought out the newly ordained Father Russ to hear my confession face-to-face. I was very nervous, and he was very calming. As I proceeded, we talked and he consoled and reassured me. I said an act of contrition, received absolution, and said my penance. Afterwards, I felt a relief that I had not experienced in years. I knew I was okay, that things would work out, and that God was there for me always.

There are no words to describe the internal feeling that comes over me now when I think of that special moment of spiritual rebirth. I am so thankful that I made use of the sacrament of reconciliation that day. It helped me rebuild my life and my faith. I am now comfortable with face-to-face reconciliation and make use of this special sacrament frequently.

Cathy A. Bloom   *Brownsburg, Indiana*

Lighter Than Air

In 1987, I was twenty years old and a cradle Catholic. I had not attended church in years and was absorbed with worldly pleasures. I seemed happy on the outside, but I was not on the inside. Something kept nudging me to go back to the faith. When I finally decided to make the move, I wanted to start clean, so I committed myself to going to reconciliation. I really didn't want to, but I knew deep down inside that I had to.

I was nervous, frightened and very embarrassed. I had to say out loud all the mean, disgusting, gross, perverted, hurtful and immoral things I had done. That was not easy.

When I went to receive the sacrament of reconciliation at St. Matthias Church in Lanham-Seabrook, Maryland, my confessor was a short, elderly priest who always wore a smile. As I struggled through my sins, I felt filthier than dung. Yet, he continued to smile without any judgment. He told me how wonderful it was that I had returned to the Church and had taken this first step in my faith journey

Now, here is the best part. Immediately after he said those words of absolution, I felt empty. My body, which had felt heavy and full of *yuck*, suddenly became lighter than air, as though someone had scooped all the yuck out of me. I had never before experienced anything like that.

When I left the confessional, I could have sworn that my feet never touched the floor; I felt as if I were floating, or walking on air. I had been touched by the awesome power of God. Today, I no longer just *go* to reconciliation, I run to it!

Eric G. Small   *Elkridge, Maryland*

Change of Heart

Relations had deteriorated to the point where contact was brief and increasingly infrequent. As the only child of a first generation Italian-American father, my role was shaped to a large degree by tradition and the Fourth Commandment. Still, I resented my status.

212

As a father of four and a military officer of some experience and responsibility, I didn't appreciate the frequent unsolicited criticism and on-the-spot guidance I received from my father. It seemed to me that I had never really measured up to my father's expectations, nor had my wife and children. Our family visits to my parents were filled with tension, bickering and frustration. Then it happened.

My aging father was *correcting* one of my children for some real or imaginary failure and I blew up. For the first time in my life, I raised my voice to my father and told him in some colorful language to "back off." It was as if I had thrust a knife into his heart. My children were shocked, he was wounded, and I felt like a heel. While the matter was dropped at the time, we parted more estranged than ever. It was clear that a dangerous threshold had been crossed.

Time and distance didn't improve the situation, and my sense of guilt grew. Telephone conversations took on the character of nuclear exchanges, and there were no winners.

This festering sore came to a head one Sunday during Mass when the reading from Ecclesiastes burned into me like hot coals. "My child, support your father in his old age; do not grieve him during his life, even if his mind should fail. Show him sympathy; do not despise him in your health and strength."

I was racked with guilt and anxiety. The following weekend we went camping and attended a church near the campsite that we regularly visited. Confession was available before Mass, and I knew I had to go. I couldn't drag the guilt around any longer.

The pastor, Father Mike Wilson, always celebrated Mass with enthusiasm, and his relatable homilies touched me. With a heavy heart, I entered the confessional and dumped the whole thing on him: forty plus years of grief and acrimony. I didn't know what to expect.

I was relieved when there were no accusing looks or harsh words said to me. Instead, Father Mike looked at me with understanding eyes and a nod or two. Then he shared a bit about his relationship with a parent, and that put me at ease. In a few brief sentences he put the whole issue into perspective.

The pain I felt was prompted by the love I had for my father, and his concern for me was prompted by his love for me. Father Mike observed that real pain can only be inflicted by people we love. It made sense, and I knew that another part of the great Christian paradox had been revealed to me. I wondered why I hadn't recognized this truth before.

Father Mike gently challenged me to be patient and less judgmental. His words of absolution washed over me like a soothing balm. I left the confessional changed, free of the spiritual luggage that I had been dragging around for years.

After that confession, I brought a new attitude into my relationship with my father. Oh, things weren't perfect, but slowly a healing occurred. In the twilight of my father's life, our roles sort of reversed. I became his advocate, his confidant, and most importantly his friend. Our last meeting was filled with laughter, tears and joy.

Some years later I told Father Wilson that I believed the turn around in my relationship with my father started with that confession nearly a decade before. Priests rarely learn of the change of heart that their care stimulates in a penitent through the sacrament of reconciliation, and I thought he'd like to hear what a difference he had made in my life.

As a deacon, I minister in a nursing home and a drug and alcohol treatment center. In these institutions, many troubled relationships between parent and child linger. I share my story, listen, and offer encouragement. Father Wilson's wise words from long ago continue to plant many seeds of hope and reconciliation in others who are experiencing difficulties in their relationships.

Eugene K. Mastrangelo   *North Beach, Maryland*

Teaching Children the Gift of Confession

by Christi Gareis

Christi Gareis is the mother of twelve children and has been happily married to her husband, Hugo, for twenty-six years. Christi has been home schooling since 1991, and over the course of time she has learned many practical tips on teaching her children the sacraments. In this article she goes beyond theory to what actually works in teaching children about the sacrament of confession.

It was through attending the preparation course for my oldest child's first confession that I made the final decision to join the Catholic Church. I had been attending Mass on and off since my early teens, and now at twenty-eight, when I heard about the forgiveness to be received and the graces gained through the sacrament of reconciliation, I longed to be able to participate in this sacrament. I was then the mother of four children and expecting my fifth, all of whom were being raised in my husband's faith, a joint decision we had made at the baptism of our first child. It was not much longer before I was faced with the necessity of introducing the concept of this very sacrament, which had drawn me into the fold, to one of our younger children. At that time, I simply reached into my heart and explained, to the best of my ability, the gist of sin and how confession helped us to heal from it. Later, as we began to home school, I became more knowledgeable of the subject and came across many wonderful resources, many of which I will share with you at the end of this article.

Timing is Important

I will begin by sharing what I actually did with many of my children the first time I thought that they were ready to begin learning about sin and the awful effect it has on one's heart. For each

215

CHILDREN AND CONFESSION

child the timing has been different, but their reaction has generally been the same—an eagerness to have their heart cleaned by Jesus. I actually had one child go to confession for the first time at the ripe old age of three. After watching many of her siblings attend confession she badly wanted to talk to the priest about what she had done wrong and the priest said "Well, if she wants to talk to me, she can." So he sat down in front of the icon by the altar and gravely listened to her little lisping lips share the woes on her heart. Of course, I have no idea what she shared, but I do know that the priest's eyes were twinkling as he listened to her, while his countenance was all seriousness!

Confession, though a simple concept, is a heavy subject to tackle, and when first faced with the difficulty of trying to impart its necessity to a young child, I felt somewhat intimidated. It happened in an *in the moment* situation. Every child reaches that stage when you suddenly realize that the innocent denial of having done something wrong is no longer simply forgetfulness on the child's part, but is, in fact, a lie. He or she has put one and one together and realized that admitting to having cut his or her baby sister's bangs is likely to end in an unhappy consequence. Most likely one was going to lose his scissors privileges. And so they lie. And in lying, they commit a sin. How was I to impart the seriousness of this that Jesus saw all and knew all and would be saddened by what they had done. Better yet, how was I do this in a way to improve the likelihood that the child would feel inspired to admit to what he had done and feel contrition without overly burdening him at such a tender age?

When faced with this for the first time a parent can feel overwhelmed, but you can start with this simple exercise and simplify it according to the age of the child.

 E-S-I As Pie

As most of us know there are five parts or steps to a good confession. An acronym a local teacher that I know uses to help her students recall them is E-S-I As Pie.

When you present this to your student or child, use the five digits on your hand as you go over them. A great idea for the young student is to have him trace his hand, label each digit, and then list below the drawing the five steps in the acronym.

 Five Easy Steps to remember

1. Examine one's conscience;
2. Sorrow for one's sins;
3. Intentions not to commit them again;
4. Accuse one's self of them to a priest;
5. Penance, carry out the penance that the priest gives.

Each of these five steps is essential for a good confession, and no one is more important than the other.

Here are the five steps broken down from an actual first confession lesson I taught to one of my young daughters when she was six years old.

I stared into my young daughter's round eyes. I cannot now recall what she was denying having done, but I do remember the heavy feeling I experienced at the knowledge that I had caught her in a fib. I also identified with that onerous feeling of having done wrong, like the time I stuffed my white undershirt into the bathroom garbage can, praying that my mother would not find it with the deep brown stains left on it from the chocolate chips I had smuggled out of the house to eat at choir practice and then forgotten 'til it was time to change for bed. I was all of, perhaps, seven years of age. Old enough to know better, but not being Catholic I was clueless about confession and the benefits that come with it: the feeling of well being that comes from a good confession and the graces to overcome the temptations of life. I was left for years with the bitter aftertaste of sin on my soul.

Squatting down in front of my daughter, I stared at her beautiful

CHILDREN AND CONFESSION

eyes that were now rimmed with tears. How, I wondered, was I to help her to confess her sin and so experience that sense of liberation that comes from doing so? At six, she was not yet old enough to receive the actual sacrament but old enough, I felt, to begin to prepare for it.

1. Examine one's conscience;

"Sweetie Pie," I started, "you know that Jesus lives in your heart, right?"

She nodded.

"Well, your heart is like the window to your soul."

I paused for a moment trying to think of how to best convey my thoughts to her. I had a sudden inspiration.

"What happens if a window gets dirty; really, really dirty?"

"You can't see through it," She lisped sadly to me.

"And the room is dark because the sun can't shine through it, can it?" I said.

She shook her head with a serious expression on her face. "No," she replied, "It's very dark if the sun can't shine."

"Well, imagine Honey, that when one tells a lie, it is like a piece of dirt getting stuck to your heart, and your heart is the window to your soul. Or how about when we are disobedient by running in the house? More dirt gets stuck on the window of our heart. Eventually the window gets so cloudy and dirty that Jesus can't see out anymore. At some point, it might get so dirty that Jesus might feel that He has to move out. You wouldn't want that to happen would you?" I asked quietly.

2. Sorrow for one's sins;

Horrified, her eyes grew even rounder. She shook her head hard, her curls bobbing around her ears. "Oh no, I wouldn't want Jesus to leave me!"

3. Intentions not to commit them again;

"That's good." I smiled to reassure her. "Jesus doesn't want to have to move out either, so he has fixed a way for us to keep the window in our heart clean no matter what we have done, no matter how much dirt we get on it. Do you want to know what it is?"

She pulled in her breath and let it out slowly. "Oh yes, Mummy, what is it?"

4. Accuse one's self of them to a priest;

"Well, we can go to confession, and we can tell the priest all of our sins, all the things we have done wrong. We can tell him about pulling our sister's hair, or cutting holes in mummy's quilt, or maybe when we have told a lie. Then Jesus, through the priest, forgives us, and our heart is washed all fresh and clean when we are forgiven. After we go to confession, our hearts are sparkling fresh and Jesus can see through so nicely again. His love is able to flow through us, helping us to be strong and to not sin so easily again."

"When can I go to confession Mummy?" my little daughter queried.

"Very soon, honey, but not yet. So while you are waiting you can talk to Jesus about the things you have done wrong and Jesus will forgive you. And as soon as you are old enough, you will go to confession and Jesus will wash your heart clean and fresh for you."

The memory of the fib she had been caught in was evidently on her mind and she wrapped her arms around my neck and whispered in my ear, "Can you help me ask Him to forgive me now, Mummy?"

Quietly we prayed together, and then she sighed a huge sigh of relief and flashed me a big grin.

"I feel so much better, Mummy. Thank you! I can't wait, though, for Jesus to wash my heart!"

I couldn't either and once she was fully prepared for it, she was eager and happy to go to Jesus in this beautiful sacrament, and when

219

she came out of the confessional, I know that her face only partly reflected the joy that we both felt, now that her little heart, the house where Jesus lived, had all of its windows clear and squeaky clean.

5. Penance, carry out the penance that the priest gives.

Following this child's first confession have been several others in our family, as well as many opportunities for me to share this story of the window in our heart and the importance of keeping it clean for Jesus to be able to see out and into our soul. I have kept to this illustration because it is so simple, and so far, all of my children have been inspired by it. But this will not necessarily be so in your family, and as I am not always the most imaginative person and like to have examples, I am including another idea that you can perhaps use as a bouncing board to leap off of.

As the basis for choosing an allegory for sin, I would focus on the idea that sin is evil and damages the soul, and look for something the child can relate to that is nasty and or repugnant. For example, garbage. Instead of suggesting to a child that Jesus is looking through a window in his heart, one might suggest when one sins, he begins to fill his heart with little pieces of garbage, and carry on with this idea of how one would want to empty his heart of all sin before it crowded Jesus out of his heart, and then explain how confession helps us to do this.

As your child gets older, you will want to expand on the examination of conscience.

Examination of Conscience

How do we help our children do a good examination of the conscience as well recognize sin and differentiate between mortal sin and venial? Typically, studying the Ten Commandments is a good idea and opens the way to using them as the foundation for careful and thoughtful examinations of conscience.

The New St. Joseph Baltimore Catechism, in both volumes one and two, have detailed explanations of the Ten Commandments, as does the fifth book, *Living like Christ, in Christ*, of *Our Holy Faith* series. For the convenience of those who do not have immediate access to any of these catechisms I will do a brief synopsis here of how the Ten Commandments can be used for a child's examination of conscience.

When we first approach the study of the Ten Commandments, it is good to begin by talking about how we have a conscience that helps us to know right from wrong, and perhaps invite your child to talk about how he feels when he has done something he knew to be wrong. In doing so, we help to make what we are saying concrete to the child.

Then we continue on to explain how the Ten Commandments are God's gift to us as a means to strengthen the voice of our conscience. This will help the child to better understand why the Ten Commandments make such a good platform for self-examination, whether before confession or at the end of the day.

When Jesus walked the earth, one of the many truths that he revealed to us was the two great commandments.

"Thou shalt love the Lord thy God with thy whole heart, and with thy whole soul, and with thy whole mind, and with thy whole strength."

And the second is like unto it. "You shall love your neighbor as yourself." (Mt. 22:38–39; cf. Deut. 6:5)

What some do not know is how perfectly Jesus captured the whole of the Ten Commandments with these two laws. In the first law, which Jesus rightly called the greatest, we have the first three commandments:

1. I am the Lord thy God; thou shalt not have strange gods before Me.
2. Thou shalt not take the name of the Lord thy God in vain.
3. Remember thou keep holy the Lord's Day.

Then the next seven he summarized in the law of love:

4. Honor thy father and thy mother.
5. Thou shalt not kill.
6. Thou shalt not commit adultery.
7. Thou shalt not steal.
8. Thou shalt not bear false witness against thy neighbor.
9. Thou shalt not covet thy neighbor's wife.
10. Thou shalt not covet thy neighbor's goods.

When we begin to walk our child through the examination of conscience we would do well to remember the penitential rite in the Mass when we pray, "I confess to almighty God, and to you my brothers and sisters, that I have sinned through my own fault, in my thoughts and in my own words in what I have done and in what I have failed to do."

Note: Generally, a child is focused more on what he has done wrong and does not think about what he has failed to do.

1. I am the Lord thy God; thou shalt not have strange gods before Me.

When one of our children fails to be obedient we will sometimes take him or her through the commandments that his behavior touches on, and ultimately we always end on the First Commandment, since if we break any of God's commandments, then we have clearly put some desire or want ahead of obeying God. In doing so, we made *desire* an idol that we have placed before *Him.*

This is a concept that is helpful to keep in mind as we help the child to reflect through the other commandments.

2. Thou shalt not take the name of the Lord thy God in vain.

After reviewing with the child the importance of only using God's name and titles with reverence, we should also discuss the importance of praying reverently as well. When we know we have failed in these areas we can confess them and ask for God's graces so we will be more reverent in the future.

3. Remember thou keep the Lord's Day holy.

Questions that help a child to reflect on this commandment can follow in this vein:

> *Did I try really hard to pay attention to Father during Mass?*
>
> *Did I interrupt Mass through unnecessary movements?*
>
> *Did I distract others (i.e. siblings) from the Mass by playing with them or whispering to them?*
>
> *Did I cooperate when getting ready for Mass or did I cause us to be late?*
>
> *Did I make every effort to attend Mass or did I try to find a reason to not have to go?*

Obviously these questions should be adapted to what the parent knows are the areas the child needs help with in staying focused in Mass, remembering that one of the benefits of the sacrament of confession is to receive God's graces to not sin more in that area of temptation. Your child's behavior in Mass will guide you in your choice of questions.

4. Honor thy father and thy mother.

Encompassed in this short, simple commandment is a host of ideas. Parents represent authority to the child, and in today's society there are others who act in lieu of the parent, chiefly schoolteachers, Sunday school instructors, as well as day-care providers or an older sibling baby sitting while the parent is out of the home.

It is important for the child to understand that these people represent the child's parent and they must answer to the parent for the child's behavior, so when the child disobeys a care taker, he is indirectly disobeying his parent. Yet, having said that, it is also important to help the child understand that he is not required to obey implicitly what a person in authority asks him to do, and that most adults will not ask a child to do something that mummy and daddy would not ask them to do; and if an adult asks him to do something your child feels is wrong, or is asked to keep a secret from you, then the child can indeed and should say no!

CHILDREN AND CONFESSION

At this time, we might also need to explain the difference between a good secret and a bad one. We don't want to tell Mummy what her birthday gift is, but we do want to tell her if we have bumped our head and the baby-sitter has asked us to keep it a secret.

As you can see, this commandment requires some time to go over and is not as simple as it first appears.

5. Thou shalt not kill.

It is rare the child that is going to commit a sin as serious as this, but do not be tempted to slip over it as there are various levels within this commandment as well.

Our body is the temple of Christ, and we are commanded to care for this body, so some of the questions we can ask young child are:

> *Have I been playing in a way that was not safe?*
>
> *Have I been eating well and not eating more sweets than I should?*

Again, knowledge of your child's habits will help you to form appropriate questions for this commandment. We should also note that the commandment does not state we shall not kill humans, it is "we shall not kill," period. For the young child it would be appropriate to point out that as stewards of the earth we are called to care for the earth and especially the animals within it. If the child has a pet that he or she is responsible for, we might include questions that cover the care of it, as well as the importance of not teasing or playing in a way that hurts our pet.

6. Thou shalt not commit adultery.

Now how do we approach this commandment with a child? How much detail you go into explaining is going to depend on how knowledgeable your child is about the intimacy between parents and how much you want to deal with this area. On the simplest level we can explain that parents are married to each other and a man is only supposed to live and sleep with his wife, and vice versa.

For the older child, though, we can deal with the need for modesty/ purity in thought and appearance and the importance of it. Again, your knowledge of your child and individual situation is going to impact the type of questions you help the child develop as their regular examination of conscience. I would also like to note that in our family, we have tried to educate our daughters about the impact that their choice of dress has on the opposite sex, and while they are not responsible for a male's behavior, they are responsible for causing an occasion of sin or temptation through their choice of clothing.

For the older child, we also want to draw his attention to the importance of staying away from impure visions such as those found in unchaste movies and/or magazines, as well as the internet. St. Maria Goretti is a good saint to us as an example as well as one for our children to pray to when in need of aid in this area.

7. Thou shalt not steal.

Here are some questions that can be used for this commandment:

> *Have I remembered to ask before borrowing a toy or piece of clothing?*
>
> *Did I take proper care of it and return in the same condition I borrowed it in?*
>
> *Have I been taking more than my share of cookies from the cookie jar?*

8. Thou shalt not lie.

Here are some ideas that can be used to develop questions for this commandment:

> *When a window was broken, did I admit to my part in the accident or did I let my friends take all of the blame by saying nothing.*
>
> *Have I told stories about playmates that were not true, in order to get attention or a laugh?*

225

Have I listened to stories about friends, true or not, and laughed at the expense of the person involved?

9. Thou shalt not covet thy neighbor's wife.

This, again, is a commandment invoking us to be pure, and when our children get to the age of dating, a commandment to give more consideration to.

10. Thou shalt not covet thy neighbor's goods.

Finally, after a few commandments that are a little difficult to bring down to a young child's level of examination of conscience, here is one that will be a little more easily dealt with. We have all admired something someone else owns, but there is a difference between admiring, and wishing you had something that another person has to the point of wishing he did not have it, and herein lies the crux of this commandment.

Children need to understand that focusing on what we do not have instead of being happy with what we do have can lead us to breaking the Seventh Commandment. It is important to help our children to practice gratitude for the things they have been blessed with and to practice humility by being happy for others who have something we like but cannot have ourselves. For children with siblings much older, this can also apply to privileges they are not yet old enough to enjoy.

Three Tips to Encourage Your Child to Make Regular Confessions

1. The best way to keep a child regularly receiving this precious sacrament is by our example. If we, as adults, do not make frequent use of this sacrament, we cannot realistically expect our children to do so.

2. Find a church that is convenient to your home so that traveling to it does not become an excuse for putting it off.

3. Some families, even though the option of anonymous confession is always available, prefer not to have to go to confession to their

parish priest. This can be especially intimidating to a young child who has yet to build the confidence that the next time Father John sees her, Father John will not be remembering how many times she had to confess recently to sneaking cookies out of the cookie jar.

Resources

I have used many. When I originally began home schooling, I purchased a prepared curriculum, but I eventually switched to using my own self-designed curriculum once I had the confidence to develop my own.

We have made much of use of the *Faith and Life* series volume two. It is a beautiful series that is filled with wonderful copies of famous paintings and photos. Still, it is good to have more than one resource on hand, and one of the many wonderful religious education resources I was introduced to was the *Our Holy Faith* series, which is built on *The New St. Joseph Baltimore Catechism*. I have also used the three volumes of this series and love the detailed explanation of the Ten Commandments to be found in the both the first and second volume.

I will note that in St. Joseph's first volume, in attempting to bring the information down to a younger child's level of understanding, they simplify it almost too much, which can occasionally confuse the child. When this happened, I would refer to the same material in volume two, in which case the child was better able to answer the questions from the study section. Because of this, I would advise purchasing both volumes together, especially if this is your first attempt to teach catechism to a child. In addition to these resources, there is also a short and simple, as well as very beautifully illustrated, *First Communion Catechism* also of the *St. Joseph* series.

Here are some online stores where one can purchase these resources:

Living Like Christ, In Christ of the *Our Holy Faith* series:

http://www.neumannpress.com/index.html

The New Saint Joseph Baltimore Catechism, volumes one, two and three available from Amazon.com as well as: http://www.catholiccompany.com).

The New St. Joseph First Communion Catechism can be purchased through:

http://www.chcweb.com, a family owned and run business called Catholic Heritage Curricula.

Faith and Life series can also be purchased from Catholic Heritage Curricula and is usually more easily found in your local Catholic bookstore than any of the other resources I have listed.

You can find more inspirational material on raising children from Christi Gareis on the web at http://mum2twelve.blogspot.com/. Special thanks as well to Shayne Prorock who contributed to this article.

The Holy Door

The phone woke me. Exhausted, I could barely stand. I shaved and headed to the hospital on Saturday, March 4th of the Great Jubilee. I walked up the hill of the Four Crowned Martyrs thinking, "The next time one of our kid breaks a neck in Rome, it's Juliann's turn to come."

When I reached the ward, the doors were open for families to help with breakfast. Rachel was out of traction, lying in a steel halo.

I was helping Rachel brush her teeth when her doctor came in and gave me a white film envelope with her x-rays. He read the letter explaining the results of the motorcycle hitting her a week earlier as she crossed the Appian Way. He said he would have signed copies on Monday for her medical transport to America, but he wanted her to have a drug other than prednisone.

An American surgeon, who, by providence, was also in Rome, had made the suggestion for her to be given prednisone. The change in medicine concerned me.

I brushed Rachel's hair until visiting hours ended.

Sisters arrived for the midday meal with Rachel. Visiting hours ended and we went for a sandwich. Knowing how busy Sunday would be as we prepared for her transport home, and knowing that I still had to reach the student coordinator about getting Rachel's luggage, I asked Sister if St. Peter's had a Saturday evening Mass.

"There is no Saturday night Mass at St. Peter's," replied Sister, "but why don't you go to confession there? We want to bathe Rachel for the trip. Go right after we are allowed in to see Rachel at three o'clock."

"Sister," I replied, "I went last Saturday before heading here and I have been too busy to sin."

They laughed, but she said, "Use the grace of the sacrament then." She leaned closer and smiled, "They have the best English confessor in the world there."

"They do?" I asked in surprise.

"It is, after all, Saint Peter's."

There was silence and she said, "His confessional says Italian, English, and Maltese. He is the only one in Saint Peter's with Maltese listed. Go in the Holy Door and then right of the altar. You're supposed to be there," she said waving a mock finger.

"Well, let's tell Rachel and then I'll go, but I have to be back by six o'clock when evening visiting hours begin."

"You will have the time you need."

We went back in and I told Rachel where I was going. She was happy about it and gave me her camera for pictures.

Arriving at Saint Peter's by taxi, I took one picture and her camera jammed. I headed up the steps.

"Through the Holy Door and to the confessionals on the left," I repeated in an exhausted whisper. I knelt at the Holy Door, said a prayer for Rachel and headed left. It was already four o'clock. Each confessional had lines.

I was searching for "Maltese" when I saw the familiar face of the American surgeon's wife. "Hi, is Len here?" I asked.

She turned around, startled. "Is something wrong with Rachel?"

"No, I'm here for confession, but I need to talk to Len."

"How did you find us?"

It was a good question.

Her husband had not heard of the medicine that the doctor wanted to give Rachel and told me to have the transport physician from the States review all medications. Then I told them that I was looking for the best English confessor in the world, and they were surprised. They mentioned the confessionals that were on the "right side" of the altar.

Those confessionals had lines, and I read the signs above the doors. I reached the next to last one. It said, "Italiano, English, Malti-bil". I knew it was the confessional I was looking for, and there was only one person in line. I tapped him on the shoulder.

"What are you doing here? Is something wrong with Rachel?" It was the student Coordinator.

"She's fine. Here for confession. The good Lord saved me a phone call."

We quickly worked out the luggage details. I asked, "Have you gone to this confessor before?"

"No," he said.

"Best English confessor in the world." At that he looked worried. "We better examine our conscience," I suggested.

We stood there for two minutes before his turn came.

Standing there, I realized my unworthiness. What an unworthy sinner I was for God to go such lengths to take care of me. Why me, when Rachel was the one suffering?

I began to cry and then advanced from crying to sobbing. No one else approached me. I was the sinner in the temple. I tried to pull myself together.

The student coordinator came out looking pale.

I went to the confessional and sobbed as I knelt at the opening. The most sonorous voice I have ever heard said, "It is all right my son."

"Father, before I confess I must tell you about my daughter," I sobbed.

"I know about your daughter," the voice sang, "Sister told me. I have been praying for her every day."

I sobbed harder and said I was dealing with too many doctors and was saying who-knows-what in Italian trying to get medical care for my daughter.

"And what else?"

There was a long pause and I told him that in my heart there was anger against the motorcyclist who hit her. He spoke with authority. "It was an ac-ci-dent. Ac-ci-dent! God did not want this to happen to your daughter."

I mentioned praying the Joyful Mysteries of the rosary.

"God does not want deals. He only wants your sorrows. That is all he wants from this. A sacrifice of nothing, nothing but your sorrows. There will be more sorrows in your daughter's case. You must accept what comes as a sorrowful mystery and offer it as a sacrifice to God. You know Italiano *corragio!* Your daughter and you must have *corragio.* Heart! Courage! Courage of the heart!"

I cried harder.

He gave me a penance and said slowly and in a whisper, "Trust in God."

I came out sobbing. One Sister who looked Maltese stood in line. Seeing my face, she became one very frightened Maltese Sister.

I knelt and began my penance. Everyone had to be looking and thinking, "Thank God, I am not a sinner like that one!" On the Our Father, when I reached "Thy will be done," the tears stopped. The grief stopped.

Unexpectedly, in the Year of the Great Jubilee, a Holy Door had been passed through, and a true confession made. The good Lord had used a horrible accident for the good of His kingdom and had removed punishments I deserved for past sins. That day in Saint Peter's knelt a modern-day Jairus accompanying Christ, hoping for healing of a bedridden daughter, and discovering, "Fear is useless. What is needed is belief." In that moment, I was given the full grace of the sacrament of reconciliation.

Michael F. Russo   *Broken Arrow, Oklahoma*

I Was Forgiven

When my husband and I were engaged to be married, he had to leave me to go to Germany with the Army. After he left, I found out I was pregnant. I wrote to tell him the news, but I didn't hear back from him for a very long time. In the meantime, I told my parents I was pregnant, and they encouraged me to get an abortion. I was nineteen years old and so confused that I did what they wanted.

After getting the abortion, I heard from my fiancé. He said he had been gone in the field when I had written to him about the pregnancy, and that was why there was a delay in his getting back to me. He said he loved me and that we would get married as soon as he returned home. I regretted having had the abortion and told him that I lost the baby. We did get married when he returned home, but it was not a Catholic wedding.

In 1997, my husband, who had been a non-practicing cradle Catholic, was coming home to the Catholic faith. I began taking RCIA classes so I could also be Catholic, and I knew I had to confess this sin that had been bothering me for years if I were to go any further in my faith development.

My husband knew I was nervous about confession and tried to comfort me. I finally went in the confessional and sat face-to-face with the priest. I was shaking and started crying as I told him what I had done. Not only was I deeply sorry about having the abortion, but I was also sorry that I'd had premarital sex and had lied to my husband about the baby. I felt as if I were nineteen again.

Then I felt as if Jesus were sitting where the priest was, telling me that I was forgiven of my sins. I felt Him telling me to let it go, that He had released me of my sins. I felt as if He said, "Welcome home!" to me.

At that moment, a peace I can't describe came over me. My husband told me later that when I came out of the confessional I had a glow about me. I told him it was because I had a good confession with Jesus.

I became a Catholic at the Easter Vigil in 1997 with my three children, and my husband and I had our marriage blessed. It was very beautiful, especially because I knew I was free of the sins that I had held in my heart for such a long time. My husband and I have been married for twenty-nine years, and we have three children and seven grandchildren. All of us belong to the Catholic Church.

Anonymous   *Oklahoma*

Twinkle in His Eye

About nine years after converting to the Catholic faith, I picked up a book that was collecting dust in the bookcase titled *Many Faces of Mary*. It was an intriguing book about the many different ways and places that the Blessed Mother has appeared in the world. The story of one woman appearing in so many different ways sounded interesting and puzzling at the same time.

It was God's good grace and nudge that inspired my wife to step into the picture when the Mary topic came up. She knew I was reading another book on Mary and recalled something in the Sunday bulletin at church about an upcoming Marian conference in Everett, about twenty-five miles north of Seattle. As God would have it, the author of the book that I was reading just happened to be at the conference.

The conference was going well, and one of the main speakers at this event was a very holy priest, Father Stephen Barham (God rest his soul). He was gentle, funny, a serious crowd pleaser, and when he laughed, everyone laughed. He had a signature laugh. Being charismatic in both the Eastern and Western Rites, he was not shy by any means.

During one of the breaks at the conference, my wife suggested going to confession since it was readily available. It had been quite awhile since she had gone, and she convinced me that it would be a good idea for me to go too.

The silent line was about forty people deep, but it moved surprisingly fast since there were several priests hearing confessions. The priests were in small cubicles in two small rooms. While in line, I briefly spoke with a little nun with a twinkle in her eye, and she mentioned that through this sacrament there were many graces and that she would pray especially for me. Well that was new for me. Thank you, Sister Marion Goyke (God rest her soul).

When it was my turn in line, there sat Father Barham, waiting. The confession began something like this: "Forgive me, Father, for I have never gone to confession and this is my first time ever since converting to Catholicism…"

The priest was very fatherly, and at the end of it, with a smile and a twinkle in his eye, similar to the one that Sister Marion had, he gave me absolution. He then slapped his knee, and jokingly and quite loudly said, "Don't wait so long between confessions and you won't have as much stuff to tell!" Then he immediately let out his funny laugh that echoed in the room, down the hall, and into the auditorium. Naturally, I was a little perplexed. Others came up later and commented on the huge laughter that they heard.

I often reflect on that experience and how the little sister prayed for me. That weekend was the beginning of my conversion of heart that soon sent me on a pilgrimage and continued growth in the beauty of the Catholic faith. God's grace continues to work in mysterious ways, but confession is always my favorite.

Ron Belter   *Kirkland, Washington*

Ask For God's Peace

My name is Breon Gonzalez; I live in Lake Elsinore, California and attend St. Frances of Rome parish. I am a Catholic convert of nineteen years, married, with five wonderful children.

Of our twenty-two years of marriage, my mother-in-law has lived with us for twenty and a half years. Some days are better than others, and I try to look at the positives.

In February of 2003, I was in a lot of emotional pain. On the outside, I was my usual bubbly, happy-go-lucky, person. Inside, my chest hurt very badly, and I was crying. My mother-in-law, when she is nice, she is really nice. However, when she is angry, she is very mean and cruel to the point of telling my children unkind things about me.

Out of respect for my husband's feelings, as this is his mother, I have dealt with this for years. This particular year it was really causing me emotional pain. I am not a vengeful person and only want peace and harmony, so I decided to go to confession. Father Martin sat and listened to my confession, as I cried my way through with trembling emotion.

I didn't go in to complain about my mother-in-law. I went for the guilt of my ill feelings towards her. Afterwards, the priest was so stunned that he replied, "Wow, some people look so happy you would never guess how much pain they are in!"

He told me to ask God for peace and off I went. I still felt the heavy pain in my chest as I left the confessional, even though I was relieved to have confessed all of my feelings and pain. I was in such a daze as I left that I almost forgot to kneel and pray for God's peace!

I knelt and prayed. When I arose from prayer, my whole body was renewed! I felt the peace run through me; the pain in my chest was gone! I will never forget the feeling of euphoria and peace that I felt that day. I was healed that day and have never felt that much pain again.

Breon L. Gonzalez   *Lake Elsinore, California*

A Memorable Day

Good Friday of 2005 changed my life. Walking out of the confessional that day I no longer felt the pain that had plagued my soul for twenty years. It was completely gone. In its place was a peace that I had never before experienced in my life. This peace was overwhelming and beautifully indescribable. I had never felt such an inner calmness.

My encounter with God's mercy that morning was so tangible that even if my life had been asked of me at that moment, I would have had no fear of facing God. I knew I had been forgiven and embraced by His love. Before that confession I had not realized the degree to which my sins had paralyzed me and controlled my life.

On that memorable day God gave me the strength I needed to honestly unload the weight of the sins that I had been carrying for many years. Then the priest gave me my penance and absolved me of my sins. The key to my profound peace was that simple.

As I left the confessional, I felt that the penance I had been given was very insignificant compared to the many years worth of sins that I had just confessed to God. I expected a penance that would take days or a week to complete, yet the priest only asked me to go to the Good Friday service that afternoon, touch the cross, and leave my sins there. It seemed too simple. However, I soon realized that this penance would play another major part in changing my life.

Later that day I joined the line of people going forward in the church to venerate the cross. When it was my turn, I placed my hand on those rough wooden timbers. It was at that moment, with tears flooding my eyes, that I grasped what Christ had done for me because He loves me so much.

As I recall that moment today, tears still stream down my face. Jesus' love for us is so deep that no matter how horrid a sin we may have committed, He is always ready to forgive us. All we have to do is come to Him with genuine sorrow and allow Him to pour His mercy upon us. When I embraced the cross that day, these words of St. Peter became real to me: "By His wounds, you were healed." (I Peter 2:24)

Suzanne Luteran   *Erie, Pennsylvania*

"2. When you enter the confessional, whether the confessional box or sitting face-to-face with the priest, you begin by saying, 'Bless me, Father, it has been (say how long) since my last confession. I am sorry for the following sins.'"

Appendix A: Making a Good Confession
   by Father Jim Van Vurst, OFM

see page A-1

The Left Confessional

I remember my first confession when I was seven years old, back in the late 1960s. The confessional at St. Boniface was very dark, and I was nervous and cold. Though I had all the prayers and *the script* memorized, I didn't know what to say for my sin, so I made one up.

During the following school years, my parents assumed that I went to confession with my CCD class, but somehow I evaded it. In my sophomore year of high school, my friend Susan shared how she had just gone to confession and how great she felt. She was persistent that I should go and get this wonderful forgiven feeling too.

I went to confession but found that it was still a very dark and cold place. I had forgotten what to say, and I didn't even remember the act of contrition. I did not have the wonderful feeling after my confession that Susan had raved about, so I didn't return to confession until my sophomore year of college.

I was at a Teens Encounter Christ (TEC) weekend in Onamia, Minnesota, when I celebrated the sacrament of reconciliation in college. It was a face-to-face confession, and it was light, but I didn't think it was much better than the dark confessional. I probably went a few more times in my college years, but the importance of confession fell out of my life. I even evaded it when the priest urged my fiancé and me to go before we got married.

About eight years later, Karen, who was a friend from church, made a comment about needing to make her obligatory confession so she could receive Communion on Christmas. I was dumbfounded.

I had gone to Mass all my life and had received the Eucharist weekly since I was seven years old, but somehow I had missed the part about needing to be in a state of grace before receiving communion. I had some serious reflecting to do. How could I continue to receive my Lord at Communion, knowing that I had sinned and not gone to confession? I prayed for courage and decided that I would go on Sunday.

I told my friend that I didn't remember exactly how to go to confession and she told me that there was a sheet hanging by the confessional that I could take in with me and read from. "How will I be able to see it in the darkness of that little room?" I asked. "Go in the left confessional; it's light enough in there to read," she said.

We belong to a small rural parish that has only one Mass a week. Father drives from another town and hears confessions before Mass begins. At the time, I had three small children and a husband who didn't see the importance of ever being early for anything. He didn't see the importance of weekly Mass either. I didn't want to tell him why he had to sit with the kids an extra fifteen minutes at church while I went to confession—something that he knew I didn't ever do.

The first week after I decided I would go to confession, we didn't arrive in time for me to go. I didn't go to Communion that day either, and did not like the feeling of not being able to receive Jesus.

The following week I prayed for courage and opportunity and got both. I went into the confessional on the left with the *instruction sheet* that Karen had told me about and knelt with my back to a window. It was not stained glass or clear. No one could see in, but the brightness of the sun flooded that little room. It was light, and I felt warm.

I heard the partition slide open and took a deep breath. "Bless me Father for I have sinned…I don't remember how long it has been…"

I doubt the priest knew of the tears I wept. I had finally found the wonderful forgiven feeling that Susan had told me about twenty some years earlier. Now I never go to confession without a couple of tissues because I cry every time. I still get that intense forgiven feeling over ten years later.

Our parish has done some remodeling and the "one on the left side" with the window is now used for storage. The remaining confessional has a light that is always on when Father is hearing confessions. I know I could go to confession in the dark now if it was necessary. I know the words, and more importantly, I know the security of God's love and the warmth of His forgiveness. Confession has changed for me. Reconciliation has changed me.

Lynda S. Lowin   *Blunt, South Dakota*

That's Everything!

I am the youngest child in a large family, and I was abused when I was young. Over time, and through a series of incidents, I discovered I suffered from dissociative identity disorder, formerly known as multiple personality disorder. It wasn't as severe as what you see in the movies; the *other personalities* didn't have different names or wardrobes.

As I worked my way through therapy and things started to come together for me, I not only became aware of terrible things done to me, but I also saw the terrible things I had done and had to answer for.

About six years ago, near the end of my therapy, I wanted to reconcile my faith with my life, so I consulted a wonderful priest in my parish. It was both a humbling and a humiliating experience.

After a few visits with this priest, I no longer needed to consult with him. Things were straightened out for me, and my questions were answered. I realized that I needed to go to confession for the things I had done in the past that had harmed others as well as me.

I consulted the same priest for confession. He absolved my sins and then added the most wonderful phrase I've ever heard, "…and that's everything!"

Many times I look back at my life and the memories are difficult. The phrase, "…and that's everything!" is my crutch and my comfort. Tears come to my eyes as I write this, just thinking of it. That priest healed me and gave me the strength to face the Lord when I die. I experienced true mercy that day.

Anonymous   *Philadelphia, Pennsylvania*

Medicine Box

I remember the first time I ever experienced the sacrament of reconciliation. It was back in the 1970s when it was called confession. I was around eight or nine years old and about to make my first Communion at St. Anne's Church in Beaumont, Texas.

I was the oldest, tallest, and largest kid in the class, and I felt very out of place and unworthy. I also felt like a failure because I thought everyone prayed more devoutly than I did at Mass. While I tried to look like I was praying, I was constantly distracted at church by looking at people's interesting shoes during holy Communion.

My little brother and I fought constantly, and I wanted to do a good job with my first confession so I wouldn't mess it up and feel like I was a failure with that too. I listened carefully to Father Hannafin, whom we called "Father Grandfather" because he reminded us of a grandpa. He was instructing us on how to do a proper confession. I was nervous and thought that if I didn't do it correctly I would disappoint Jesus again and be doomed.

As I nervously waited for my turn to enter the confessional, I resisted listening to the previous penitents telling their sins. We had no doors on the confessionals back then; curtains covered the entrance to the small, dark, cubicle-like confessionals.

After I went inside, I knelt and made my confession to the priest through the screen that separated us. It turned out that I didn't need to be nervous after all! When I went back to the pew to do my penance, it literally felt like the weight of all those sins was lifted off my shoulders. I felt free, physically and mentally.

It is now thirty-three years later and I still remember the wonderful feeling I had from my very first confession. I believe the Lord put His arm around me, reassuring me of His love and forgiveness. Now when the weight of the world is on my shoulders, I just go into the *medicine box* and God will listen and help me.

Janis M. Hairgrove   *Beaumont, Texas*

Smell the Roses

I had been an extraordinary minister of holy Communion for over a year and had known the power of Christ present in the most holy Eucharist. However, when we moved across town and got involved with all the hustle and bustle that comes with settling into a new home, I gave myself an excuse to skip Mass for several weeks.

My heart ached. My soul ached. I missed the real presence of Christ in the Eucharist, and I knew I was putting further distance between myself and the Lord every time I chose not to attend Mass. But I continued to allow my distractions to overshadow the deep desire I had to reunite myself with Him.

I think I missed Mass for six weeks straight. I felt hollow and empty. I knew I had to reconcile myself to God before I could receive Him again, but it wasn't easy to admit to Him that I had been lazy and selfish. Finally, I got on my knees to prepare myself to receive the sacrament of reconciliation. I called on the intercession of Our Lady and St. Therese to help me make my confession.

As I entered what would be our new parish home, a friendly face greeted me. A woman directed me toward the confessional and I walked right in. Previously, my reconciliations had been face-to-face with the priest. As a convert, I had seen the traditional confessionals with a screen in the movies, but I had never used one in my ten years as a Catholic.

All the movies in the world could not have prepared me for what was going to come next. As I knelt in front of the screen, the space went black and I was enveloped in total darkness. In that moment, the world and its troubles disappeared. I knew that the Lord was with me, and silent tears of sorrow spilled down my cheeks. I missed Him and longed to be reunited with Him.

"In the name of the Father, and of the Son, and of the Holy Spirit," I whispered as I crossed myself. From the other side of the screen, Father Vince Rogers' kind and gentle voice guided me through my confession. He reminded me of the infinite mercy of God and of Christ's desire for me to join Him at Mass, and that I could begin anew.

Father Rogers understood how my choice to skip Mass had separated me from God, and he understood the deep sorrow that accompanied that choice. He reminded me of the suffering Our Lord had endured on my behalf and asked me to consider whether one short hour a week was too much for Christ to ask in return. Of course, I knew it wasn't.

My silent tears continued as I received absolution and left the confessional. Tears of sorrow turned to tears of joy as I grasped the magnitude of the mercy I had just received. A smile broke out across my face and my heart swelled with gratitude as I left the church. I had a new life in Christ, and I intended to never again take that for granted.

For weeks afterward, I smelled roses during the consecration. I will probably never know for sure if the scent was just the perfume worn by women sitting nearby, but I don't think it was. Instead, I choose to believe that it was a reminder that Our Lady and St. Therese were there with me, surrounding me with their sweet aroma as the darkness had surrounded me in the confessional.

Lara Muse   *Agency, Missouri*

My Thoughts...

My wife and I taught kindergarten classes at our church. Each year we would give the children a guided tour of the church and point out what each item in the church was for. One year, as we were showing the children our confessional, one child asked, "Which side is for the men and which side is for the women?"

Fr. Anthony R. DiMaggio

Five Minutes

When I was working at the Newman Center at the University of Utah, I was asked to help with first reconciliation at a neighboring parish, St.Theresa's. There were a large number of children ready to make their first confession, as well as a sufficient number of priests. One of the priests was a very stern and tough speaking former military chaplin.

All of the priests went to their appropriate places. I was assigned the reconciliation room. After I heard a few confessions, a little boy entered and began his confession. I welcomed him with joy and assured him of God's mercy.

"Bless me, Father, for I have sinned. This is my second confession. It has been five minutes since my last confession."

"Five minutes," I hollered. "What sins did you commit in five minutes?"

"Father," the boy said sincerely, "I made my first confession with Father (the military chaplin), and he made me so mad that I thought I better confess again."

I was taken aback. I explained to him that the priest is used to working in a military setting and is just more rough.

I told him that the sacrament of penance ultimately leads to joy, because the Lord forgives our sins and we experience joy.

"Your second confession is fine," I said, "and the Lord will forgive you and fill you with peace."

The boy smiled. He was relieved that he was forgiven.

"For your penance, say a prayer for priests," I told him.

When the boy left, I thought how wonderful it was that this first penitent felt comfortable to go to confession immediately after his first one. He trusted in the Lord and the Lord gave him peace and joy.

Then, I had to chuckle because that was the first and only time that I had heard, "Bless me, Father, for I have sinned; it has been five minutes since my last confession."

Father Thomas Kraft, O.P.   *Seattle, Washington*

Never Give Up

I was raised a Lutheran in theory, but not in practice, as our family did not go to church or do much of anything in a religious way. When I was eight years old, my aunt got married in a Catholic Church. I was very impressed with the beautiful ceremony of the Mass. It was my first experience of being in a Catholic Church. The priest was very nice to me; he asked me questions about school and made me feel very welcome. His thoughtfulness left a lasting impression. From that moment on, I knew the Catholic Church was where I belonged.

This did not agree with my mother at all. She would get very upset if I mentioned anything positive about the Catholic Church and would state very forcefully that it would be over her dead body if I became a Catholic. Needless to say I didn't mention it to her very much.

When I was sixteen years old and in my last year of high school, my parents moved across town. I started the new high school, but after two days of being in a totally strange environment, with no friends or teachers or students I knew, I announced to my mother that if I had to go to that school I was dropping out.

My parents worked out an arrangement for me to stay with my boyfriend's parents (he was away in the military) so that I could be in my old school with my old friends. The mother of my boyfriend was a faithful Catholic and went every Sunday to Mass. Since I had never been in a family that went to church services on a regular basis, this was very beautiful to me. I would go to Mass with her, and I loved it. Then, because

I planned to get married to my boyfriend, his mother suggested that if I wanted to take instructions to become a Catholic, I could do that.

I did not tell my mother about this, but I took the instructions and became a Catholic. I did not have a problem with confession at all. In the Lutheran Church, they believe in confession to God privately, but to me the confessional box in church was very private. What was the difference?

My Catholic faith became very important to me, but unfortunately, I had many problems to work through. I started drinking and couldn't quit. It clouded my thinking, my judgments and my social life. At one point, I thought I was pregnant and went for an abortion. It turned out that I wasn't, but later, at the age of eighteen, when I was trying to make things right with God, I knew that I was as guilty as if I had done it and so needed to go to confession.

The priest was having a bad day. At least that is what another priest years later would tell me. I went into the confessional very contrite, nervous and upset, but wanting to be right with God. The priest listened to my whole confession until I got to the part about how I had considered an abortion, and then he went ballistic. He refused to give me absolution. It was something, he yelled at me that I would have to live with until Judgment Day!

I was in shock and very upset. I went away with a much bigger problem than what I came with! I talked to several priests after this, and though they informed me that when a person makes a good confession, with a contrite heart, absolution cannot be denied. I did not have the courage to attempt confession again. Well, I did try once at a penance liturgy, but the priest there would only give me a blessing and not absolution. After this, I made up my mind I would not try again though I kept seeking the Lord's compassion in other ways. I still continued to be active in the Church. I joined the choir, helped with the music, and even did some teaching.

But God never gives up! Finally, in his mercy and kindness, He sent a monsignor into my life as a friend of my husband's. My husband and Monsignor would often go fishing together, and many times he would come over for dinner. Through their friendship, I became secure enough to ask him for an appointment for confession. He readily arranged for me to meet with him in the library at our church. I was very nervous and thought, "Here we go again. Nothing has changed and I'm letting myself in for it one more time!"

However, because I knew this priest as a friend and was familiar with him in a family setting, it was quite different. He gave me complete absolution. I felt as if the weight of many years were totally lifted and carried away. I was so relieved and so happy.

I now no longer have a problem going to confession and find much solace in being able to go regularly to unburden my troubles and problems. God is good!

Carol A. Rusch   *Sun City, California*

Mysterious Touch that Gave Courage

This true story took place in the late 1970s while I was teaching at our Franciscan seminary, Duns Scotus College in the suburbs of Detroit, Michigan. The chapel of St. Anthony and the college building were modeled after the Franciscan Basilica and friaries in and around Assisi.

One of the most important ministries we had in our chapel was that of hearing confessions. Every day, except Sundays, we heard confessions in the mornings from nine to eleven, in the afternoons from two to five, and in the evenings from seven to eight. People came from all over the city and surrounding areas.

This story was told to me by a lady following her confession. She had been away from the sacraments for many years and recently had found *making a new start* more and more on her mind. The thoughts would not go away. And so, one summer afternoon, she gathered up her courage and drove to our chapel to make her confession. But, the closer she got the more scared she became.

She parked her car and headed toward the chapel. Leading to the chapel from ground level, there were twelve large and long steps. In her state of mind, those steps looked like the steps to the gallows. There was no way she could go up. Instead, she decided to follow the lovely wooded pathways that went around the chapel and college; it was not a short walk. She walked, and walked, and walked. Back and forth, back and forth as the thoughts raced through her head, "Do I really want to do this? Maybe I should wait and come back next week? Maybe…"

Finally, she had enough courage to go up the stairs. She was not certain that she would actually go to confession. Just get up the stairs! That was her first task to accomplish. It was after five o'clock in the evening when she finally reached the chapel. Only a few people were waiting in the pew to go to confession. She knelt at the end, still not sure that she would actually make the move to the confessional when her turn came. After the first person and then the second entered the confessional, she was alone in the pew. She told me, "Father, I know I was alone, but when the last person came out of the confessional, I felt a nudge on my left arm, like someone gently poking me with his elbow, and a voice said, "Okay, you're next."

She told me later that when the nudge and the voice came, she got up without a thought and went into the confessional. She was surprised that even though she had been away from church for such a long period, it didn't take much time. When she came out of the confessional, she looked for the person who touched her arm and there was no one. "Father," she exclaimed, "there were no cars in the parking lot. No one was in the chapel. Who could it have been?"

I am convinced that God, in some mysterious way, allowed her to experience His touch and His call. How? Who knows? Grace comes in mysterious ways. I'm not sure that she needed her car to get home that evening; she was so happy she easily could have floated without touching the ground.

Fr. Jim Van Vurst, OFM   *Cincinnati, Ohio*

Communal Confession with Owl Head

Some of the best days of my priestly vocation were spent with the Indians on a mission in Arizona near the Mexican border. The Indians loved to give everyone nicknames; they gave me a number of them, and one of them was "Owl Head," since I made priestly visits at odd hours of the night because of sickness or other situations.

One story stands out in particular that shows quite clearly how I lived up to this grand name. In the days before group reconciliation services were popular, I was introduced to the method by necessity.

Late one evening, after I had gone to bed and was peacefully sleeping, I awoke with a start to hear the mad pummeling of a horse racing up to my abode. As I scrambled out of bed to see what was up, I found a young, worried and breathless boy who told me to come quick because his grandparents were sick and in need of a priest.

I quickly got dressed, grabbed my priest kit, and jumped into my pick-up, leaving the boy to follow behind more sedately with his horse. I knew where the village was—way out beyond all traces of civilization on a bare, desert road with sagebrush and cactus. It took me some time to get there, but when I arrived at the small adobe hut, barely discernable in the darkened landscape, I made my way inside.

It was a typical Indian home with thick adobe walls that made up one large room in which the mother and father, kids and kitchen lived on one side, with a big double bed shoved against the wall on the opposite side in which resided the grandparents. They were both too ill to get out of bed. The room was lit by a single coal lantern that flickered warmly in one corner and cast dancing shadows against the opposite walls. Both grandparents wanted to confess and receive anointing of the sick. I knew that in their weakened condition there was no way they were going to be getting out of the bed to give the other any privacy. Nor did it occur to the rest of the family to go out into the dark night to give them any, either.

If they wanted confession, fine, get on with it, I told myself. First I listened to the elderly lady's sins while her husband propped himself up weakly on one elbow to listen. After every sin his wife confessed, he would nod his head up and down and say, "Uh-huh, Uh-huh," in total agreement as to what she had done. I rather think he might have reminded her if she had forgotten anything. I gave her absolution and then turned to the elderly man while now his wife propped herself up on her elbow to listen carefully to what he confessed. The same thing happened in reverse. Every sin he confessed, up and down would bob her head and she would say, "Uh-huh, uh-huh," in total agreement with every rotten thing he had done. Once I had heard both of their confessions, I then anointed them with holy oil as I administered the sacrament of the sick to them.

Then something beautiful happened. When I gave each of them Communion, placing the Lord gently on each tongue, a very sweet and gentle transformation came over both of them. It was such a profound change that the room seemed to glow with God's presence.

After I had done all that I could for the sick couple, the rest of the family insisted that I must stay and have something to eat. The rich, good smell of deer meat cooking over the fire had greeted me upon entering, making a pleasant contrast to the stank, burning fumes of the coal lamp. I was hungry and soon was greatly enjoying a big plate of venison and tortillas and enjoying the warm company of the rest of the family. Before I had finished, someone came from another Indian home and wanted me to go to their house to bless someone else. It was still night but "Owl Head" needed to be on his way.

Fr. Maurus Kelly, OFM   *Santa Barbara, California*

A Simple Tutorial for Making a Good Confession

Note from Sr. Patricia:

In collecting stories and helpful tips for making good confessions, I received an email from Martha Ervin. She told me that when she was a new convert she had had questions about confession, and so she went to an online site at www.americancatholic.org. On their "Contact Us" page they had a place where you could send in a question and it would be answered by a priest. She shared with me the question she asked and the wonderful reply she received that still continues to help her today.

Below is her question, along with the reply she received.

I am a convert and joined the church in 1994. I continue to struggle with the sacrament of reconciliation/confession, and my insecurity keeps me away from the Eucharist. I need confession lessons.

Thanks for this forum and your kind attention.

Martha Ervin

Hello, Martha,

I'm so glad you wrote because I want to help you and make this as easy as possible for you. Keep in mind that all priests go to confession themselves; they are not exempt, obviously. So, I'll give you the procedure and you can jot it down or copy it from this email and use it. I'll do it in a series of steps.

1. It is good to take a few minutes before confession to reflect on your life since the time of your last confession. You don't have to start going over all of the sins that you confessed already—they are already forgiven. We all have regrets about past sins, but you don't need to confess them again. And if you forget some sins that need

to be confessed, it's okay. They are already forgiven by your intention to confess them. Remember that the Lord's forgiveness is for all of your sins.

Usually, if there is something really bad that you need to confess, it will come to mind. I find that if we reflect on our relationships with ourselves, our families, and others, we commonly see that we fail in charity, through gossip, and sometimes in lying. You never need to go into detail; it isn't necessary. Nor do you need to remember exactly how many times you committed that particular sin—just in general.

2. When you enter the confessional, whether the confessional box or sitting face-to-face with the priest, you begin by saying, "Bless me, Father, it has been (say how long) since my last confession. I am sorry for the following sins."

3. Some examples of typical sins are: I was unjustly critical of a family member and caused hard feelings. In order to avoid embarrassment, I lied twice. I became angry at a fellow worker and showed my dislike towards him. Struggles with sexuality are always difficult to confess, but a person can say something like, "I have struggles with the virtue of purity and confess I am guilty in thought or deed."

4. We conclude our confession by saying, "I am sorry for these and all the sins of my past life and I ask God's pardon and penance of you, Father."

5. The priest might give you a word of advice, ask you to say a prayer such as an Our Father as a sign of our contrition, and then ask you to make an act of contrition. (see examples on next page)

6. For this you can say, "O my God, I am sorry for all my sins because they have offended you and my neighbor. I promise to try not to sin again in the future. Amen."

That's all there is to it. I would also suggest that during Lent you attend one of your parish's communal penance services. They are wonderful, because they bring together a group of people, all brothers and sisters in the Lord, all of whom by their very presence are part of God's family, asking for forgiveness.

Finally, you should not stay away from Communion unless there is something really, really, serious bothering you. We all struggle with ordinary human sins and frailty, and we should never let that prevent us from receiving Communion. Each of us approaches the Lord knowing we are fragile and sinful. That's why we go to receive Him in the Eucharist—not because we are perfect, but because we are imperfect. We simply ask the Lord to feed us and help us on our journey. I hope this helps. God bless you.

Fr. Jim Van Vurst

Act of Contrition

O my God, I am heartily sorry for
having offended you, and I detest
all my sins, because of Your just
punishments, but most of all because
they offend You, my God, who are
all-good and deserving of all my love.
I firmly resolve, with the help of
Your grace, to sin no more and to
avoid the near occasion of sin.

Act of Contrition 2

Forgive me my sins, O Lord, forgive me my sins;
the sins of my youth, the sins of my age, the sins of my soul,
the sins of my body; my idle sins, my serious voluntary sins;
the sins I know, the sins I do not know; the sins I have concealed
for so long, and which are now hidden from my memory.
I am truly sorry for every sin, mortal and venial,
for all the sins of my childhood up to the present hour.
I know my sins have wounded your Tender Heart,
O My Savior, let me be freed from the bonds of evil through
the most bitter Passion of My Redeemer. Amen.
O My Jesus, forget and forgive what I have been. Amen.

The Ten Commandments

Comments by Father Pat Umberger

The First Commandment

I am the Lord your God; you shall not have strange gods before me.

Do we truly love God above all, or do we sometimes give greater importance to things of this world: money, image, looks, clothes, popularity or selfish desires?

Do we claim to have good values, but often bend or abandon them in order to fit in and be "part of the group?"

Do we turn to God in thankful prayer, or do we pray mostly when we want something?

Do we really want to be transformed by the will of God, or do we just use our religion in order to "look" like good Christian people?

The Second Commandment

You shall not take the name of the Lord in vain.

Do we show disrespect for God's name by misusing it out of frustration or anger or to look "tough" to others?

Do we hesitate to mention God's name in appropriate situations, in conversations with friends and family members?

Do we continue to learn about God by paying attention in Church, Religion Class and through reading the Times Review and paying attention to Catholic periodicals, articles on religion in the secular press and television programs?

The Third Commandment

Remember to keep holy the Lord's day.

Do we come to Church to celebrate the Eucharist on Sundays and Holy Days? Do we attend Mass only when it is convenient or when it will make us "feel good?"

Do we participate in the Eucharist by praying and singing, or do we simply sit as spectators and wait to be entertained?

Do we pay close attention to the Word of God and open ourselves to God's call to allow His word to take effect in our lives?

Do we acknowledge the "true presence" of Christ in the Eucharist and receive Holy Communion with respect and reverence?

The Fourth Commandment

Honor your father and your mother.

Do we help bring peace and happiness to our families, or are we disrespectful of others and a source of hurt and division for those who are closest to us?

As parents, are we generous and patient with our children? Do we spend time with them and give them the attention they need? Do we set responsible limits for them and make sure they follow rules that will help them grow into responsible adults?

Are we willing to say "no" to our children, or are we more likely to ignore problem behavior and hope it will "go away?"

Do we listen to our children carefully and treat them with respect?

As children, are we loving, respectful and obedient to our parents? Do we appreciate the many sacrifices they make for us? Do we say "Thank you" and "I love you" often enough?

Do we do our chores without being asked, or do we wait for our parents to become upset before we move away from what we are doing?

Do we listen to our parents' reasoning when they say "no" to us?

The Fifth Commandment

You shall not kill. *

Have we injured another person through carelessness or fighting?

Have we placed ourselves or others in danger because of reckless use of alcohol or other drugs? Have we caused difficulties for ourselves or others because of their use?

Have we risked our lives by driving or riding with someone under the influence alcohol or other drugs?

Do we strive to forgive those who have hurt us, or do we hold on to resentment and desire for revenge?

Do we use our powers of influence well, especially our voting rights, in order to fight war, oppression, abortion and injustice, or do we allow those evils to continue by our apathy and our silence?

Have we been violent or abusive either in action or in speech? Have we been verbally abusive to our children or other family members?

Do we share what we have with those in need? Do we support the life and mission of the Church by responsible stewardship - sharing our time, talent and treasure?

Do we bring our Christianity to every day situations, or do we stand on the sidelines and complain about every flaw we can detect in others?

*Those who have had, procured or assisted in an abortion, see the end of this Examination of Conscience.

The Sixth Commandment
You shall not commit adultery.

Do we respect the dignity of the human body and the holiness of Christian marriage? Do we show that respect in our speech, or are crude language and jokes often part of our conversations?

Do we understand and appreciate the gift of our sexuality as a means of expressing our love [and God's love] in the Sacrament of Marriage?

Have we been faithful to our marriage, priestly or religious vows? Do we keep our commitments simply because we said we would, or do we seek to nourish ourselves and others through our lifetime commitments?

Have we dishonored our bodies by fornication, impurity or unworthy conversation or thought leading to impure actions?

Have we encouraged others to sin by our failure to maintain good moral standards?

The Seventh Commandment

You shall not steal.

Do we respect the property of other people? Have we stolen, damaged or vandalized the property of others?

Have we cheated at work or in school? Have we encouraged others to sin by pressuring them into helping us cheat?

Are we honest and hardworking in school and at work?

Are we faithful to our promises? Can we be trusted?

The Eighth Commandment

You shall not bear false witness against your neighbor.

Have we lied to stay out of trouble or to avoid a difficult situation?

Do we gossip about others? Have we damaged the reputation of another person by exaggeration or making up stories about them?

Can we be trusted with a secret?

Do we stand up for those unjustly accused, or are we merely a channel through which rumors pass, whether or not they are true?

The Ninth Commandment

You shall not covet your neighbor's wife.

Have we weakened or damaged our marriage commitment through our obsession with another person?

Do we respect the commitments of others and help them remain faithful to their promises?

Do we treat our marriages casually in our conversations and attitudes? Have we said or done anything which made a mockery of our sacred promises?

The Tenth Commandment

You shall not covet your neighbor's goods.

Are we satisfied with what God has given us, or are we jealous of those who seem to have more?

Do we try to prove we are better than others by bragging or buying more things?

Do we appreciate our own good qualities, or do we constantly compare ourselves with others and become resentful or bitter?

Do we cope well with the problems that confront us and maintain our Christian hope in spite of hard times and difficulties?

Do we truly "seek first the Kingdom of God" in our lives and place our trust in Him?

Do we reflect the peace, hope and joy of a people redeemed and made holy by the Blood of Christ?

*The Fifth Commandment is where we deal with life issues. Having an abortion, procuring one, or assisting at one are grave matters. The wisdom of the Church has shown that many find it difficult to forgive themselves in these situations. Fathers of children who have been aborted seem to have as many difficulties as mothers. Most dioceses provide means (in many places called "Project Rachel") to help them deal with the complicated issues involved so they can move on with their lives. After-abortion support is also available at: 1-800-401-6494. Know that you are very much in our prayers! Another grave Fifth Commandment issue involves supporting or helping to procure abortion, supporting euthanasia, etc. by talk, action, taking a person to procure an abortion, influencing legislation, directly or indirectly. Such things put our souls in grave danger. Those participating should not receive Communion until they've had a change of heart, confessed that sin and left it behind.

Questions & Answers

The questions below have been answered by several priests who graciously consented to give their educated and prayerful answers. Each of the priests selected has been hearing confessions for many years.

Q 1.—We were told by our parish priest some years ago when communal penance was accepted, that it wasn't necessary to elaborate on how many times the sins were committed, only that one had contrition for his sins. Also, he said that a general description was all that was necessary, say for instance, a sin such as impurity could cover many types of sin in that category.

A If you went along with the instructions of your pastor, then be assured that your sins have been forgiven. For pastoral reasons, perhaps because of the large number of penitents present and the small number of confessors, he felt justified in keeping confessions as brief as possible. Under normal circumstances, sins of impurity (which you mentioned) would have to be confessed more specifically. Impurity embraces lust (desire), masturbation, fornication, pornography, prostitution, and adultery. (2nd edition of *The Catechism of the Catholic Church*, p.564, 2528). Those specific titles can be confessed without going into details. Some general idea as to numbers should be given as well; e.g., two times a week, or month, or year, so the confessor can tell whether the sin is habitual or just a momentary lapse of weakness. His advice to the penitent would change accordingly.

Q 2.—How does one confess to very embarrassing personal sins of a sexual nature without telling the priest what he or she has done. Won't Jesus forgive those kinds of sins anyway if one confesses to him personally?

A It is embarrassing to confess personal sins of a sexual nature. You will not be telling the priest anything he has not heard already. In moral theology, he has covered all possible sins of a sexual nature and has heard it all long before he even sits in a confessional.

The embarrassment can be minimized by simply stating the category of sin and the approximate number of times it was committed. There is no need to go into details; in fact, we are dissuaded from going into specific details. The Church bends over backwards to make confession as easy as possible by allowing the penitent to go anywhere and to any priest he or she wants to, and also to go anonymously by entering the confessional where the priest cannot see the penitent.

Finally, keep in mind that the priest also has to go to confession if he is foolish enough to commit sin. He understands your situation and your embarrassment, and he will be compassionate.

As far as confessing to Jesus personally—that is not an option. Jesus is the one offended by our sins, and He stipulates the terms of reconciliation, not the offender. After His resurrection, He appeared to His apostles and said, "Peace be with you. As the Father has sent me, so I send you." He then breathed on them and said "Receive the Holy Spirit. Whose sins you forgive are forgiven them, and whose sins you retain are retained." (John 20:22-23) This clearly implies confession, because the apostles were not mind readers, and only sinners know what their sins are. Jesus has every right to demand we humble ourselves by confessing our sins to His representatives (priests) as part of our penance for sin. The sinner does not stipulate the terms of reconciliation.

We can always tell God that we are sorry, and it is good to do so frequently. However, only a perfect act of contrition can take away sin outside of confession. Perfect sorrow means that we are sorry for offending God because He is so good and deserving of our love. We are sorry solely because we have offended Him and not because of any punishment that may befall us because of sin: e.g., we deserve to be punished and because we are afraid of going to hell. There must be no selfish motivation involved, and that is difficult for most humans. Imperfect sorrow (selfishness involved) is sufficient for forgiveness of sin in the sacrament of reconciliation.

Q3.—How often should a senior go to confession? I pray an act of contrition every single night before sleeping, just in case I might not make it to the morning.

AThe church mandates that anyone having committed a serious sin must go to confession at least once a year during the Lenten season. However, keeping in mind the efficacy of the sacramental graces of confession, we should all be going to confession more frequently. A good norm for those in their golden years would be once a month. It is not necessary to have sinned before going to confession. If the penitent is not aware of any serious sins, the procedure would be to tell the confessor how long it has been since the last confession and state that he or she has not committed any serious sins and mention some venial sin or a sin of the past in some general way; e.g., against the Fourth or Sixth Commandment. That will provide the confessor with sufficient matter for absolution, and the penitent will receive the sacramental graces to overcome temptations and remain in the state of grace.

It is always good to say an act of contrition, not only each evening, but any time we slip and commit any sin. It helps to remind us where we stand in our relations with God and makes us more aware of the dangers of sin.

Q4.—What will a priest think of me when I confess something I am particularly ashamed of? Will a priest ever think badly of what I have done and change his opinion of me?

AThe priest does not get personally involved with the sins of the penitent. People sin against God and not the priest. Besides, it is the job of the priest to be the mediator between God and the sinner. One of the most satisfying feelings for a confessor is to realize that he has been instrumental in bringing another member of the mystical body of Christ back to God. It is one of the sacred duties of a priest. In moral theology, the seminarian acquires knowledge of all the possible sins people can commit. Nothing a penitent does can possibly scandalize the priest. He has heard it all in the classroom before he even enters the confessional. If anything, he has great admiration for a penitent who humbles himself or herself in order to return to God's grace. Besides, it is unlikely that the confessor will recognize the penitent in the confessional, unless the penitent makes a face-to-face confession.

Q5.—Must one confess a sin if the sin was never actually committed, not because he or she did not want to commit the sin, but because the person did not get the opportunity to do so?

AJesus reminds us that anyone who lusts after a woman has already committed adultery in his heart. If the will gives in to a temptation, and the person plans to commit an action that is sinful, sin takes place in the mind even before the action itself takes place. The will has already committed itself to sin. Sinful thoughts are simply confessed as having entertained sinful or improper thoughts.

Q6.—Can a non-Catholic go to confession? If a non-catholic wanted confession because he or she were in a critical state of health, could that person receive confession and anointing of the sick?

ATechnically speaking, if a person is validly baptized he or she is baptized into the Church which Christ founded upon the apostles, and the person would be entitled to the sacraments. However, for the sake of unity within the church, and out of reverence for the sacraments, church law prohibits non-Catholics from receiving the sacraments.

In the case as proposed by the questioner, where a non-catholic is ill or in danger of death and asks for confession and the anointing of the sick, it would be a pastoral decision. I would hope that most priests would respect the request of a non-catholic under these circumstances. Church law would yield to the higher law, charity.

Q7.—I was raised Catholic. I haven't attended a Mass in over forty-five years. Can I still go to confession?

A Of course, someone away from the church for forty-five years can still go to confession. All that is required is sorrow for his or her sins and a firm purpose of amendment. God is happy to embrace a lost sheep, no matter how long he or she has been away.

Q 8.— I struggle with certain temptations and find myself falling into the very actions I pray so hard not to do. I went to two different priests and got two different reactions. How can two priests in the same Catholic Church say almost the opposite?

A Keep in mind that priests are human. Just as some fathers are disciplinarians in dealing with their children and other fathers are more compassionate in dealing with theirs, so too we have disciplinarian and compassionate confessors. It has nothing to do with the gravity of the sin.

The conditions for serious sin are simple:

1. The offense against God must be a serious violation of God's law.

2. The person committing the act must be aware that is it a serious violation of God's law.

3. The will of the offender must be acting freely without any pressure or fear.

The sad experience you had with the first priest is not common. He might not have been feeling well, or been under some pressure, or might just have been having a bad day. The confessor does have an obligation to instruct the penitent and to help form a true conscience. This can all be done in a compassionate way. You have the right to seek out a confessor who is more to your liking.

It is important to realize that overcoming habits of sin takes a long time and is not accomplished in just a few confessions. It is the cumulative effect of many confessions, and the sacramental grace that comes with the sacrament of reconciliation, that will eventually help break those habits. It means going to confession on a regular basis; e.g., every week, or at least every month. With God's help, nothing is impossible. We have to keep at it.

Q 9.— If Jesus forgives us the second we admit we have sinned, why do we have to go to a priest for the formality?

A Just admitting that we have sinned does not take away sin. We have to be sorry for sin and have a firm purpose of amendment (the intention of not sinning again).

God is the one offended by our sins, and He stipulates the terms of reconciliation. Jesus laid down the terms for reconciliation when, after His resurrection, He appeared to his apostles and said: "Receive the Holy Spirit. Whose sins you forgive are forgiven them, whose sins you retain are retained." John 20:22-23. These words of Jesus imply confession. How can the apostles forgive someone's sins, without knowing what those sins are? Therefore they must be confessed first.

Through the Holy Spirit, by baptism, we are all incorporated into the mystical body of Christ (the Church) and our sins harm the entire church to which we belong. Jesus made it clear that is it only by confessing to an official representative of the church (the priest) that sins will be forgiven.

The Church teaches that only a *perfect* act of contrition (sorrow) will take away sin. That means that our sorrow is motivated solely because we have offended God, who is infinitely good and undeserving of our offense, and not because of any selfish reasons; e.g., because we are going to be punished or because we are afraid of going to hell.

Q 10.—Is it a sin to have great fear in withholding detail to the priest regarding a past sin you know is grievous?

A We are not supposed to go into great detail in confessing our sins. We are to mention the specific category of the sin, and give some general notion as to the frequency of the sin, so the confessor can determine whether it is a habit or just a moment of weakness, and give appropriate advice. Confessing one's sins is difficult enough, without having to go into details.

Q 11.—Why do we have to confess to a priest? Especially to priests who themselves are flawed?

A Priests don't cease being human because they happen to be ordained. They carry around with them the same weaknesses and temptations that everyone has. Yes, they can and do sin at times, but that does not mean they have lost the powers bestowed on them at ordination. They can still validly consecrate bread and wine into the Body of Christ at Mass and give valid absolution in confession. They have to go to confession for their sins like the rest of us and seek counsel.

We go to a priest for confession because that is what Christ requires for forgiveness of our sins. John 20:22–23. God stipulates the terms for reconciliation, not the sinner. We can't tell God how He is going to forgive our sins. He lays down the rules! None of us feel really comfortable in going to confession. That is part of the penance for having sinned.

Q 12.— If a person returns often for the same sin or problem, what do you say to help him or her?

A I encourage him or her to come frequently with the same problem, so that with the accumulative effect of the sacramental grace that comes with the sacrament of reconciliation, he or she may gain the strength to finally overcome the temptations to sin. It is the same thing a doctor does with patients who come to him frequently with the same physical ailment. It cannot be cured in one visit, or with just one application of medicine. It takes a lot of visits and a lot of medication and pills before a persistent infection or illness heals. This is also true when it comes to healing a predominant tendency to sin. It takes a lot of work, persistence, and grace (through confession) to overcome this predominant tendency to sin. I also encourage him not to lose hope, because with God's help and grace, nothing is impossible.

QUESTIONS & ANSWERS

Q 13.—I am a divorced Catholic who is remarried. I was married in the Catholic Church the first time, and that lasted fifteen stressful years. The second time I was married in a courthouse. This marriage is strong, and we're approaching fourteen years of happiness.

I cannot receive the sacraments since I broke the rules of our religion, but I do attend Mass every Sunday. At my church, if you are not of the Catholic faith or a Catholic who can not receive communion for any reason, you are invited to go up and cross your arms over your chest to receive a blessing; I do this since I cannot receive the blessed sacrament.

My question is this: Can I still go into the confessional booth & profess my sins to the priest even though I can not be granted absolution? I still feel very Catholic, and I love our Church so much.

A You mentioned that your first marriage lasted fifteen stressful years. This suggests that there was something wrong with the marriage from the beginning. Have you ever tried to have that first marriage annulled? If there were something lacking in the beginning of the marriage essential to a marriage contract, such as if one partner's intention was not to have children, or if he or she were just getting married with no intention of making the marriage last until death, or if one married just for monetary reasons, then the marriage contract was null from the beginning. Seeking an annulment for that first marriage would be the perfect solution to your problem.

By all means, continue to go to Sunday Masses and to practice your faith as far as you able; and yes, go up for the priest's blessing during communion time with your arms crossed.

There would be no point in going to confession if the priest cannot give you absolution. True sorrow is necessary for absolution and that means to have the intention of not committing the sin again. That would only be possible if both you and your present husband promised to live as brother and sister and not avail yourselves of "marital rights." That might be asking too great a sacrifice from both of you.

Q 14.—How can I ever go to confession if I am married but was not married in the Catholic Church? Because of my non-catholic husband, this situation is not likely to change.

A If, as you say, your marriage situation is not likely to change, the only thing you can do is to observe the external obligations of your faith, like going to Mass on Sundays and holy days of obligation, fasting, abstaining from meat during the Fridays of Lent, etc., and do the best you can. You cannot go to confession without a true purpose of amendment.

Q 15.—My mother and I have not spoken for over one year. She decided that my husband and I were taking money from her. Wholly untrue. Also she feels that we were going to put her in a nursing home. Again untrue. But she has a bevy of friends from church who have trouble with their children, and she has taken on their woes. Let me say it's been a rocky sixty-seven years for me with her. She's never really approved of anything connected with me, including my husband. She has a real dislike for him.

The worst part is that we live in the same neighborhood, and she has a next-door neighbor, much younger than she, whom she has taken into her confidence. She speaks to my son, to whom she has confided that I am the one at fault. Anyway, I went to confession, and the priest seemed to feel that because she is my mother, I should make every effort to reconcile. I have been unable to follow his advice and have not gone to confession or church since. His take on it was that I am having trouble with my faith because of this situation with my mother. It's very hard to be rejected time and again. This is the very short version. Suffice it to say, because of this situation, my health has taken a downward swing and I now need to take a higher dose of blood pressure medication and an anti-anxiety prescription.

My question is, if you decide to ignore a parent for the rest of your life in order to regain your quality of life, can you be forgiven in confession. Would I have to keep confessing this situation?

A Please keep in mind the difference between reconciliation and forgiveness.

It takes willingness on both sides for reconciliation. Your mother seems to be unable or unwilling to reconcile. You cannot do anything about that. You can, however, forgive her meanness, because she is your mother and because God wants you to forgive her. If she is not speaking to you, you don't have to seek her out but can still send her Christmas and birthday cards to show her you are thinking about her. People who harbor hatred and anger make themselves sick and destroy themselves. Once your forgive her, despite all she has done to harm you, you will find peace with God and within yourself, and your blood pressure will get back to normal. Once you forgive her in your heart and confess that sin, you need not mention it again in confession.

Q 16.—I have not gone to confession for over thirty years, and I am seventy-five. I just don't think I will ever have the courage to do so, especially when most confessionals seem to be face-to-face now. Will we ever have *general confession*?

A People have been away from confession for more than thirty years and have come back again without too much trouble. God is happy to embrace you, especially because you have been away so long. Remember, Christ is the Good Shepherd who leaves the ninety-nine sheep to search for the one lost sheep.

A confessor takes Christ's place in the confessional. Remember, you have not offended the confessor, and he is only too happy to have you return to the flock. There are still plenty of confessionals in operation these days. I suggest that you make a good review of the past thirty years, make an act of contrition, go into the confessional and say, "Bless me, father, for I have sinned. I have been away from confession for thirty years and would like you to help me through this confession because I don't know where to start." The priest will then ask you questions, and all you have to say is "yes" or "no." He will lead you through the essential parts of confession.

Q 17.—I have a question concerning confession that has bothered me for some time. Are there specific prayers one must know and recite when in confession? When I was a child, we were taught a formal procedure with prayers said in the correct format. Since then I have forgotten many of them and feel uncomfortable when going to confession now.

A The format for confession has not changed. First, make an examination of conscience to recall your sins (and they need not be serious sins), and then make an act of contrition, telling God you are sorry for your sins because you have offended Him who is so good and undeserving of our offenses. Firmly resolve not to sin again, and ask God's forgiveness. In the confessional, say "Bless me, father, for I have sinned. It has been x number of months or years since my last confession. I am single or married and these are my sins…"

After the priest gives you absolution, he will give you some prayers to say, and if he should give you a penance (prayers to say) with which you are not familiar, tell him so and ask him to please substitute those prayers for other prayers that you do know.

Q 18.—If I made a *general confession*, or any confession, sincerely confessed and was sorry for all my sins, and then after the fact remembered a sin that I'm not sure was confessed at some point in time, do I then have to *again* confess this sin?

A You have asked a common and a very good question. The simple answer is, "no." The *only* time you go back over past sins, forgotten or doubtfully forgotten, is when you are sure that it was a mortal (serious) sin, and you are absolutely sure that it was *deliberately* held back in confession. We have to trust in the mercy of God, Who will forgive us of any sins we may have forgotten in confession. Once we start going back over past sins, we will keep bringing old skeletons out of the closet. This leads to scrupulousness—a terrible spiritual affliction.

Q 19.—Is it okay to write out your sins on a piece of paper, so you won't forget any of them, and bring the list to confession with you?

A There is nothing wrong with writing out your sins on paper so you won't forget them. I suggest however, that you write them in a code known only to yourself. You might lose the paper and have someone else find your list of sins.

Q 20.—Is there any practice we can do to build courage for any right action, but particularly to confess shameful acts, besides prayer? I believe I know most of the reasons why I should not be fearful, but how can I become more courageous?

A Ask God to give you the courage you need to make a good confession. Remember also that you will not scandalize the priest. He has heard all the sins humans are capable of committing, even before he ever sat in the confessional. In moral theology all this was explicitly covered. Keep in mind also that you have offended God by your sins, and not the priest. The priest is merely an instrument of God in the confessional. A lot of the embarrassment of confessing is taken away, if we confess properly—that is, mention the category of sin (without going into explicit details). We are not supposed to be explicit or go into details in confession. The priest understands your embarrassment because he too has to go to confession, and he sympathizes with the penitent. Last but not least, most priests consider being instrumental in the forgiveness of sin in the sacrament of reconciliation as one of the greatest gifts of the priesthood (after that of offering the Holy Sacrifice of the Mass).

Q 21.—My question concerns the frequency of going to confession. What are some guidelines as to the frequency of receiving the sacrament of reconciliation? I'm aware that the Church expects us to go at least once a year. My sins are always before me, and a lot of times I'm aware that I'm confessing the same ones again, although not as many offenses as prior times. I usually go every three months, but is that sufficient?

A The frequency of confession is a very personal thing. I know of some people who go to weekly confession, even though they do not have serious sins to confess. They appreciate the importance of the sacramental graces of the sacrament of reconciliation and use it to their advantage. The confessor is also a spiritual director, and frequent confession helps him know where you are in your relations with God and enables him to give you better guidance. If you are comfortable with going to confession once every three months, by all means continue to do so. In the seminary, we had to go to confession every week.

Q 22.—Are our venial sins forgiven when we attend Mass? Should we confess them anyway *if* they are already forgiven from attending Mass?

I had a priest tell me he would not hear me confess the sins of my past when I tried to end my confession saying, "I am sorry for the sins of my past, especially…." He stopped me, saying it would be a sacrilege to do so. Has that changed from what we once learned as the format for confession? (I am old, sixty-five years old.) So many changes….

A The rules for confession of venial sins have not changed. If there are no serious sins to confess, we have to at least provide some matter for absolution, and that means mentioning some sin of the past (mortal or venial) in a general way. It is still acceptable to conclude your confession with the formula, "…for these sins and any that I may have forgotten, I ask pardon of God and absolution from you." Perhaps your confessor noted a touch of anxiety in your voice and stopped you because he was afraid you might be on the road to becoming scrupulous—a terrible spiritual affliction, which can easily lead to doubting the mercy of God. If you want to receive the graces of the sacrament and have no serious sins to confess, simply say, "Bless me, father, it has been *x* number of weeks, or months, since my last confession. I have no serious sins to confess at this time, but I am sorry for my past sins, especially those against the Fourth, or Sixth, etc. Commandment." This practice will enable you to get the cumulative benefit of the graces of the sacrament of reconciliation as often as you wish.

Q 23.—What can you say to a person who has stopped going to confession because of an experience of rebuke from the priest during confession?

A Go to another priest. That priest may have had a rough day, or may have misunderstood what the person said. You must realize that you go to confession to talk to God, and you are telling him the sin. True, He already knows the sin, but God wants to give us the confidence and trust that He has in another human being. The priest is an ordinary person.

Q 24.—How do I convince children and their parents that it is important for them to go to confession?

A Impress upon the youngster and his parents that he is not going to a priest, a human being; he is going directly to God and asking God through the instrumentality of a priest to forgive him for his sins.

Q 25.—Sometimes I am tempted not to go to confession, and because of this I keep postponing it. How can I start?

A Remember, it is a matter of your spiritual life. You go to Communion regularly, and confession is one of the ideal preparations to go to Communion; therefore, if you to want to receive Communion in the best possible way, with all the benefits, graces and privileges that the Lord gives, you must prepare for it. If you are hesitant about going to confession, I just say, "Go to confession!" Go to another priest if that is of any help.

Q 26.—If you go to confession and must always confess the same fault or sin, what is the point of going?

A Put the responsibility of your conversion on God! Keep on mentioning your sins, failings and weaknesses until the Lord releases them.

Too many people think that they have to hurry through confession because there are others who are waiting, so it is much easier to mention the same things because they do not have to give it much thought, so they just try to word it in a different way. This is not good. It is not a matter of being a catalog; it is a matter of getting some advice also to help you not do it again. Let the priest ask you questions. Answer as honestly as you can. The priest can counsel you on how to take steps to overcome your sins.

Q 27.—Is thinking about hating someone a mortal sin?

A Learn to say a prayer for that person, because we don't know what you hate about that person, and we don't know why that person is that way. First of all, it is your personal intuition, and secondly, ask yourself, "Do I want to hang on to it?" I would turn to the Lord and say, "Lord, I hope you are never mad at me, like I am at this person." Make it human in your every day life.

Q 28.—Do I have to confess wishing I were dead?

A This is a cowardly attitude and an escape of all things. The Lord has a special thing for you to do. Maybe a year or so from now, the Lord will need you to do something special; now if you are wishing you are dead, you are throwing the Lord off.

Q 29.—Do I have to confess that I am unhappy living?

A When a person confesses this, he is unhappy with the situation he is in, not with living. It is instinctive in all of us to want to live; we run to every doctor or person we can to help us so we can live.

Q 30.—Is taking a long time in the confessional selfish if there is only half an hour and people are waiting?

A Ask the priest if you can have more time after Mass or at another time. I always say if you have the time and you want to wait, I will give you all the time I can. But still, remember that you are number one with the Lord right now in the confessional, and therefore you are in the Lord's time.

Q 31.—I believe the desire of many of us is to live in close union with God and with others. Unfortunately, we find ourselves hoarding grudges against each other and yet feel no sense of remorse. How can you help?

A Pray for that person. Not a long prayer, but just a short ejaculation will help.

Q 32.—Some people have a problem making a confession to a priest who is known to them. What advice could you give?

A I never remember who goes to confession to me. It is a matter of a good, solid, spiritual visit. The priest hears hundreds of confessions; the Lord gives us the ability to not remember people's sins. We pray before the confession and we pray after the confession that the Lord gives us the ability not to remember what people say. Confession can make a priest very happy in that people have trust and confidence in him, so therefore you are doing him a favor.

Q 33.—What questions should I ask myself in order to make a good confession?

A I would start by looking at my relationship with my beloved God who, as the Blessed Trinity, dwells within me at the center of my being. It is a relationship of love. How have I treated my beloved? Where have I been careless in communicating with God? Am I holding out on this beloved God in any way? Am I carving out an area of my life that is against the wishes of my beloved God? Looking at the example of Jesus, am I using that as a guide to being a good beloved to God in a consistent way in my daily life? Are there any parts of my life that are lived as if God did not exist? They may not be evil; they are just places where I have not invited God to be and share and take possession.

With this foundation, I would look to see where I seem to have the most trouble. What do I need to work on the most? These thoughts will include my relationship with other people. If I bring these main points to the priest in the sacrament of reconciliation, then he can guide me to a positive way of acting more fully out of love in relating to God, myself, and my fellow human beings.

Q 34.—Why do some priests not have you say the act of contrition?

A There are several possible reasons for that. If you receive the sacrament of reconciliation as part of a public penance liturgy, for example in Advent or Lent, the act of contrition is already said in common before the people go to the priests for confession. Or the priest may presume that you have made an act of sorrow in preparation for the sacrament. This is certainly a valid assumption since we come to the sacrament to receive forgiveness, and that means we are sorry for our sins. Have you ever reflected on the fact that we really have our sins forgiven before we come to the priest because we have told God we are sorry as we prepared? The actual confession brings us to the special presence of the merciful Christ, who envelops us in an embrace of blessings and special help to avoid those sins for the future. We also have the help and counsel of the priest, who can guide us towards better love and abandon to our beloved God. A final reason I can think of for the priest's not asking for the act of contrition is the fact that he may see clearly in listening to your confession that you are expressing sorrow in almost every other word. He may find this quite sufficient. The guidelines for confessing our sins do mention the need for the act of sorrow, but as you can see, there are different ways to perform that very important action that we, as penitents, make as we receive from Jesus the assurance of forgiveness and help for the future.

Q 35.—Why do guilty feelings remain behind after we have confessed our sins and have received forgiveness?

A It is strange, indeed, that once we have received the forgiveness of God, and we know that God has forgiven our sins and has forgotten them, we still feel guilty. Our feelings sometimes have a different way of looking at things. We know that our feelings don't know God or the things of God. They just know us and whether or not we are feeling good. They know if we have to defend ourselves, or survive some crisis, or have some unwanted pain. If we do something evil, our feelings may or may not have guilt. It all depends on how these feelings of ours were trained as we grew up. It is good to have a feeling that we have done wrong when, in fact, we have done something wrong. That helps us to work to repair the wrong by asking for forgiveness or making amends. However, the feelings may have their own agenda when we have done some particular wrong. Then they will feel guilty even though we have received forgiveness. In this case our feelings need to heal. We may have to express feelings of remorse or sadness over the forgiven sin so our feelings can share in that forgiveness. Sometimes the sin stirs up feelings from the past not even related to the present situation. It is a feeling that needed healing in the past, and we didn't take care of it for some reason. In any case, once we know that it is a matter of feelings only, we can deal with the feelings in a respectful but firm way, and usually the guilt will gradually fade away.

Q 36.—How do you get over the fear of going to confession?

A The fear of going to confession probably comes from a bad experience in confession when we were young. Those early impressions at a tender age tend to go rather deep into our feeling memory. It could also be as simple as being afraid of a small, enclosed space. With the modern spacious confessionals, this is less of a problem. If a past experience gave rise to the fear, we need to work with the memories of the unpleasantness and experience again the fear, so that we can bring it up to date. Now the terrible priest who so embarrassed you or scolded you unkindly is nowhere around. You are safe from him or anyone else who might have made those confessional experiences so unpleasant. Then you can gradually get your feelings to get over it. In this process you may need to release some old anger you are carrying against these persons. While thinking of the unjust actions against you, you can release the anger by any number of practices. Some people release anger by writing about the whole thing and then tearing up the paper. Others, while thinking about the one who hurt them, will bang a ball on the ground. Others find beating up a pillow for a few seconds does the job. The feelings of anger should diminish. If they come back later, do the same thing over again. We come to heal our feelings, and then come to have a gentle but effective control over our feelings of anger and fear. Hopefully, they will no longer make it so difficult to experience the gift of the sacrament of reconciliation.

Q 37.—What are the regulations about where and how to receive the sacrament of reconciliation?

A The sacrament can be experienced in any number of places, times, and circumstances. Taking a walk with the priest is a great way to experience the sacrament if it provides privacy and a calm atmosphere that help the reconciliation. We can receive it face-to-face or through a screen, as many still prefer. We can receive it in the hospital, and if there is a patient in the next bed, the priest merely asks you to express sorrow for your sins without mentioning them. There are lots of ways to receive this sacrament. Communal sacrament of reconciliation is popular especially in Lent and Advent. Some parishes have it once a month. It is a sacrament for people, and therefore, adapted to people's needs.

Q 38.—What is sin, really? How do I know it is sin; how can I tell the difference between a mistake and a real sin?

A This is a good question, because we as human beings can never be perfect. Our human nature has too many complexities, and we operate on too many fields in our modern life to do everything perfectly. We will make mistakes. There will be errors in judgment, misreading of people, or a slip of the hand or the lip. We forget something, and it hurts another person. We did not intend that. Not all these human weaknesses or failings are sins. Someone may demand that we apologize for something we did that caused difficulty even if we did not intend it. Part of our apology may be our explaining that we never intended to hurt or inconvenience him. Sometimes something we do innocently causes another to get very angry. That doesn't make it a sin, because we did not intend to cause the anger. We were surprised by it. It is not any sin on our part, even though we may feel somewhat guilty, because what we did caused such anger. A sin is when we choose to do something to hurt another, or ourselves, or when we set our will against what we know is God's will for us.

Since our God is our most beloved, we can be assured that we can never sin seriously without knowing it. If we are holding out on God in any significant way, God will somehow let us know it so we can change that behavior. If we practice making God, our beloved, the center of our lives, instead of ourselves, we will be occupied with what pleases God. We will not be so preoccupied with sin, which tends to put the focus on us. Finally, when we are in doubt about something we are planning or are doing, it is good to seek the advice of a trusted friend who will keep the conversation in confidence, or mention it to the priest when we go to receive the sacrament of reconciliation.

Q 39.—What do I do if I believe firmly in my conscience that something is not a sin, but I know the Church teaches differently?

A When we find ourselves in this situation, we need to check a couple of things. First, our conscience could be wrong or misinformed. We need to look at that carefully. Once we are fairly sure we have a well-informed conscience we need, secondly, to look at the action in question. There are a number of laws of the Church that are put forth as the general law or norm for all in the Church. However, in applying the law to our particular situation, and being conscious of the real purpose of that law, we may find that it does not apply in our situation. Or, as may be the more common case, there is another principle of moral behavior that, in our experience, overrides the original law. We can make a moral judgment based on that, and there is no sin. Again, if this is a serious matter, it helps to seek the counsel of a priest or other well informed person who can talk with us as we make that decision. The general laws of the Church do not always envision every situation that may come up. Thus we may have to judge carefully, with help, what God's will is for us in this particular situation. Since God is our most beloved God, He will appreciate our efforts to judge wisely and lovingly in these human actions.

Q 40.—Is it a sin to have great fear in withholding details from the priest regarding a past grievous sin? It would be confessing in general, but not from the depths of all the pain you know your sin has caused.

A When we confess a serious sin in the sacrament of reconciliation, we need to give the priest enough detail so he knows what the sin was about and, generally, how many times it was committed, and any special circumstances that would affect the nature of the transgression against God's plan for our lives. If a person confesses a sin of adultery, it means that at least one party to the sin was married to another person. If both parties were married to other persons, this is an important circumstance to mention. If the sin of adultery resulted in the breakup of a stable marriage, and it causes subsequent terrible anguish and pain to that family, that is another circumstance that needs to be addressed in the confession. These circumstances enable the priest to help the penitent know how to proceed for the future and how to bring peace to his life again. It may be helpful to bring up to the priest the pain that the adultery has caused the penitent. Or maybe the adultery has nothing but positive feelings about it, but the penitent knows it is wrong. Mentioning this to the priest enables him to be of more help in this difficult situation. Finally, a sin may be so unpleasant that the penitent really can't talk about it. Just confess it in that way, with a general indication of the seriousness and nature of the sin, and the priest will be very understanding and helpful. Remember, the priest in the sacrament of reconciliation represents Christ, our most loving and merciful brother.

Q41.—Are there specific prayers one must know and recite in confession? The childhood formulas are forgotten now, and it makes it uncomfortable to go to confession.

AThere are a few formulas that we can use for the sacrament of reconciliation; however, we must remember that the sacrament is a meeting with Christ through the priest. Thus, it is a loving meeting, full of the lavish mercy and goodness of God to encourage us to dedicate ourselves all the more fully to living out God's wishes in our everyday lives. As a priest who has heard confessions for many years, I would say that any greeting is just fine. It just needs to include about how long since your last confession, and I need to know that you are there to receive the sacrament. After confessing your sins, listen to the words of the priest. He will give you some prayers or actions (a penance) to help you make up for the sins by acts of love and dedication to God and kindness to other people. Somewhere in the confession you need to express sorrow for the sins. Many people do that after accepting the penance from the priest and before the priest offers the prayer of absolution. Finally, a word of thanks is appropriate, and, if you wish, a word or two about how the confession helped you. This helps the priest know that, indeed, he has helped you in this beautiful sacrament.

Q 42.—What if you have been away from confession for years, and on returning have trouble counting the number of mortal sins, for example, as in missing Mass on Sunday for years, or living in adultery for a long time?

A You are speaking of a very happy occasion when someone comes back to God with sorrow for his or her sins. The priest will be most happy, I am sure, to help you make the confession for those long years. The priest will be able to judge the nature and number of sins when you say, "I did not go to Mass for all these years." Or, "I lived with my husband in a civil marriage for thirty years." He may ask you some questions. He wants to help you bring out those things that really stood in the way of your relating lovingly with your beloved God. As I mentioned, it is a happy occasion, and heaven rejoices over a sinner coming to forgiveness. It is not as if there is a computer hard drive within us that can bring up every event of the past. It is a matter of looking at the main things that stood in the way of a free and loving relationship with God, with ourselves, and with our fellow human beings. After this first confession in a long time, it is good to continue to receive this sacrament of reconciliation from time to time so we can stay in touch with spiritual helps and guidance. Long habits are hard to break, and they may need special attention. We also may need special encouragement to keep moving along this blessed road of peace and greater oneness with Christ Jesus and the most Holy Trinity within us.

Authors by Location

Australia
Andrea Ellen Bentham, *Logan Central, 61*
Rachel S. Williams, *Melbourne Victoria, 145*

Canada
Alberta
Frances M. Rychlo, SFO, *St Albert, 100*
British Columbia
Denise R. Buckley, *Comox, 140*
Joan Ann Pogson, *Saanichton, 60*
Ontario
Dale T. Bisanti, *Bramalea, 203*
Pete Vere, *Sault Ste Marie, 59*

England
Daniel A. Longland, *Devon, 17*

Kenya
Bernard M. Kago, *Thika, 168*

Nigeria
Margaret J. Akpan, *Calabar, 209*

United States of America
Alabama
Yvonne J. Nihart, *Seale, 66*
Arizona
Fr. James W. Modeen, *Tuscon, 144*
Theresa Carol Pettis, *Casa Grande, 205*
California
Anonymous, *Los Angeles, 49*
Candice Franicis, *Escondido, 19*
Breon L. Gonzalez, *Lake Elsinore, 235*
Sylvia A. Green, *Pasadena, 105*
Fr. Maurus Kelly, OFM, *Santa Barbara, 250*
Carol A. Rusch, *Sun City, 246*
Colorado
Kelly M. Westover, *Centennial, 197*
Connecticut
Anne Caron, *Newington, 208*
Florida
Susan M. Barber, *Jacksonville, 26*

Rose Mary Danforth, *Jacksonville, 42*
Amanda Mason, *Jacksonville, 81*
Dale Recinella, *Macclenny, 187*
Georgia
Brenda R. McCloud, *Canton, 104*
Hawaii
Suzanne Ching, *Honolulu, 25*
Illinois
Fr. Gary C.Caster, *Washington, 107*
Robert J. Decker, *Maryville, 170*
Catherine A. Nelson, *Gurnee, 58*
Rita F. Prenavo, *Chicago, 92*
Indiana
Cathy A. Bloom, *Brownsburg, 210*
Jeanne M. McClure, *New Albany, 91*
Kansas
Jean M. Heimann, *Wichita, 149*
Annette Sosa, *Hugoton, 124*
Louisiana
Bonnie Taylor Barry, *Sunset, 162*
Mary Grisaffi, *Gretna, 186*
Maine
Danielle M. Sabine, *Greene, 120*
Maryland
Anonymous, *Derwood, 166*
Nancy H. Cioffi, *Chesapeake Beach, 69*
Eugene K. Mastrangelo, *North Beach, 212*
Eric G. Small, *Elkridge, 211*
Massachusetts
Anonymous, *Bedford, 128 & 138*
Gail M. Besse, *Hull, 167*
Bonnie Doherty, *Haverhill, 132*
Melissa Shaw, *Millbury, 137*
Michigan
Lou Therese Anthony, *Flint, 121*
Susan Kay Newberry, *Lansing, 62*
Lisa A. Stechschulte, *Owosso, 46 & 184*
Minnesota
Tim A. Drake, *Saint Joseph, 159*
Mary Jo McCarthy, *Pequot Lakes, 198*
Mariann Otto, *Lester Prairie, 87*

United States of America, *cont*

Mississippi

Frances D. Huck, *Picayune, 41*

Missouri

Lisa M. Coleman, *Lee's Summit, 80*

Lara Muse, *Agency, 243*

New Mexico

Virginia Schmuck, *Portales, 110*

New York

Joan M. Beebe, *Rochester, 21*

Paul J. Gwozdz, *Poestenkill, 102*

Virginia E. Heim, *Copake, 64*

Fr. Edward R. Wolanski, CP,
Shelter Island, 3 & 127

Leodones Yballe, *Rochester, 29*

Catherine M. Zubrovich, *Freeport, 155*

North Carolina

Connie A. Andretta, *Denver, 83*

Carmen Creamer, *Jacksonville, 65*

Jacqueline D. Henry, *Carolina Shores, 44*

North Dakota

Sandra L. Nicolai, *New Rockford, 204*

Ohio

Anonymous, *Johnstown, 88*

Anonymous, *Twinsburg, 98*

Lois M. Bruce, *Maumee, 189*

Fr. Charles Foeller, *Mt. Gilead, 147*

Katherine P. Hoff, *Marion, 158*

Linda L. Lochtefeld, *New Bremen, 11*

Jeanne C. McGuire, *Columbus, 52*

Molly N. O'Connell, *Mason, 180*

Judith Smedley, *Portland, 119*

Mary K. Soyka, *Salem, 6 & 181*

Jessica A. Zajac, *Northfield, 86*

Fr. Jim Van Vurst, OFM, *Cincinnati, 248*

Oklahoma

Anonymous, *McAlester, 232*

Michael F. Russo, *Broken Arrow, 229*

Oregon

Maureen Paloma, *Tigard, 178*

Lucy O. Scholerman, *Bay City, 23*

Fr. Gary L. Zerr, *Keizer, 99*

Pennsylvania

Anonymous, *Philadelphia, 241*

Craig N. Glantz, *Philadelphia, 5*

Darlene E. Graver, *Strasburg, 27*

Suzanne Luteran, *Erie, 236*

Carol Ann Matz, *Hazleton, 177*

South Carolina

Amanda S. Abbott, *Beaufort, 18*

Lynda S. Lowin, *Blunt, 239*

Texas

Anonymous, *College Station, 70*

Pauline L. Bludau, *Victoria, 50*

Dora C. Gallardo, *Uvalde, 40*

Janis M. Hairgrove, *Beaumont, 242*

Marcel R. LeJuune, *Lubbock, 89*

Virginia

Toni I. Leach, *Oak Hill, 139*

Janet L. Smith, *Gainesville, 131*

Utah

Pauline Wilson, *Stansbury, 108*

Washington State

Anonymous, *Seattle, 148*

William R. Baxter, *Spokane, 67*

Julia Becker, *Spokane, 143*

Ron Belter, *Kirkland, 234*

Fr. Thomas Kraft, OP, *Seattle, 245*

Joseph M. McDonald, *Colfax, 156*

Joanne McGoldrick, *Spokane, 7*

Mary, *Tacoma, 8*

Angela Schweig, *Spokane, 122*

Most Rev. William Skylstad, *Spokane, 1*

Lisa A. Wehrman, *Tacoma, 195*

Wisconsin

Jane M. Adams, *Fitchburg, 24*

Maureen E. Ozminkowski,
New London, 200

Index

I N D E X

A Catholic Guide

PREPARING FOR THE SACRAMENT OF RECONCILIATION

Companion to

101 INSPIRATIONAL STORIES OF THE SACRAMENT OF Reconciliation

SISTER PATRICIA PROCTOR, OSC
& FATHER ALBERIC SMITH, OFM

ISBN: 0-9728447-6-7
Price: $6.95

***If you have enjoyed reading this book,
you may be interested in our
confession workbook guide:***

Preparing for the Sacrament of Reconciliation.

This workbook is for adults. It's a solid, honest guide to bring your faith and walk with God into a maturity that will help you face your problems, obstacles and difficulties with greater understanding and acceptance. It will show you what doors you need to open and move through to find greater peace, joy and energy in your day-to-day life, your relationship with others and your walk with God.

The workbook is set up to provide guidance for monthly confession for a year. Every month you will examine these four areas by answering seven to eight questions under each of these topics:

1. My relationship with God.
2. My relationship with self.
3. My relationship with family and friends.
4. My relationship with difficult people.

When they are completed you will have carefully examined what needs to be confessed and what needs to be worked on.

For more information visit www.confession101.com and click on "Workbook".

The workbooks can be purchased from Saint Anthony Messenger Press at:

1 800 488-0488

or on the web at

www.americancatholic.org.

Three More Great Books
from the Catholic Inspirational Series

At Your Local Catholic Bookstore
or from Saint Anthony Messenger Press
www.americancatholic.org
1 800 488-0488

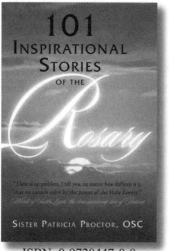

ISBN: 0-9728447-0-8
$12.95

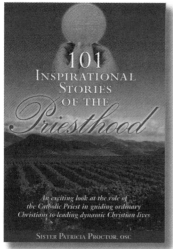

ISBN: 0-9728447-3-2
$12.95

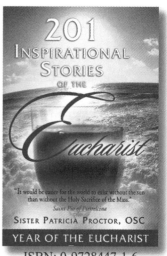

ISBN: 0-9728447-1-6
$14.95